Echoes of the Divine:

Unveiling Prayer in the King James Bible

A Profound Exploration of Prayer's Universal Significance for Believers and Seekers Alike

by Gary E. Risenhoover

TABLE OF CONTENTS

Hey there, Awesome Reader!

Welcome to a rollercoaster of ideas, insights, and captivating stories that will grab your attention from the very first page! This book didn't just appear overnight; it was born from countless hours of sleepless nights, deep dives into research, spirited debates, and the burning desire to share something truly electrifying with you.

Long before this book took shape, there was a spark—an itch to explore uncharted territories and challenge the ordinary. We embarked on a mission to unravel complexities and turn them into a thrilling narrative that not only informs but dazzles and inspires. Every chapter you're about to dive into carries the heartbeat of that mission.

The research process was nothing short of an adventure itself. It led us down winding paths, meeting brilliant minds, and uncovering fresh perspectives that gave this work its unique flavor. We sifted through mountains of data and stories, peeling back layers until we found the essence that makes this topic pulse with life.

Our goal? To deliver a book that's not just another read, but an experience. One that grabs you by the collar and drags you through new ideas, making you laugh, think, and maybe even question what you thought you knew. We want you to feel the adrenaline of discovery on every page.

You'll notice a mix of storytelling, facts, and lively commentary—crafted deliberately to keep you hooked. This isn't dry textbook territory; it's a living, breathing conversation we're inviting you to join. Imagine us sitting across the table, firing off thoughts and bouncing ideas in a way that's casual, sincere, and packed with punch.

As you turn each page, keep your curiosity wide open. Let your mind roam free with the sparks this book will ignite. You're not just a reader here—you're an explorer charting a course through thrilling intellectual landscapes.

Don't be surprised if you find yourself eagerly racing ahead or pausing thoughtfully to soak it all in. Both reactions are exactly what we aimed for. Your engagement is the fuel that powers this book's spirit.

Thank you for trusting this journey. The fact that you're here, ready and willing, means the world. Now buckle up because we're about to dive deep, break molds, and uncover truths that might just change how you see everything.

Ready? Let's get started. Adventure awaits within these pages, and it's just for you.

Fuel your curiosity and enjoy the ride!

Gary E. Risenhoover

The Sacred Canvas: Painting Prayer in the Language of the King James Bible

The Majesty of KJV Prose

In the grand tapestry of sacred scripture, few threads shimmer with as much enduring brilliance as the language of the King James Bible. Its majestic cadence and poetic grandeur have not only shaped religious thought and devotion but have also elevated the very act of prayer into a profound artistic expression. To engage with the King James Bible (KJV) is to enter a realm where words are more than mere vessels of meaning; they become instruments of transcendence, resonating with a sacred music that stirs the soul and elevates the heart. This subchapter invites you to immerse yourself in the rich and majestic prose of the KJV, exploring how its rhythmic and poetic language transforms prayer into an art form—one that transcends time and tradition, inviting every reader into a sacred dialogue that is at once ancient and immediate, intimate and universal. At the heart of this exploration lies an essential truth: prayer within the KJV is not simply speech or petition. Rather, it is a sacred artistic expression, akin to a beautifully composed hymn or a masterful painting, where rhythm, imagery, and sound conspire to lift the spirit beyond the mundane and into the realm of divine encounter. The KJV, with its arresting blend of simplicity and grandeur, employs stylistic devices such as parallelism, repetition, and metaphor with remarkable finesse—each device weaving a sonic and visual tapestry that evokes awe, reverence, and an almost palpable sense of sacred presence. The initial step on this journey is to attune the ear and the heart to the unique musicality of the KJV's English. It is a language shaped during a time when speech was as much an oral as a written art, and when poetry and prayer were deeply intertwined. The translators of the KJV, under the reign of King James I in the early 17th century, not only sought accuracy but also literary beauty, crafting a Bible designed to be read aloud in congregations, to echo within the stone walls of churches, and to inhabit the inner sanctuaries of individual souls. This spoken heritage remains palpable, even centuries later, in the rise and fall of KJV verse—a majestic cadence that both calms and stirs, that quiets the mind yet awakens the spirit. Consider the opening lines of the Book of Psalms, a collection widely regarded as the spiritual heart of biblical prayer. Psalm 23, the Shepherd's Psalm, is one of the most celebrated passages, its language imbued with gentleness and assurance. Yet its power lies not only in the comforting message but also in its elegant poetic structure: "The Lord is my shepherd; I shall not want. He maketh me to lie down in green pastures: he leadeth me beside the still waters. He restoreth my soul: he leadeth me in the paths of righteousness for his name's sake." These opening verses utilize parallelism—a cornerstone of Hebrew poetry mirrored perfectly in the KJV. The repetition of "He" at the start of each line creates a rhythmic pulse that echoes both God's steady presence and the psalmist's unwavering trust. The balance of images—the green pastures, the still waters, the restored soul—packages spiritual sustenance into sensory experience, inviting the reader to visualize and almost feel the peace and care provided by the divine shepherd. Here, prayer becomes not a mere statement but a sacred song, a carefully constructed layering of sound and image that evokes calm and confidence. The effect is magnified still further by the KJV's use of formal diction and archaic verb forms—"maketh," "leadeth," "restoreth"—which impart a solemnity and timelessness that transcend ordinary speech. These linguistic choices do not hinder understanding; rather, they frame the prayer as something removed from daily chatter, raised instead on the altar of reverence and sacred tradition. The cadence carries the words forward in a stately procession, inviting the reader or listener to step into a sacred space, a spiritual twilight where the familiar and the eternal meet. Parallelism is not the only stylistic feature that deepens the majesty of KJV prayer.

Repetition, when artfully applied, intensifies meaning and imparts a meditative quality that invites the soul's extended dwelling within sacred sound. In the Lord's Prayer (Matthew 6:9-13), repetition underscores key petitions. It infuses the prayer with solemn rhythm: "Our Father which art in heaven, Hallowed be thy name. Thy kingdom come, Thy will be done in earth, as it is in heaven. Give us this day our daily bread. And forgive us our debts, as we forgive our debtors. And lead us not into temptation, but deliver us from evil." Here, we see not mechanical repetition for mere effect but a deliberate echo of divine will and human need. The repeated invocation of "Thy" draws focus again and again to God's sovereignty, underscoring the prayer's core orientation toward the divine. The rhythm pauses and flows, creating a sacred dance between petition and worship. Each successive line builds upon the last, like phrases in a musical composition that call the listener deeper into reflection and surrender. Further adding to the transcendent quality of KJV prayer is its frequent deployment of metaphor. Biblical prayer within this tradition does not merely describe spiritual realities but evokes them through imagery that invites full sensory participation. Take, for example, the metaphor of God as "rock" and "fortress," a recurring theme throughout many psalms. Psalm 18:2 declares: "The Lord is my rock, and my fortress, and my deliverer; my God, my strength, in whom I will trust." The "rock" here is not just a stone but an emblem of stability, endurance, and protection—qualities that resonate deeply with any who seeks refuge amidst life's storms. The fortress conjures a vision of impregnable safety, a sanctuary where one can stand unshaken. The metaphor is vivid, tactile; the mind can almost feel the rock's roughness and hear the echo from the fortress walls. In this way, the KJV prayer language becomes a sensory portal, transporting believers into a lived experience of divine shelter. A particularly profound example of metaphor's spiritual and poetic artistry in the KJV emerges in the Song of Solomon, which, while often interpreted in various ways, is steeped in imagery akin to the soaring heights of prayer as adoration and longing: "Thy love is better than wine; Because of the savour of thy good ointments thy name is as ointment poured forth, therefore do the virgins love thee." (Song of Solomon 1:2-3)Though the context is a lyrical conversation of love, the language resonates with the ecstatic yearning and intimate communion often found in prayer. Love is transformed into a sensory experience—taste, scent, touch—each line an offering of devotion that reaches beyond words into embodied worship. Through such imagery, prayer in the KJV transcends propositional meaning, becoming a living artwork evoking all senses and all the longings of the human heart. Within these rich examples, we begin to perceive the foundational theme of the KJV prayer as a sacred art form—one that invites a profound reverence and aesthetic appreciation. It is prayer not only to be spoken or read but to be savored, meditated upon, and experienced as an encounter with the divine that is as much felt as understood. This artistic dimension aligns closely with the biblical vision of prayer as more than communication: it is communion. It is an act that transforms the one who prays, shaping the inner landscape as new spiritual realities dawn. This dawning, this spiritual awakening, can be sensed as the reading moves deeper, like the slow descent of twilight, when the day's light softens, and hues deepen—a moment pregnant with mystery, expectation, and grace. The language of the KJV, like the twilight sky itself, is layered with texture and color. The rise and fall of syllables create an auditory landscape to which the soul naturally responds—its cadence offering rest, its poetry inviting awe. Imagine reading Isaiah 40:31 aloud: "But they that wait upon the Lord shall renew their strength; They shall mount up with wings as eagles; They shall run, and not be weary; And they shall walk, and not faint." Here, the rhythm is steady and uplifting, echoing the soaring metaphor of the eagle's wings. The imagery invites the reader into a palpable spiritual vision of renewal and empowerment. The repetition of the future tense "shall" engenders a certainty that is both comforting and inspiring. As the words roll forth, a sensory layering occurs: the strength of wings, the motion of running and walking, the rising above weariness—all painted vividly in the mind's eye while stirred in the heart. This is the majesty of the KJV prose: it meets the reader/emitter at the threshold of art and worship, creating a space where prayer is lived within the cadence of language itself. The prose is both an invitation and a mantle—an invitation to enter a sacred dialogue, a mantle of solemn beauty that dignifies every word and every breath as an offering. The musicality of KJV prayer deserves special attention. Unlike prose that is prosaic or dry, KJV prayer resonates like a song, marked by its melodic rise and fall, cadence, and stress patterns aligned in harmonious balance. This musicality arises from the skilled interplay of several techniques: from the alliteration of consonants and the assonance of vowels to the metrical pacing of phrases and the measured repetition of key words and themes. Take, for instance, the Book of Lamentations, which, while sorrowful, is a masterpiece of poetic lamentation and prayer: "How doth the city sit solitary, that was full of people! How is she become as a widow! She that was great among the nations, and princess among the provinces, How is she become tributary!" (Lamentations 1:1)The repeated question "How" at the start of three lines creates a rhythm that both mourns and pauses, allowing the reader to inhabit grief fully. The juxtaposition of the city's former greatness with present desolation is rendered with a poetic precision that evokes the senses: the sight of a deserted city square, the silence of forgotten streets, the heaviness of loss—all captured in a cadence that is at once mournful and memorable. This kind of musicality functions not only to enhance memorability but also to evoke spiritual and emotional resonance. It transforms reading or reciting prayer into a participatory event where sound and meaning become inseparable—a lived musical experience echoing in the soul. As readers journey through this sacred linguistic landscape, they encounter what might be called the "sensory layering" of KJV prayer—where sound, rhythm, imagery, and emotion branch and intertwine. The twilight hues of spiritual awakening—softening, deepening, mysterious, and illuminating—are reflected in the interplay of language. Each phrase invites the ear to listen, the mind to contemplate, and the heart to respond. The effect is holistic, drawing the whole self into encounter and transformation. Beyond the purely literary, this layering reflects a deeper spiritual principle: prayer is not simply an intellectual exercise or a utilitarian means to an end. Rather, it is a holistic act of communion with the divine, touching mind, body, and spirit. The KJV's majestic prose enfolds this principle in its very texture, demanding that the reader approach prayer not only with intellect but with aesthetic sensibility and emotional openness. What then does this mean for us today, for contemporary readers and seekers of all backgrounds? The majesty of the KJV prose, far from being an archaic curiosity, offers a guiding pathway—an invitation to rediscover prayer's power as sacred art. In a world often characterized by haste and distraction, the intentional cadence of KJV prayer can draw us back into moments of reverence and stillness, where the heart's desires meet the divine gaze in luminous dialogue. To engage with the KJV is to enter a realm where language is sacred clay, prayer its sculptor's hands, fashioning beauty and meaning from silence and breath. It is to stand beneath a vast canopy of spiritual twilight, awash in the colors of ancient song and sacred story, invited to voice the unutterable, to dwell within mystery, and to be shaped anew by the echoes of the divine. In embracing the majesty of KJV prose, we accept both the challenge and the gift of prayer as sacred art—an art that does not merely communicate but transforms; that does not simply ask but worships; that lifts words from earth to both echo and invoke heaven. It is a language that calls us into awe and invites us to listen, to speak, and ultimately, to be changed. Thus, in the sacred cadence of the King James Bible, prayer is revealed as a living masterpiece—crafted with echoes of grandeur, woven with the artistry of poetic devices, and illuminated by the mystical light of divine communion. It is the echo of human longing and divine response—a symphony of words that forever invites us to step closer, breathe deeper, and enter the majestic dance of Spirit and soul.

Symbolism and Sacred Imagery

In the vast and majestic tapestry of the King James Bible, prayer is often articulated not merely in words but through the rich symbolism and sacred imagery that infuse its verses with a depth and texture beyond the literal. This symbolism serves as a divine language, a conduit through which the ineffable mysteries of God's presence and human longing are rendered visible and tangible. To step into the prayers of the KJV Bible is to enter a realm where light and shadow intermingle, where the elemental forces of water and air breathe life into supplication, and where the radiant dance of celestial bodies mirrors the soul's journey toward communion with the divine. These images are far more than poetic embellishments; they operate as spiritual signposts—portals opening onto the hidden realities of grace and transformation. In this sacred dialogue between the human and the holy, prayer emerges as a living, breathing canvas, painted with colors and textures that resonate in the quiet spaces between words.Light and shadow form among the most primal and powerful symbols threaded throughout biblical prayers. Light, in the Scripture, is a universal emblem of divine presence, purity, and revelation. From the opening chapters of Genesis, light distinguishes itself as the first creative act of God—"Let there be light" (Genesis 1:3)— marking the genesis of order from chaos and the dawn of spiritual illumination. In prayers recorded in the King James Bible, light frequently emerges as a metaphor for God's guidance, protection, and sanctifying power. The Psalmist, for example, invokes this imagery vividly: "The Lord is my light and my salvation; whom shall I fear?" (Psalm 27:1). Here, light is not simply a physical phenomenon but a symbol of existential assurance and divine defense against the encroaching darkness of fear and despair. Contrasting with light is the motif of darkness and shadow, which in biblical prayer carries its own complex layers of meaning. Shadows often indicate the presence of trouble, temptation, and the unknown; yet, intriguingly, they also emphasize the protection and refuge found in God's care. Psalm 23's famous reference to "the valley of the shadow of death" (Psalm 23:4) illustrates this paradox. While the valley is fraught with peril, it is within this shadow that God's presence is palpably felt as a shepherd—guiding, comforting, and sustaining. This duality of light and shadow in prayer captures the dynamic tension between vulnerability and divine shelter, casting prayer as both an act of honest confrontation with darkness and of hopeful seeking toward divine illumination. Water, another elemental symbol, courses through the prayers and sacred texts of the King James Bible as a bearer of life, purification, and renewal. It is at once a physical necessity and a spiritual token of cleansing and rebirth. The Psalms frequently employ water imagery to express the soul's deep thirst for God: "As the hart panteth after the water brooks, so panteth my soul after thee, O God" (Psalm 42:1). This vivid image encapsulates prayer as a yearning for sustenance and restoration, on both a corporeal and spiritual level. Water appears also in the rituals of purification and sanctification—baptism being the paramount example—as it symbolizes the washing away of sin and the rebirth into newness of life. In the texture of KJV prayers, water's symbolism extends to evoke the mysteries of the Holy Spirit as a living, flowing presence that animates and transforms. The Spirit is often likened to rivers and streams that refresh the barren spiritual landscape, giving rise to parched souls now blooming in the presence of God's grace. This motif invites the believer into an experiential understanding of prayer as a continual source of life-giving energy, a sacred immersion into the divine that cleanses and consecrates. Incense forms another deeply evocative element in the symbolic vocabulary of biblical prayer. Its rising smoke is universally understood within the biblical milieu as a fragrant offering to God, a visible sign of worship and intercession ascending heavenward. In the King James Bible, incense is imbued with significance both tangible and mystical. The Psalmist declares, "Let my prayer be set forth before thee as incense; and the lifting up of my hands as the evening sacrifice" (Psalm 141:2). This passage positions prayer itself as an aromatic sacrifice, a sweet-smelling gift pleasing to God, carried on invisible yet fragrant currents toward the divine throne. The incense's curling smoke symbolizes the ethereal quality of prayer—simultaneously weightless and palpable—bridging the earthly and celestial realms. It evokes a sensory dimension that invites the worshiper's entire being into prayer: the visual of smoke ascending, the imagined scent of holiness, the tactile awareness of hands lifted in supplication. This multi-sensory language enriches our understanding of prayer as an embodied act, embraced fully in sight, sound, and scent, and thus as a transformative encounter that engages the total self. Celestial bodies—the sun, moon, and stars—stand as majestic icons within the sacred imagery that frames biblical prayer in the King James Bible. They represent divine order and cosmic authority, reflecting God's sovereign reign over the universe. In prayers, these luminous bodies frequently serve as metaphors for divine constancy and illumination amidst life's uncertainties. Psalm 19 celebrates the heavens as a proclamation of God's glory: "The heavens declare the glory of God; and the firmament sheweth his handywork" (Psalm 19:1). This imagery suggests that prayer is not confined to the individual soul but is part of the grand cosmic harmony, aligning the petitioner's voice with the celestial chorus of creation praising the Creator. Moreover, stars serve as emblems of hope and as a testament to God's covenantal promises. Abraham's prayerful faith is linked intimately with the promise of descendants as countless as the stars: "Look now toward heaven, and tell the stars, if thou be able to number them: and he said unto him, So shall thy seed be" (Genesis 15:5). This cosmic metaphor enshrines prayer as a bridge between earthly longing and heavenly assurance, inviting believers into a sacred narrative that stretches beyond time and space. Beyond these elemental images, the King James Bible's prayers are imbued with a nuanced portrayal of the Divine Presence that is both ambient and intimate, elusive and yet tenderly near. This presence is often depicted through atmospheric imagery—vaulted heavens, mounting clouds, trembling earth—that envelops prayer in a sacred aura. For instance, the psalmist's descriptions of God's majestic entry or the trembling of the earth before His holiness evoke the awe-inspiring backdrop against which prayer unfolds. Such imagery situates prayer within the larger frame of divine grandeur, reminding the petitioner of God's transcendent majesty and sovereignty. Yet, alongside this majestic portrayal exists a contrasting depiction of intimacy—moments of grace's subtle touch revealed in whispered assurances and gentle dwelling. Prayers such as Hannah's or David's reveal a God who listens attentively, responding to the quiet cry of a humble heart and meeting believers in their solitude and brokenness. This juxtaposition of the vast and the personal in the divine presence crafts a multi-dimensional spiritual landscape, where prayer is both profound conversation and a tender encounter, echoing through the halls of eternity and nestled in the quiet chambers of the soul. Understanding prayer as a multi-sensory painting further deepens when we consider the roles color and texture play in the biblical imagination. The KJV's poetic language invites readers to "see" prayer vividly—not only through words but as a living tableau painted with hues of gold, purple, and crimson, and textures ranging from rough sackcloth to smooth alabaster. These colors are not arbitrary; they carry theological weight, pointing to concepts such as royalty, sacrifice, humility, and divine favor. Purple, the color of kingship, often signals the presence of God's sovereign authority. Crimson, reminiscent of blood and sacrifice, evokes the cost of redemption and penitence. Likewise, the tactile sensations of sackcloth and ashes symbolize mourning, repentance, and the human condition's frailty. This chromatic and tactile imagery bridges the gap between spiritual abstraction and sensory experience, making prayer a vivid reality accessible to the heart's eye and touch. It turns prayer into a sacred art form—a canvas where scents, colors, sounds, and textures converge to create a holistic spiritual atmosphere. In this sacred silence between verses, where words fall away yet meaning lingers profoundly, the soul encounters an echo of the divine that transcends the spoken petition. As we explore the sacred imagery further, it becomes clear that these symbols are not static; they are dynamic, inviting active participation and meditation. Each image calls forth different emotional hues—hope, reverence, longing, awe, surrender—engaging the believer's entire being in a dance with the divine. For instance, the rising incense captures the movement of the soul's ascent, while the shadows reflect places of struggle that, paradoxically, deepen one's reliance on God's light. Water's gentle flow becomes a reminder of renewal and the ever-present possibility of spiritual rebirth, while the steadfast stars affirm the enduring faithfulness of God's promises. Moreover, this symbolic language connects believers across time and culture, providing a shared vocabulary of faith that transcends linguistic and denominational boundaries. The symbols labor as a communal heritage of spiritual expression, allowing readers and worshippers from diverse backgrounds to tap into a wellspring of meaning that speaks directly to the human longing for connection—to a sacred reality that both humbles and exalts. The sacred imagery in the King James Bible also functions as a theological lens through which one can discern facets of God's nature and His relationship to humanity. Light reveals God as source and guide; water speaks to the renewing and cleansing power of grace; incense embodies prayer's role in mediation and worship; celestial bodies display the cosmic dimension of divine sovereignty; and the intimate ambience of God's presence assures the believer of a God who is near even in the deepest solitude. It is within this dense symbolic fabric that prayer is revealed not merely as speech but as an encounter. Each symbol acts as an invitation—an opening of a window into the divine mystery where seekers gather to be seen, heard, and transformed. The imagery draws the participant from the surface of words into the depths of spiritual experience, urging a contemplative posture that hears the whisper beneath the shout and sees the light beyond the shadow. In considering how these images operate together, it is helpful to reflect on prayer as a multi-sensory painting—a living mosaic of sensory and spiritual perception. Imagine, for a moment, a prayer as a canvas laid before the soul: the first strokes are faint beams of dawn's light breaking through shadow's grasp, symbolizing hope's birth. The middle section is textured with flowing streams—water that refreshes the thirsty heart, soaked in somber hues of repentance symbolized by sackcloth, yet touched by the warm gold of forgiveness. Wisps of incense curl upward, invisible yet sensed, creating movement and scent that connect earth to heaven. Above all, shining stars punctuate the night sky, steadfast beacons guiding the way. In this painting, the Divine Presence is both the artist and the muse, simultaneously holding the canvas and inspiring the strokes. It is a living composition where colors and textures do not merely decorate but speak, breathe, and pulse with meaning. The sacred silence between verses becomes the space where these images resonate most deeply, where prayer ceases to be a mere recital and becomes an encounter—an unfolding mystery that invites the heart to listen and the spirit to dance. Thus, as readers engage with the symbolic tapestry of the King James Bible's prayers, they are invited into a multi-dimensional spiritual journey. This journey reveals prayer as a sacred art that transcends words and reaches into the very essence of human experience, drawing all who seek into the embrace of divine mystery. Through light and shadow, water, incense, and celestial bodies, prayer becomes a holy canvas—an echo of the divine spoken not only with lips but with the language of the soul itself.

Auditory Reverence: Prayer as Song and Breath

In the vast tapestry of scriptural expression found within the King James Bible, prayer emerges not merely as a series of words or petitions but as a living soundscape—an auditory reverence that pulses with life and breath. This soundscape stretches beyond the written text into the realm of voice, cadence, and silent breath, forming a sacred song that fills the soul's horizon. To encounter prayer in this manner is to engage with it as a dynamic, vibratory experience—one that transcends the intellectual and touches the very essence of human existence. It invites us to listen deeply, to attune ourselves to the holy resonance that emerges when speech and spirit dance together. The King James Bible, celebrated for its majestic poetry and rhythmic flow, presents prayer in a form that is inherently musical. The carefully chosen words and phrasing resonate with timeless cadence, conjuring musicality even before one utters them aloud. This poetic quality is neither accidental nor ornamental; it is integral to the sacred purpose of prayer, shaping how it moves through the breath, the body, and the heart. The auditory texture of prayer invites participation not simply as an act of reading or reciting, but as a soulful breath—a sacred song informed by ancient rhythms that echo through generations. At the heart of this exploration lies the physiology of speech and breath—the primal mechanics by which prayer takes form and meaning. Before words coalesce into coherent ideas, they emerge from the breath, carried on the vibrations of vocal cords, shaped by the lips and tongue in a symphony of bodily cooperation. Breath, in this sense, is the invisible thread connecting earth to spirit. This sacred wind animates prayer as a living utterance. When we consider prayer as a song, the breath becomes the melody bearer, the pulse underlying each utterance, while the spoken words are the notes that articulate the human desire for communion with the divine. In the King James Bible, the psalms offer a profound example of this intersection between voice, breath, and sacred song. Many of the psalms function as hymns, prayers, or cries, each crafted to be spoken or sung aloud. Consider, for instance, Psalm 42: "As the hart panteth after the water brooks, so panteth my soul after thee, O God." The vivid metaphor evokes not only the yearning contained within the words but also the rhythm of panting breath, the very sound mirroring the soul's desperation and longing. Here, the act of prayer is inseparable from its vocal expression; the cadence and breath work in harmony, enabling the soul's ache to reverberate audibly. The King James translators, cognizant of this auditory dimension, rendered the Scriptures in verse and prose that flow with a deliberate meter and balance, often recalling the musical tradition of the Hebrew originals. The repetition of sounds, the parallelisms, and the alliterations are not decorative—they serve to anchor prayer within a sonic framework that amplifies its emotional and spiritual impact. When read aloud, these prayers ripple with rhythm, encouraging a meditative immersion that engages listeners and pray-ers alike in a participatory act. The sound becomes a sacred vessel, a channel through which the spirit communes, transforms, and heals. Yet, prayer spoken is not only about the presence of sound but also the sacred space carved by silence. The pauses between words, the rests in the rhythm, the inhalations of breath—all these create a fertile ground where the divine may speak and the soul may listen. In the tradition of the King James Bible, moments of silence punctuate the spoken prayers as much as the words themselves carry meaning. This interplay of sound and silence forms a pattern akin to music's phrasing—a breathing that honors the mystery beyond the utterance. To cultivate devotional prayer, one must learn to inhabit these silences, to breathe into them as fully as into the spoken word, recognizing that the stillness holds a sacred presence equal to the sound. For the modern reader and pray-er, cultivating an awareness of this auditory dimension is a pathway to deeper engagement. The experience of prayer becomes more than recitation; it becomes a meditative practice, an active listening to the divine music within oneself and the sacred text. By reflecting on the cadence, inflections, and even the sounds of the vocalized prayers in the King James Bible, one enters into a transformative dialogue in which voice, heart, and spirit intertwine. This enlivened awareness can cultivate a prayer experience that is immersive and sustaining. Engaging with prayer's auditory reverence invites several layers of reflection. First, there is the sonorous beauty of the language— the lyricism and stately flow which announce the presence of the sacred. Readers are encouraged to vocalize the prayers not only with their lips but with their hearts, allowing the words to resonate deeply within. Second, there is the reverberation in the body—the subtle vibrations in the chest and throat that accompany breath-filled speech, connecting the physical self with the spiritual yearning embodied in the words. Finally, there is the silence that enfolds the voiced prayer, inviting stillness and receptivity— spaces where the unheard becomes heard, where the soul listens for answers unspoken. To assist individuals in cultivating this profound engagement with prayer's auditory form, practical exercises rooted in scriptural passages may serve as a gateway. These exercises seek to deepen the connection between voice, breath, and devotion, establishing a living foundation for ongoing spiritual practice. Begin by selecting a passage from the Psalms, such as Psalm 23 or Psalm 51, or other prayers in the King James Bible rich with rhythmic cadences. Read the passage aloud slowly, observing the natural inflections and melodious qualities of the words. Notice how the breath flows in and out, how the voice rises and falls with the phrasing.Next, repeat the reading focusing on breathing deliberately. Inhale fully before beginning a line, allowing the breath to fill the body and mind. As you articulate each word, feel the voice vibrating through your throat and chest. Pay close attention to the spaces between lines, breathing into silence, allowing the pauses to deepen your receptivity. Then, explore chanting a portion of the passage soft and slow, embracing the song-like quality of scriptural prayer. Let your voice ride upon the natural rhythms and repetitions of the text, treating the speech as a sacred melody. Notice how the harmonizing of breath and word fosters a sense of calm and centeredness. Afterward, sit quietly in silence, allowing the vibrations of the vocalized prayer to settle within your being. Notice what feelings, insights, or spiritual touches arise in the quiet space beyond sound. This silence is as much a part of the prayer as the spoken word, inviting your spirit into a deeper communion beyond language. Finally, reflect on the experience in writing or meditation. How did focusing on breath and sound alter your perception of the prayer? Did the act of vocalization and attentive listening bring fresh meaning or emotional movement to the ancient words? Through these intentional practices, prayer ceases to be a static recitation and transforms into a dynamic spiritual gesture that engages the whole person—body, breath, voice, and spirit. It becomes a sacred song echoing through the corridors of time, a living dialogue formed not only by meaning but by the very act of sounding. This approach aligns closely with the biblical tradition where prayer and song often merge. The Psalter itself was designed for liturgical chanting and communal singing, reinforcing the inseparability of prayer and sacred music. Likewise, the New Testament references the use of psalms and hymns in worship and prayer (Ephesians 5:19, Colossians 3:16), underscoring how the early Christian community embraced prayer's musical dimension as a vital expression of faith. Moreover, understanding prayer as song unveils the transformative power embedded in its auditory quality. Psychologically and physiologically, intentional vocalization regulates the nervous system and evokes a sense of peace or reverence. The rhythmic breath and melodic speech soothe anxiety, center attention, and open the heart toward divine connection. In this way, the form of prayer allied with its content creates a holistic encounter that shapes the individual's spiritual and emotional landscape. In reflecting on these truths, readers are encouraged to view the King James Bible not solely as a written relic but as a living manuscript meant to be vocalized and heard. Through listening and speaking its sacred prayers aloud, one participates in a tradition that transcends time—a lineage of faith where every utterance becomes an offering, every breath a hymn, and every silence an invitation to divine presence. By nurturing an appreciation of prayer's auditory reverence, one cultivates a richer, more embodied spirituality. Words become not just ideas but instruments of sacred resonance. Breath turns into the melody of life itself, weaving together the human and the divine in an intimate dance. The soul's horizon, once merely conceptual, expands into a soundscape filled with holy song, calling each individual to join in the eternal chorus of prayer. As a living foundation, this focus on the sound and breath of prayer prepares the way for subsequent chapters which explore prayer's visual, tactile, and communal dimensions. It anchors the reader in the experience of prayer as a holistic act—embracing voice, body, and spirit—thus enriching the spiritual journey in profound and enduring ways. In summary, prayer in the King James Bible is not only theological content but a sacred song born of breath and silence. It invites the believer and seeker alike to discover the deep consonance between word and spirit through auditory reverence. Engaging consciously with these sacred sounds, one steps into the timeless flow of faith, where prayer becomes both a personal and universal melody echoing across human history.

Echoes at Dawn: The Genesis of Prayer

Primal Cries in the Wilderness

In the earliest dawn of human experience, before towering temples and sacred scriptures were etched, before ritualistic liturgies shaped the fabric of worship, lay the primal cries of humanity — unadorned, raw, and suffused with the vast burden of existence. These first utterances, scattered like fragile sparks in the wilderness of Genesis, are not merely historical footnotes but foundational echoes in the soul's first-reaching toward the divine. They pulse beneath the surface of recorded scripture as humanity's tentative dialogue with the sacred, reflected most poignantly in the brief yet profound prayers and acts of Cain, Abel, and Enos. It is here, in these primal moments, that prayer reveals itself in its purest form: a sacred breath escaping from the very heart of human longing, uncertainty, and hope. To stand in the presence of these earliest prayers is to feel the weight of being alive — at once vulnerable, bewildered, and yearning for solace or favor beyond human capacity. Cain's cry, Abel's offering, and Enos's invocation together weave a tapestry of human seeking, illuminating an ancient spiritual impulse that transcends the bounds of culture, language, and time. In what follows, we journey closely with these biblical figures, unearthing the emotional landscapes and spiritual impulses that shape their utterances. We situate these moments as archetypal beacons lighting the dense forest of humanity's earliest understanding of and yearning to connect with the divine. The story begins, inevitably, with the first children of Adam and Eve: Cain and Abel. The narrative in Genesis 4 is brief but laden with profound spiritual and emotional resonance. Abel, as the keeper of sheep, brings an offering of the firstlings of his flock. Cain, the tiller of the ground, presents the fruits of the soil. The text states: "And in process of time it came to pass, that Cain brought of the fruit of the ground an offering unto the Lord. And Abel, he also brought of the firstlings of his flock and of the fat thereof." (Genesis 4:3-4, KJV). Though terse, this moment contains the kernel of prayer itself: a reaching out through gifts, an acknowledgment of a power beyond self, and an implicit request for acceptance and affirmation. The motivations underlying Cain and Abel's offerings reveal early human nuance in how the sacred is approached. Abel's offering is accepted, described in the vague but powerful phrase "the Lord had respect unto Abel and to his offering." Cain's offering, however, finds no favor: "But unto Cain and to his offering he had not respect." The stark contrast invites the reader into a profound emotional space — one laden with disappointment, confusion, and the painful eruption of alienation. What might Cain's inner prayer have been? Though unvoiced explicitly, one imagines it was a desperate cry of a misunderstood soul: a plea for acceptance, love, and justice. His subsequent anger and despondence — "his countenance fell" (Genesis 4:5) — lay bare the rawness of human vulnerability when spiritual efforts seem futile. In remarkable ways, Cain's response to rejection introduces an elemental truth about prayer and the human spirit: that prayer is not always met with clear answers or affirmation, yet it compels the seeker forward. The story reveals an archetype of spiritual wrestling and inner turmoil, where unanswered cries fuel sorrow, regret, and ultimately tragedy. The wilderness here is both outer and inner — a dark terrain where cries echo back unanswered, where the sacred feels distant, and uncertainty reigns. Abel's offering, in contrast, hints at a prayer of trust and surrender. While the text is silent about Abel's words, the very act of offering "the firstlings of his flock" carries deep symbolic weight. Offering the "firstlings" connotes giving the very best, a heartfelt consecration of life's preciousness to the divine. Abel's silent prayer may be seen as a trembling act of love and faith — a gesture transcending literal words but pregnant with devotion and hope. This kind of prayer sets a formative precedent: prayer as a wholehearted giving that acknowledges dependence on a higher reality. As Genesis unfolds, the story swiftly progresses to Enos, the grandson of Adam and Eve. Genesis 4:26 describes a pivotal development: "And to Enos was born a son: then began men to call upon the name of the Lord." This statement marks perhaps the earliest explicit reference to calling upon God, situating Enos's generation as the point at which communal acknowledgment of the divine takes a formative shape in human history. The phrase "began to call upon the name of the Lord" implies an expansion from individual offerings to collective invocation — a birth of prayer as a shared human endeavor. This moment crystallizes the transition from isolated spiritual seeking to communal worship, embodying the universality of prayer. The wilderness of solitude gives way to the clearing of community, where voices converge in longing and recognition. Yet, even here, the emotional texture of calling upon the divine retains its ancient intimacy — touching on hope amidst hardship, confession amidst frailty, and yearning amidst the uncertainty of the human condition. Enos's fatherhood and his children's response to the divine name evoke the deep human yearning for connection, meaning, and guidance. Examining the King James phrasing in "then began men to call upon the name of the Lord" deepens our understanding. The verb "call" suggests a dynamic, reaching out — a vocal and spiritual act of lifting the self beyond immediate needs towards recognition of a power greater than man. "Upon the name of the Lord" emphasizes that prayer is directed not just to a distant deity but to a name that carries the essence and presence of the divine. Names in biblical thought are not mere labels; they embody character and presence. Calling upon God's name thus symbolizes invoking the fullness of divine relationship, mercy, and covenant. The archetypal resonance of these earliest prayers is profound. Cain's inner cry reflects the anguish of rejection and the danger of spiritual disconnectedness. Abel's offering manifests faith in surrender and devotion, cultivating a tender relationship with the sacred. Enos's initiation of calling upon God's name signals the birth of conscious, collective awareness of and reliance upon divine presence. Together, they dramatize the multifaceted nature of human prayer: cry, sacrifice, invocation — all facets of the soul's attempt to bridge the abyss between mortal limitation and infinite grace. This triad of expressions also shapes a template for the emotional textures underpinning all prayer. Pain, hope, gratitude, longing, fear, and surrender swirl beneath the surface of these primal calls — emotions as old as humanity itself, yet as perpetually fresh as each new human heart that reaches upward. The wilderness, an apt metaphor, is both literal and figurative. The earliest humans lived among forests and open lands, facing the wild unknown. Spiritually, the wilderness encapsulates the terrain of uncertainty, loneliness, and searching in which prayer begins. It is significant that these primal cries arise not from certainty or imposed doctrine but from profound experiential realities. They emerge from recognizing human vulnerability amid vast cosmic mystery. In Cain's rejected offering, the spiritual seeker confronts unfulfilled longing; in Abel's accepted gift, the seeker finds fleeting solace; and in Enos's invocation, the human reaches for relationship with a promise of divine presence. Each step uncovers prayer's function as an embodied, urgent act: a reaching out that embraces the whole person — mind, body, and spirit. Reflecting on the universal Seeker's voice inherent in these early prayers, one perceives a continuous thread that binds all humanity through time and culture. Regardless of creed or context, the act of prayer mirrors the same essential impulses — yearning to be seen and heard, seeking guidance in darkness, offering love and gratitude, wrestling with doubt and pain. These elements resonate deeply with the rawness of Cain's cry, the faith in Abel's offering, and the communal invocation that begins with Enos. To engage with these verses in the King James Bible is to encounter a language that conveys these emotional nuances with grace and gravity. The solemn cadence and archaic rhythm give voice to ancient longings, forging a bridge across millennia between contemporary readers and their ancient spiritual ancestors. The deliberate choice of words — "offering," "respect," "countenance fell," and "call upon" — turns scripture into a vessel of living breath, carrying the weight of human prayer in its infancy. Moreover, within these early prayers, we glimpse the embryonic understanding of God not just as a cosmic judge or creator but as a living presence relationally engaged with humanity. The narrative's portrayal of favor and rejection, acknowledgment and alienation, signals that prayer is simultaneously a spiritual act and a dialogue of the heart. It is this relationality — fraught, tender, hopeful — that cements prayer's status as a universal human expression transcending time, culture, and creed. The scene is set for all subsequent prayer: the wilderness as place and condition, the cry as voice, the offering as gesture, and the name as presence. These primal interactions echo endlessly within the human spirit's quest to touch what is holy and eternal. From the primitive, imperfect expressions of Cain, Abel, and Enos arises a foundational truth: that prayer, at its core, is humanity's immutable cry into the vast unknown — a cry that, though often unanswered in clear ways, continues to resonate across generations as a beacon of hope, surrender, and communion. In conclusion, the earliest biblical prayers, brief as they may be in scriptural text, carry immense weight in their symbolic and spiritual reach. They embody our shared origins as seekers standing at the edge of the unknown, grappling with the mysteries of existence and the yearning to be seen, heard, and embraced by the divine. Through these primal cries in the wilderness, prayer emerges not as a distant formalism but as the ancient and abiding breath of the human spirit, calling, offering, and invoking across the ages. It is here, in these first sacred dialogues, that the timeless dance of prayer begins — a dance that continues within each seeker's heart, radiant with the possibility of encounter, transformation, and peace.

Patriarchal Intercessions: Abraham, Isaac, and Jacob

In the opening chapters of Genesis, three towering figures emerge whose lives are deeply intertwined with the advent of prayer in the biblical narrative: Abraham, Isaac, and Jacob. These patriarchs are not only the founding fathers of Israel but also the earliest exemplars of covenantal communication with the Divine. Their prayers provide a profound window into the nature of human-divine interaction—a dialogue marked by trust, petition, struggle, and transformation. As we traverse the complex emotional landscapes of these prayers, we witness a gamut of spiritual expression from the earnest pleas of Abraham to the intimate wrestling of Jacob, each revealing a unique facet of the evolving relationship between God and humanity. This subchapter seeks to delve into these intercessions with careful scriptural reflection and heartfelt contemplation, revealing how ancient voices speak with undiminished power to every seeker engaged in the timeless quest for divine connection. Abraham: The Voice of Faith and Intercession. Abraham stands as a seminal figure whose life is punctuated by moments of profound prayerful encounter. From the earliest narrative in Genesis, his relationship to God is framed by covenant—an agreement that undergirds the unfolding drama of divine promises and human response. The intercessory prayers of Abraham reveal a steadfast trust in God's faithfulness, tempered by an intimate and transparent communication that does not shy from bold petitioning or challenging the Divine will. One of the most striking examples is Abraham's intercession on behalf of Sodom, found in Genesis 18. Through this dialogue, the patriarch exemplifies a prayerful posture characterized by audacity and compassion. When confronted with the impending destruction of the city, Abraham stands in the gap, pleading with God: "Wilt thou also destroy the righteous with the wicked?" (Genesis 18:23, KJV). This question represents more than mere legalistic bargaining; it is a profound moral appeal rooted in the character of God as just and merciful. The tone here is one of respectful boldness. Abraham approaches God with reverence yet does not hesitate to inquire, negotiate, and reason. His prayer reveals a relational trust that acknowledges divine sovereignty while inviting God's justice to reveal itself through mercy. The rhythm of this intercession is measured; Abraham moves incrementally from fifty righteous people to ten, seeking a threshold for divine clemency. This measured pleading captures the tension between human advocacy and divine prerogative—a tension that continues to resonate in intercessory prayer across generations. Beyond the words, the narrative situates

Abraham's prayer within a larger covenantal framework. The promises made to him—that his descendants would be numerous and that through him all families of the earth would be blessed (Genesis 12:2-3)—infuse his prayers with weighty expectation. His intercessions are not isolated petitions but embedded within a trust-bound relationship. He is not a supplicant knocking at a distant door but a friend who walks with God, as the text later affirms, "Abraham called upon the name of the Lord" (Genesis 12:8). This phrase, simple yet profound, encapsulates an ongoing life posture of seeking and naming God's presence. Moreover, Abraham's prayers are suffused with hope even amid uncertainty. His dialogue with God over Sodom acknowledges the reality of judgment but also opens a space for divine mercy to flourish. Here, the prayer navigates the fragile balance between human desire for justice and the recognition of divine mystery. It serves as a model for modern spiritual seekers, illustrating that prayer is not passive acquiescence but an active engagement with the Divine will—open, honest, and persistent. Isaac: The Quiet Continuity of CovenantCompared to Abraham's vigorous intercession, Isaac's prayers in the Genesis narrative are more subtle, often overshadowed by the grander stories around him. Nonetheless, Isaac holds a vital place in the unfolding covenantal story and in reflecting a quieter, though no less sincere, mode of prayerful engagement. Though explicit prayers from Isaac are sparse, his life and actions imply a steadfast adherence to the covenant and a mode of prayer characterized by patience and trust. After the death of Abraham, Isaac's repeated re-digging of the wells his father had dug (Genesis 26) serves as a metaphor for a continual, faithful re-connection with the sources of covenantal blessing. This physical action reflects an internal posture of persistence and trust that undergirds prayer itself—the willingness to seek God's provision and presence anew, even when the source seems impeded or contested. Isaac's prayer is perhaps best gleaned from the quiet moments where he encounters God's reaffirmation of the promises. In Genesis 26:2-5, God appears to Isaac and commands him not to go down to Egypt but to stay in the land, promising to bless and multiply his descendants. Isaac's receptive response, though not recorded in words, is manifest in his obedience and faith. Here, prayer reveals itself not only as spoken words but as the lived experience of waiting, listening, and aligning with God's purposes. The emotional tone of Isaac's approach to the Divine is one of reflective trust amid prolonged uncertainty. Isaac inherits the covenantal promises but lacks many of the dramatic experiences that marked Abraham's journey. His path models a quieter resilience, a faithful endurance that marks the daily rhythms of spiritual life. For contemporary believers and seekers, Isaac's example encourages a prayerful posture that embraces patience and quiet confidence, underscoring that not all encounters with God are marked by vocal outpouring; some reveal themselves in steadfastfulness amid the ordinary. Jacob: Wrestling and Transformation in PrayerIf Abraham's prayers reflect pleading and Isaac's endurance reveals quiet trust, Jacob's narrative is the story of wrestling—both literally and figuratively—with God. Jacob's encounters with the Divine poignantly capture the complexity of human-divine relations, blending fear, hope, struggle, and ultimately transformation. His experience elevates prayer from petition to a profound spiritual engagement that shapes identity and destiny. The iconic moment of Jacob's wrestling in Genesis 32:22-32 is a vivid portrayal of this dynamic. On the brink of encountering his estranged brother Esau, Jacob spends the night wrestling with "a man," a mysterious figure revealed to be God or an angel of God. The physical struggle is more than a fight; it is a symbolic representation of Jacob's internal wrestling with fear, guilt, and his relationship with God. Jacob refuses to release the one with whom he wrestles until he receives a blessing. This stubborn grasp, this refusal to let go without divine affirmation, epitomizes a prayer of persistence born out of deep anxiety and hope. This encounter leaves Jacob forever changed; God renames him Israel, "for as a prince hast thou power with God and with men, and hast prevailed" (Genesis 32:28). The name change is more than a personal transformation; it marks the birth of a people, embodying a legacy of enduring engagement with the Divine. Jacob's wrestling prayer captures the raw human experience of seeking God in the midst of uncertainty, fear, and moral complexity. Jacob's prayers throughout Genesis also reveal a pattern of candid expression. Unlike the sometimes formal tone of covenantal promises, Jacob's voice often expresses vulnerability and directness. When he later prays for protection during famine (Genesis 46:3-4), he recalls God's promise to be with him, illustrating faith grounded in remembrance and hope. Moreover, Jacob's entreaties often contain a note of wrestling with divine silence and perceived absence. For instance, in the encounter at Bethel (Genesis 28:10-22), Jacob dreams of the ladder reaching to heaven and hears God's promise reaffirmed. Yet his waking response is marked by a solemn vow, underscoring humanity's desire to forge commitment amid uncertainty. Prayer here is transactional and relational, imbalanced, and deeply human—bridging the mysterious ways God engages with the world and the yearning of the human heart. The Poetic Resonance of Patriarchal Prayer The prayers and intercessions of Abraham, Isaac, and Jacob resonate not only as historical narratives but as poetic articulations of the spiritual journey. The King James Bible presents these prayers with a cadence and language that highlight their enduring beauty and depth. For example, Abraham's pleading over Sodom echoes the rhythm of supplication found in Hebrew poetry—with repetitive questioning that builds tension and emotion. Jacob's wrestling episode breaks into a liminal space of raw vulnerability and triumph, marked by the terse, potent blessing that follows. The silent prayers of Isaac, expressed in faithful obedience, contain their own poetic pulse—a quiet, steady flow beneath the more explicit words of others. This poetic quality invites readers to experience these prayers as living texts—texts that engage the imagination, evoke empathy, and invite participation. They do not simply report historical petitions but invite us into the felt presence of sacred dialogue. The very language of these prayers carries echoes that ripple through centuries, touching the universal human experiences of hope, fear, petition, and transformation . The Divine Presence: Elusive, Yet Faithful. Throughout the patriarchal narratives, the portrayal of God's presence is subtle, fluctuating between revelation and concealment. The Divine appears as both a faithful companion and an elusive mystery—a presence that invites relationship yet maintains an inscrutable otherness. Abraham's sense of God is of a covenant-making God who listens, judges, and acts with justice and mercy. At times, such as when wrestling with the fate of Sodom, God's responses reveal a willingness to engage in human dialogue. Yet, God's presence remains sovereign and ultimately inscrutable, as Abraham's questions do not presuppose full understanding but faith in divine goodness. Isaac's sense of the Divine is quieter, more trusting. He experiences God's promises as a steady underpinning but one that does not always come with dramatic signs. This underscores a form of divine presence that is steady, reliable, fostering endurance rather than dramatic display. Jacob's experience embodies paradox—the encounter with God is both intimate and enigmatic. The physical wrestling is a confrontation with mystery itself, where blessing and struggle co-exist. The elusiveness of God in these narratives invites participants into a deeper wrestling with faith, accepting that divine presence may not be fully grasped but is nonetheless intimately involved. This portrayal aligns closely with modern spiritual experience, where God's presence often feels both near and far, comforting and challenging. The biblical depiction of God as a divine companion who at times hides yet remains faithful models for spiritual seekers, an invitation into trust amid uncertainty . Parallels to the Modern Spiritual Quest The patriarchal prayers from Genesis speak across millennia to the inner experience of every spiritual seeker. Abraham's bold intercession, Isaac's quiet endurance, and Jacob's wrestling with God encapsulate central themes of the spiritual journey: trust, persistence, struggle, and transformation. Modern readers recognize in Abraham the courage to question and plead for justice in a world beset by suffering; in Isaac, the grace of patient faith amid ambiguity; and in Jacob, the raw, often painful engagement with doubt and hope that reshapes identity. These narratives affirm that prayer is not merely formulaic speech but a living interplay of the human heart with the divine mystery. Moreover, the emotional nuances—from pleading to silent waiting, from wrestling to covenantal assurance—mirror the varied moods of contemporary prayer life. They provide models for engaging with God that allow for doubt, honesty, and complexity, rather than sanitized piety. The patriarchal prayers invite seekers to bring their whole selves—fear, hope, curiosity—to the sacred dialogue. In a world often marked by spiritual searching and longing, the experience of these covenantal intercessions encourages a re-imagining of prayer as a deep, transformative encounter rather than mere ritual. They remind us that prayer is a universal language of desire and surrender, shaped by relationship and covenant, persistent in hope, and open to transformation. ConclusionThe intercessions of Abraham, Isaac, and Jacob stand as foundational echoes at the dawn of prayer in biblical tradition. Each patriarch contributes a distinctive voice: Abraham's plaintive, bold petitions; Isaac's enduring, quiet faith; and Jacob's impassioned wrestling with God's enigmatic presence. Together, they map the contours of covenantal trust and human yearning, revealing a relationship with the Divine that is dynamic, multifaceted, and deeply personal. Their prayers, richly textured in language and emotion, invite us into a sacred dialogue that transcends time and culture. They affirm that prayer is not merely a religious act but the very expression of the human soul engaged in search, surrender, and the continual unveiling of divine presence. This ancient constellation of voices continues to shine, guiding believers and seekers alike toward a deeper understanding of prayer's universal significance as both yearning and encounter, struggle and blessing, silence and revelation. In contemplating the patriarchal intercessions, modern readers find an echo of their own spiritual journeys—reminders that prayer is at once wrestling and trust, persistence and hope, and ultimately, the sacred thread that weaves human hearts with the eternal Divine.

Gary E. Risenhoover

Voices of the Prophets: Early Messengers' Intercessory Roles

In the ancient world of the King James Bible, prayer emerges not merely as a personal utterance but as a profound act of intercession—an embodied plea that traverses the space between humanity and the divine. This is nowhere more evident than in the voices of the prophets, early messengers whose prayers assume a communal and national scope, bearing the weight of shared destiny upon their shoulders. These prophets, among them Moses, Samuel, and Elijah, sculpt prayer as a form of spiritual agency—a daring conversation that seeks to mediate between human frailty and divine sovereignty. Their intercessory roles invite us to contemplate prayer's power and complexity, highlighting its enduring relevance for believers and seekers in our own time. From the outset, Moses stands as one of the most poignant exemplars of intercessory prayer within the biblical narrative. His relationship with God is marked by a unique intimacy and boldness. Time and again, Moses steps into the breach, pleading on behalf of the Israelites, who are vulnerable amidst trials and frequent rebellion. The tension is palpable: Moses confronts not merely the physical dangers his people face but also the moral and spiritual jeopardy resulting from their failings. When the Israelites worship the golden calf during Moses' prolonged absence on Mount Sinai, his prayerful intercession embodies both fervent advocacy and righteous indignation. He implores God to remember the promises made to the patriarchs, to preserve His covenant, and ultimately to spare the people from annihilation. Moses' prayers reveal a deep understanding of divine justice tempered with mercy. He recognizes God's holiness and wrath, yet his intercession is suffused with a yearning for forgiveness— not simply for the sake of the people's survival but as a testament to God's own character as a covenantal God. This interplay between justice and mercy forms the heart of prophetic intercession throughout the biblical tradition. Moses' courage to stand in the gap, often risking his own status and safety, sets a paradigm: intercessory prayer involves the urgent, often agonized, assumption of responsibility for others before God. Samuel amplifies this discourse of intercession in a dramatically charged context of transition for Israel. As the last judge and the first prophet to anoint a king, Samuel's prayers are steeped in both political and spiritual significance. His role straddles the line between divine messenger and grassroots advocate, entrusted to vocalize God's will but also to plead for divine favor amid a nation's existential challenges. The biblical account recounts how Samuel intercedes for the people following their rebellion and demand for a human king—a decision that displeases God, signaling a moment of national disobedience and a departure from God's direct rule. Yet, Samuel's commitment to intercession perseveres. When the Philistines threaten Israel's borders and God's judgment looms, Samuel prays with earnest intensity, seeking divine intervention and mercy. His prayers are neither easy surrender to fate nor casual requests; they embody a complex dialogue wrestling with the consequences of sin and the hope for redemption. Through Samuel, prayer becomes a conduit where divine justice confronts human frailty—a spiritual practice exhibiting humility and audacity in tandem. The prophet's intercession also models the necessity of acknowledging communal sinfulness while retaining hope for restoration, a delicate balance that echoes across epochs. Elijah's intercessory prayers, radiant with dramatic power and prophetic authority, further illuminate the role of the prophet as mediator. Set against the backdrop of rampant idolatry and political turmoil in the northern kingdom of Israel, Elijah's prayerful encounters with God are marked by confrontation and revelation. His bold appeals for divine intervention—such as on Mount Carmel, where fire descends to consume the sacrifice, demonstrating God's supremacy over Baal—capture prayer not only as a spiritual exercise but as an existential battleground for truth and justice. Elijah's prayers express the tension between despair and hope. When he flees from Jezebel, fearing for his life, he prays in solitude, revealing a human dimension of vulnerability mingled with determination. His intercessory role is not limited to public pronouncements but encompasses private dialogues that nourish resilience and faith. With Elijah, prayer transcends mere supplication; it is a prophetic act charged with expectancy, invoking God's active presence in the midst of crisis. These examples of prophetic intercession illustrate prayer as a courageous undertaking, requiring faith to voice difficult realities and to trust in God's redemptive purposes amid uncertainty and judgment.Lyrically, the prayers of these prophetic figures resonate as profound echoes of human craving for connection amid divine otherness. Their words embrace lament, petition, confession, and praise, weaving a tapestry that captures the breadth of spiritual experience. The poetic qualities of their prayers deepen their impact, inviting readers into a contemplative space where the sacred and human intertwine. This dimension of prophetic prayer enriches its theological significance, enabling it to function simultaneously as a spiritual practice, a negotiation of justice, and a form of activism. Scholarly insight into the intercessory roles of these prophets reveals the multi-layered nature of their prayers in historical and cultural contexts. Prophetic intercession emerges not in isolation but as embedded within a covenantal framework wherein the prophet acts as mediator between God and God's people. This intermediary role is politically charged, the prophet's prayers carrying the weight of communal identity and destiny. Through their petitions, prophets challenge both divine and human actors, embodying tension and reconciliation in the same breath. The tension within prophetic prayers stems from the dual awareness of God's sovereignty and human responsibility. Prophets pray to God as the ultimate judge and merciful redeemer. They confront divine wrath for communal sin while pleading for forgiveness, revealing prayer as a dialogue of paradoxes—a calling into account and an appeal for grace. This dialectic is part of the prophetic vocation's essence: to hold accountable, to intercede, and to foster hope. For the contemporary Seeker, these ancient intercessions reverberate with current-day significance. In an era marked by social fragmentation, injustice, and uncertainty, the prophetic model of prayer challenges individuals and communities to embrace intercession as an act of solidarity and courage. To pray as Moses, Samuel, or Elijah is to risk vulnerability, to confront uncomfortable truths, and to maintain hope amid turmoil. It invites prayer beyond private devotion toward active engagement with communal realities. Intercessory prayer thus emerges as not only a spiritual discipline but a form of resistance to despair and complicity. It calls upon the Seeker to embody a voice for the voiceless, to plead for mercy in the face of judgment, and to hold a balance between justice and compassion. The prophets teach that prayer is an act of courage, a bridge spanning the distance between human imperfection and divine holiness. Moreover, these prophetic voices affirm that intercession involves deep attentiveness to the divine will, even when it demands confrontation and lament. Prayer is not a simple request for personal desires but a radical openness to God's transformative purposes. Through their prayers, prophets embody the potential for renewal inherent in the human-divine encounter—an encounter that invites participation in the sacred work of healing and restoration. In reflecting upon the intercessory roles of Moses, Samuel, and Elijah, the Seeker encounters a rich tapestry of prayer's universal dimensions: anguish and hope, accountability and grace, justice and mercy. This tapestry invites a reimagining of prayer as an active, participatory dialogue—one that requires courage to engage honestly with suffering and sin, and an unwavering faith in a higher purpose beyond present circumstances. As we listen to the voices of these early messengers echoing across the centuries, we are reminded that prayer's genesis is not merely individual or private but communal and prophetic. It is a calling to stand in the gap, to bear the burdens of others, and to advocate with persistence and humility before the divine throne. These echoes at dawn continue to inspire from the shadowed past into the illumination of present and future, inviting all who seek to embrace the sacred task of intercessory prayer as an enduring expression of faith and love. In sum, the prophetic dimension of prayer as active intercession presents a vivid narrative of dialogue between heaven and earth. Moses' bold petitions for mercy, Samuel's fervent pleas amid national crisis, and Elijah's powerful confrontations with falsehood articulate prayer as a courageous and complex vocation. Their prayers navigate the interplay of justice and mercy, judgment and compassion—a tension that remains deeply relevant as a spiritual and ethical challenge today. As the Seeker contemplates these prophetic voices, the universal significance of intercessory prayer shines forth: a vital, courageous dialogue bridging human frailty and divine sovereignty, inviting all who yearn for transformation to link their voices in humble, hopeful appeal.

Sacred Dialogue: Prayer as Communion with the Divine

Conversations Beyond Words

In the vast tapestry of human expression, prayer stands as one of the most profound and intimate dialogues ever woven—a conversation not only of words but of heartbeats, silences, and the very breath of the soul. To encounter prayer simply as a monologue of requests or a repetitive recital is to miss its deeper dimension: prayer is, fundamentally, communion. It is a sacred exchange in which the human spirit encounters the Divine Presence, an interaction that transcends language, shaping itself within the hushed spaces where words fall away and the soul's yearning is met by a divine embrace. When the King James Bible speaks of prayer, it offers more than formal supplications or petitions; it reveals moments of stillness and surrender that invite us into a shared space beyond speech. The Psalms, a treasury of poetic prayers, often move from articulate pleas for help to unspoken lamentations, from jubilant praise to contemplative silence. Similarly, the New Testament presents Jesus Himself as the model of a one whose prayer life unfolds not merely in words, but in profound communion—the kind that glimmers like candlelight in the darkest recesses of the spirit, flickering with shared presence. This subchapter seeks to explore prayer as this very intimate dialogue: an encounter that does not always require, or even honor, the confines of spoken language. Here, prayer becomes a conversation beyond words—where sighs, silences, and the mere posture of the soul communicate a language of trust, surrender, and listening. It calls the believer and seeker alike into the tender mystery where human frailty meets divine tenderness, where spiritual yearning merges with God's attentive gaze. To understand prayer as a conversation beyond words, one must first recognize that language, while powerful, is inherently limited—especially when it endeavors to express the transcendent. The prayers recorded in the King James Bible, particularly in the Psalms, often give voice to tumultuous emotions that defy simple articulation. In Psalm 42, for example, the psalmist cries out, "Why art thou cast down, O my soul? and why art thou disquieted within me?" Here, the prayer is a raw and vulnerable outpouring, an engagement with God's presence marked not just by words but by an aching silence that lies beneath the cry. Such moments reveal prayer as a sacred dialogue where lament itself is a form of speech, yet also a surrender to the spaces where words fail. Further, there are times in the Psalms that speak to the soul's resonance with God's presence—an experience steeped in silence that invites listening rather than speaking. Psalm 46 declares, "Be still, and know that I am God." In this stillness, the "knowing" is not conveyed through argument or evidence but through an interior listening that emerges only when one ceases to fill the space with human noise. The sacred dialogue here is one of receiving, an opening of the soul that allows the Divine to commune without interruption. This theme of listening and presence is echoed in the New Testament, especially in the life and prayers of Jesus Christ. While many of His prayers are recorded—such as the Lord's Prayer or His words in Gethsemane—the Gospels also suggest the profound value Jesus placed on silent communion with God the Father. For example, the Gospel of Luke records Jesus withdrawing "into the wilderness" or "upon a mountain to pray" (Luke 5:16, 6:12), often alone, where the communication with God transcends words. These instances invite us to consider prayer not only as verbal communication but as an attentiveness to God's presence that may be experienced in silence, in solitude, and in the very act of waiting. In the Upper Room discourse of John's Gospel, Jesus consoles His disciples by promising the Spirit—"the Comforter"—who will dwell within them and guide them into "all truth" (John 14:26). This promise points to an evolving form of prayer where the Holy Spirit communicates internally, speaking through the language of the heart and spirit beyond mere words. The Spirit's indwelling invites believers into an ongoing dialogue where spiritual intuition, deep peace, and spiritual insight form a communion far richer than spoken language alone can depict. Prayer as conversation beyond words is thus not a retreat to silence for silence's sake, but a purposeful entry into the sacred stillness where the soul's deepest longings are visible only to the Divine. It is a flickering candlelight in the sanctuary of the heart, whose glow reveals the contours of intimate presence. This image of prayer calls us to understand that God encounters us not only when we speak eloquently but even when we are mute, weary, or simply present.---The scriptural witness reveals that prayer's deepest communion occurs in a mysterious interplay of presence and surrender. Consider the story of Hannah in 1 Samuel 1, whose silent prayer in the temple is described as moving God's heart though "her lips moved, but her voice was not heard" (1 Samuel 1:13). This moment embodies the unspoken prayer—a communication so profound it transcends audible speech. Hannah's inner groaning reaches God's compassionate ear, a testament that prayerful dialogue invites the soul to speak in the language of presence, trust, and longing. There is something universally human about the need to express what cannot be fully uttered. The biblical language of sighs, groanings, and unspoken cries recognizes this. Romans 8:26 paints a vivid picture of the Spirit that "helpeth our infirmities: for we know not what we should pray for as we ought: but the Spirit itself maketh intercession for us with groanings which cannot be uttered." Here, the divine presence participates in prayer, transforming the inarticulate depths of our hearts into a language that reaches God. This is a sacred dialogue of empathy, where the Spirit becomes the translator of unspoken prayers—a poignant reminder that even when human speech fails, divine communion remains unbroken. The experience of prayer as more than words invites a shift in how believers conceive their relationship with God. It invites a movement away from a simplistic model of asking and receiving toward an enriched understanding of dwelling in the presence of God. Contemplative traditions within Christianity, rooted deeply in the biblical text, have long recognized that the soul's true nourishment emerges not from incessant speaking or demanding but from the silent communion wherein God's presence is both offered and received. To pray in this way is to participate in a sacred dance—sometimes "uttering" the heart's deepest needs, other times simply "being" before God in an embrace of stillness.---Cultivating space for prayer beyond spoken language requires intentionality and openness. In the cacophony of modern life, silence is often elusive. Yet, the scriptures encourage us to seek solitude and quiet as holy ground for dialogue with the Divine. Jesus' instruction to "enter into thy closet, and when thou hast shut thy door, pray to thy Father which is in secret" (Matthew 6:6) models this practice. The "closet" can be understood not only as a physical space but as a metaphor for the inner sanctuary of the soul, where distractions fall away and authentic conversation with God can unfold. Creating this sacred space often begins with simple acts of presence: being still, breathing deeply, attuning oneself to the rhythm of God's nearness. It implies surrender—releasing control over the content, flow, or outcomes of prayer. Instead of demanding from God, one learns to listen. This posture of listening invites us into the trust that God's presence accompanies us even when words are absent or insufficient. The Psalms again provide a reservoir of imagery and insight on this spiritual posture. In Psalm 62:1–2, the psalmist declares, "Truly my soul waiteth upon God: from him cometh my salvation. He only is my rock and my salvation; he is my defence." Waiting upon God here is not a passive act but an active, expectant presence filled with trust—a silence pregnant with hope. Such waiting becomes an integral form of prayer where intimacy is born not from the quantity of words but the quality of attention. Jesus' own life exemplifies this balance between speaking and silent communion. His prayers, as recorded in the Gospels, fluctuate between powerful petitions and peaceful resting in the Father's presence. In John 11:41–42, before raising Lazarus, Jesus prays aloud but concludes, "I knew that thou hearest me always." This statement expresses a relationship grounded neither in repetitive speech nor in anxious pleading but in steadfast confidence that communion is constant, intimate, and wordless if need be. The metaphor of candlelight flickering in a sacred space within the soul captures beautifully the essence of prayer as communion. Candlelight is gentle and uneven—it does not blind or demand but softly illuminates, creating a space where shadows and light mingle. In this sacred interior where prayer dwells, human presence—fragile and finite—meets Divine Presence, eternal and boundless. The flickering flame symbolizes the dynamic, living nature of this dialogue: sometimes steady and bright; at times wavering and faint; yet always offering warmth and illumination. This flicker of prayer, held in the quiet heart of communion, points to the tender mystery that prayer is not solely transactional but transformational. Each moment of silent presence before God subtly shifts the contours of the soul. Trust deepens, surrender unfolds, and listening opens the heart to receive new life. The scriptures affirm that such encounters shape us, slow the pounding nervousness of the flesh, and awaken us to a richer existence in God's fellowship. In contemplating prayer this way, believers and seekers alike are called to approach prayer not merely as an activity or obligation but as an ongoing conversation that honors both speech and silence. There is sacred language in sighs and groans, in breath held and released before God. Such moments are not emptiness but fullness—presence without the clutter of words—that speaks deeply of the inner life of faith. To embrace prayer as conversation beyond words is to acknowledge that Divine communion often dwells in the unseen. The Apostle Paul's vision of spiritual reality underscores this: "For now we see through a glass, darkly; but then face to face" (1 Corinthians 13:12). Much of our prayer life on this earth is veiled, comprising feelings and longings that find expression in incomplete language or in silence. Yet, the promise of divine presence assures us that these moments matter profoundly. The silence within prayer is not God's absence but a holy space where our spirits meet His—the sacred room where mutual love dwells. This awareness invites readers of the King James Bible—and all who seek a deeper spiritual life— to foster practices that nurture such silent dialogues. Practices such as contemplative meditation, attentive breath prayer, or simply resting in

God's presence without an agenda become ways to enter into the sacred dialogue beyond conventional language. These disciplines cultivate a heart posture of surrender and listening, enabling the Divine to speak in the depths where words cannot reach. The scriptural tradition offers countless examples and affirmations that God desires relationship more than ritual, presence over performance, and communion beyond words. The ancient Hebrew understanding of prayer, integrated into the spiritual rhythm of the biblical text, encompasses sighs, cryings, and silent meditations alike. Thus, prayer's universal significance transcends cultural or religious boundaries—it is an expression of humanity's deepest impulse: to connect with the sacred mystery that undergirds all existence. In closing, the experience of prayer as conversation beyond words is a call to return again and again to the sacred spaces within. It is an invitation to place aside anxious striving and incessant speech and instead rest in the flickering presence of the Divine One who listens, understands, and loves without condition. This dialogue, tender and mysterious, moves beyond the boundaries of spoken language into the realm where trust is nurtured, surrender embraces, and soul communes with Spirit. May all who seek prayer's true essence discover that in moments of silence, sighs, and stillness, they are not alone. Rather, they dwell in holy conversation—one heart to Another—where human and Divine Presence merge in mysterious but tender intimacy. This is the echo of the Divine within us, the silent song of communion that prayer calls us to hear and cherish beyond words.

Surrender and Trust in Prayer

In the quiet spaces between our breaths, within the chambers of the heart that yearn for assurance and peace, prayer emerges not merely as a recitation of words but as a profound act of surrender. It is in this yielding—an offering of oneself to the unknown mysteries of divine will—that prayer reveals its deepest power. The King James Bible, with its majestic blend of poetry and narrative, gives voice to a myriad of souls who, bound by uncertainty yet buoyed by faith, embody this sacred paradox. Among these voices, the figure of Hannah stands luminous, a beacon illuminating how surrender and trust intertwine to create a spiritual freedom that transcends circumstance.Hannah's story, nestled within the pages of 1 Samuel, unfolds like a sacred choreography of hope wrestled free from despair. Childless and heartbroken, she approaches the tabernacle with a silent anguish that soon breaks forth in vehement prayer. Her words are raw, her plea urgent, yet within this toil of spirit there is something profoundly instructive: the gesture of surrender that undergirds her supplication. She makes a vow, committing the fruit of her petition—a child—to the service of God, a covenant that both acknowledges her limited control and proclaims unwavering trust. In this act, her prayer is not a demand imposed upon the divine; rather, it is a yielding, a tender release into the hands that hold all things. This tension between human agency and divine sovereignty pulses throughout biblical accounts of prayer. The believer prays in earnest, pouring forth desires, hurts, and hopes, yet simultaneously embraces an attitude of openness to the answer that may not align with personal will. Such disposition requires a relinquishment that is neither passive resignation nor fearful capitulation, but an active, courageous entrusting. It reflects a faith that does not clutch desperately at outcomes, but rests in the assurance that the divine purpose, however obscured, is good and will ultimately bring renewal and peace. The King James Bible's rich poetic cadence accentuates this interplay beautifully, inviting readers to meditate not solely on the content of prayer but on its movement—the flow between the self and the Divine. Consider the psalms, where the psalmist often cries out in lament and sorrow, yet shifts seamlessly into declarations of trust. "Commit thy way unto the Lord; trust also in him," exhorts Psalm 37:5, creating a rhythm where surrender births confidence. The act of committing here is a metaphor of laying down baggage, releasing the burdens we carry, and allowing divine guidance to direct the path. It is a deliberate choice to relinquish control while simultaneously claiming the strength born from divine intimacy. In surrender, the believer encounters a paradoxical liberation. The relinquishment of control is not loss but gain; it is the unshackling of the soul from the tyranny of anxious striving. This spiritual freedom shines forth most clearly when prayer ceases to be a means of manipulating divine will to human ends, and becomes instead a channel of communion—a sacred dialogue where the heart listens as much as it speaks. To surrender in prayer is thus to enter a relationship where vulnerability is met with grace, doubt with assurance, and confusion with clarity. The narratives of other biblical figures deepen this understanding of prayer as yielding trust. Abraham's intercession for Sodom teaches an imploring boldness that simultaneously respects divine justice. Moses' prayers in the wilderness echo a persistent dependence amid uncertainty; his dialogues with God reveal an intimacy forged through honesty and openness, not mere ritualistic adherence. Even Jesus, in the Garden of Gethsemane, models the ultimate surrender: a heart fully aligned with the Father's will, petitioning firmly yet submitting wholly. "Not my will, but thine, be done," He prays, embodying the profound truth that surrender does not negate personal desire but elevates it into divine harmony. This emotional landscape of prayer—between heartfelt yearning and the calm surrender to divine sovereignty—is where the human spirit is most deeply engaged. The delicate balance calls forth a trust that must be continually nurtured, for it is in the fragility of this balanced stance that growth occurs. The reader is invited not merely to witness these biblical testimonies, but to inhabit them, allowing the poetic expressions to resonate within their own experience. Here, the heart finds a language for its own struggles and longings, discovering that surrender in prayer is a pathway to transformation. Surrender does not erase the difficulty of waiting or the pain of unanswered questions; rather, it rests in the sacred tension, holding both despair and hope in the same breath. This duality echoes through the words of Hannah as she moves from anguish to assurance, from pleading to praise. It is a dance that invites patience—to wait upon the Lord, trusting that in His timing, the broken shall be mended, and the empty places filled. To yield fully in prayer is to open oneself to the mystery of divine timing and purpose, a mystery that challenges the human impulse for certainty and control. This openness is a spiritual posture of humble expectancy, a readiness to accept whatever response unfolds. It acknowledges that the divine wisdom guiding human lives often transcends immediate understanding, yet it fosters a peace that surpasses all reason. The King James Bible does not shy from portraying the rawness of such surrender. The psalms, for instance, repeatedly voice the anguish, the laments, and the cries of abandonment, yet these emotions are embedded within a context of trust and hope. Psalm 42:11 asks, "Why art thou cast down, O my soul? and why art thou disquieted within me? hope thou in God: for I shall yet praise him for the help of his countenance." The intimate invitation here is to recognize emotional turmoil without losing sight of the trust that sustains prayer's journey. Such poetic wisdom calls every believer and seeker to a meditation on their own posture before the divine. Can one relinquish the urge for total control, embracing instead the freedom of surrender? Can the heart learn to trust a sovereign God, who though unseen, is intimately aligned with the deepest good of creation? It is within this tension that prayer finds its transformative power, a power not reliant on the bending of divine will to human desire, but upon a spiritual alliance born of reverence, love, and unwavering hope. This subchapter, then, is an invitation to explore the sacred dynamics of surrender and trust in prayer—two aspects so interwoven that they form the very fabric of a faithful spiritual life. Drawing inspiration from biblical exemplars like Hannah, our prayers become less about commanding answers and more about entering into a relationship where authenticity, vulnerability, and persistence converge into sacred dialogue. Such dialogue honors the mystery of the divine will while embracing the human longing for connection and healing. As readers journey deeper into this understanding, they discover that surrender in prayer is far from weakness; it is the source of true strength. It is the courageous act of laying down one's burdens and expectations, stepping into uncertainty with a heart open to divine guidance. In this yielding, there is a profound rebirth—a soul unburdened, a spirit restored, and a life aligned with the eternal purpose from which all blessings flow. Thus, the paradox of control and surrender becomes a sacred dance in which prayer is both expression and encounter, petition and praise, lament and hope. It is the melody of trust that ceases to demand and begins to listen, the music of a heart harmonizing with the Divine. In this harmony, prayer fulfills its highest calling—a communion not only of voice but of spirit, a surrender that leads into the freedom of divine embrace. By embracing this delicate balance, believers and seekers alike enter a space where prayer transcends circumstance, becoming a transformative expression of faith and hope. It is here, in the yield of trust, that the soul tastes the true essence of prayer—a sacred dialogue marked by surrender, rich with possibility, and alive with the presence of the Divine.

The Divine Presence Among Us

In the quiet sanctuary of prayer, beyond the spoken words and the fervent yearning of the soul, there lingers an ineffable presence—one that cannot be fully captured by language but is keenly felt as the very atmosphere in which prayer breathes and moves. This presence, the Divine Presence among us, is not merely an idea or a theological construct; it is the living reality that embraces the human heart in its moments of seeking, surrender, and communion. It is at once majestic and tender, vast and intimate, a subtle grace that colors every prayerful encounter with hues both luminous and gentle. To approach the Divine Presence is to step into a realm where time slows and the boundaries between heaven and earth blur. It is an ambient character woven into the fabric of prayer itself, a presence that neither demands nor overwhelms but lingers like the soft glow of dawn before the sun fully rises. In this sacred space, the soul senses a nearness that transcends physicality, a nearness that becomes the very air we breathe as we speak to God, listen for God, or simply rest in the stillness of holy communion. The King James Bible, with its majestic cadence and enduring imagery, offers profound glimpses into this presence. Time and again the Scriptures invoke not only the words spoken to God but the palpable nearness of God's Spirit, imbuing moments of prayer with a weighty, almost tangible reality. The psalmist declares, "Thou art about my path, and about my bed, and spiest out all my ways" (Psalm 139:3), painting an intimate portrait of divine watchfulness and care that surrounds the believer continually. Here, the Divine Presence is not distant or detached but intimately engaged, enveloping the believer's daily journey with a tender but majestic vigilance. The presence of God, as revealed throughout the biblical narrative, often dwells in spaces of profound quiet and reverence. Moses encountered this presence not in the storm or tempest but in the still, small voice upon the mountain (1 Kings 19:12). The tabernacle, and later the temple, was consecrated as a dwelling place for God's glory—a place where heaven touched earth and the divine presence settled visibly and palpably among the people. Yet, the prophets and psalmists remind us that this presence is not confined by walls of stone. It is as pervasive as the air itself, as close as our next breath. Consider the experience of the prophet Ezekiel who, by the river Chebar, saw the throne of God borne above living creatures, radiant with indescribable glory (Ezekiel 1). Though heavenly and overwhelming, this vision reveals the complexity of Divine Presence —one that can overwhelm the senses yet also draw the heart into worship and awe. In this overwhelming majesty, there is also a deep softness. We glimpse this balance when the Psalmist writes, "He healeth the broken in heart, and bindeth up their wounds" (Psalm 147:3). The Divine Presence is both a consuming fire and a healing balm, igniting our spirits and soothing our sorrows. To experience this presence today, in our personal prayers and communal worship, is to inhabit a sacred tension between mystery and familiarity. It is to feel the hush of grace mingled with the chorus of longing, the weight of divine majesty held alongside the warmth of tender love. This duality is reflected in the King James Bible's rich lexicon—words like holy , glory , mercy , and comfort point us toward an encounter with a presence that is at once otherworldly and profoundly personal. Let us pause here, inviting the reader to lean into a moment of contemplative stillness. Close your eyes and breathe deeply.

Imagine a vast canopy of endless sky stretching above and within you—a canopy that simultaneously shelters and reveals. Sense the silent stirring of something far greater than yourself, an invisible presence that presses gently against the edges of your awareness like a soft wind bending the branches. This presence neither demands nor flees but waits in patient grace to be met. Feel the comfort of this Divine Presence—majestic yet tender—wrapping softly around your heart. Such an invitation mirrors the biblical portrayal of prayer as conversation with a God who inhabits the fullness of heaven and yet dwells within the depths of the human soul. The Apostle Paul, writing to the faithful, reminds us that "the Spirit itself beareth witness with our spirit, that we are the children of God" (Romans 8:16). In this mutual indwelling—the Spirit in us and we in God—lies the essence of Divine Presence. It is not distant theology but an experiential truth accessible in every moment of sincere prayer. Moreover, this presence activates an awareness beyond words. Sometimes in prayer, the soul speaks in silence; the tongue is still, but the spirit communes. This silent dwelling is not emptiness but fullness—a space where the Divine Presence saturates all that we are. The Psalmist echoes this experience: "Be still, and know that I am God" (Psalm 46:10). The stillness is not an absence of activity, but the sacred soil where the Divine Presence is sensed most clearly, where one's entire being is arranged around the divine mystery as a flower opens to the morning light. It is this atmospheric richness—the intertwining of majesty and tenderness, silence and speech, transcendence and immanence—that gives prayer its profound texture. Prayer, then, is never a solitary act of speaking into the void; it is an encounter with one who is present in the depths of our being and the heights of eternity. Every utterance and every silence becomes a thread woven into the great tapestry of sacred dialogue. To deepen this awareness, let us return to biblical imagery, harvesting from the rich soil of poetic metaphor to paint the contours of Divine Presence. In Isaiah's vision, the seraphim call out in worship around the throne: "Holy, holy, holy, is the Lord of hosts: the whole earth is full of his glory" (Isaiah 6:3). The repetition of "holy" intensifies the experience of divine otherness, while the earth's filling with glory speaks of presence that saturates the entire cosmos—impossible to see fully but impossible to ignore. In this cosmic fullness, the Divine Presence is the eternal source from which all life springs and the final destination to which all souls turn. Yet, even as the heavens declare God's glory, the biblical text does not overlook the tender nearness of God to the lowly and brokenhearted. The psalmist's words offer reassurance: "The Lord is nigh unto them that are of a broken heart; and saveth such as be of a contrite spirit" (Psalm 34:18). Here the majestic presence becomes intimate, almost palpably close—a refuge and sanctuary. The divine gaze is not cold or distant but compassionate and attentive, attuned to the subtle cries of the soul. Such imagery invites us to experience prayer not simply as a practice but as an inhabited space. Imagine yourself entering a vast cathedral, but not one built of stone and mortar—one crafted from light, breath, and silence. As you step into this sacred place, the air is thick with the presence of grace, and you become aware of being held in a circle of unseen but tangible love. Every whispered prayer, every rising sigh, is caught by this presence and folded into the eternal song of creation. In our modern world, often marked by noise, haste, and fragmentation, this sense of divine nearness can feel elusive. Yet, the King James Bible's enduring resonance guides us back to the sacred center. Its majestic language calls us to "lift up your hands in the sanctuary, and bless the Lord" (Psalm 134:2), beckoning us into spaces where the Divine Presence is more than a theological concept—it becomes an atmospheric reality, a living embrace. The mystics and poets throughout the ages have sought to give voice to this experience, translating the biblical metaphors into modern language that awakens the senses. Consider the words of one contemporary poet who writes:> "Between each breath, a space enfolds, > Where whispers of the sacred fold. > Not thunderous but soft and near, > The presence comes—a silent seer."Here, the Divine Presence is a quiet witness, a gentle reality that neither demands fanfare nor is diminished by silence. It is a presence sensed in the subtle movements of the soul, an ambient grace that saturates moments of prayer and unfolds into daily life. We might also draw from the imagery of light that pervades the biblical text. "Thy word is a lamp unto my feet, and a light unto my path" (Psalm 119:105) speaks not only of divine guidance but of a presence that glows softly in our darkness. This light is neither blinding nor distant, but suffuses the environment of prayer with warmth and clarity. In moments when prayer feels difficult or the soul weary, allowing this light to fill the interior rooms of our heart can be a profound solace—the calm certainty that we are not alone. To help the reader embody this experience, try now a brief contemplative exercise:Sit quietly, with your eyes closed or softly focused. Begin by breathing slowly, deeply. Allow your awareness to settle on the rise and fall of your breath. As you inhale, imagine drawing in a gentle light—a presence both majestic and tender. As you exhale, release tension, doubt, or any sense of distance. Invite this presence to fill the space around and within you. Picture it as a soft glow, like dawn's first light touching the sleeping earth. Sense it as a loving companion, patient and near. Wait in the stillness without expectation, simply resting in the reality that something greater than yourself is here, now—present, watching, listening. Let your heart open like a flower unfolding to the sun. As you step back into the world of words and actions, carry this felt sense of divine nearness with you. Know that prayer's power does not lie solely in the petitions we voice or the doctrines we affirm but in this quiet communion—the delicate yet enduring presence that embraces us with infinite grace. This presence, as the Scriptures reveal, is not an abstraction but a person—the living God who chooses to dwell among us. The prologue of the Gospel of John declares, "And the Word was made flesh, and dwelt among us" (John 1:14). The original Greek term for "dwelt" (ἐσκήνωσεν, eskenosen) literally means "tabernacled" or "pitched a tent." This signals not a fleeting visitation but a deliberate, intimate abiding. The Divine Presence is not confined to distant realms but pitches its tent within human history, within human hearts, inviting all into a shared dwelling of sacred conversation. In light of this, every prayer becomes a sacred meeting place, a holy threshold where heaven grazes earth and the infinite touches the finite. The sense of divine presence that pervades these moments is neither grandiose nor faint—it is an atmospheric richness that transforms the very quality of our spiritual life. It fills the emptiness with hope, the silence with comfort, and the longing with assurance. To pray, then, is to enter not just into speech but into presence. The prayers of David, Hannah, Solomon, Mary, and countless others are testimonies to this—living expressions of hearts communing with a God who is both transcendent Sovereign and near Father, awe-inspiring Majesty and tender Comforter. They reflect the fullness of an encounter in which the divine mingles with the human, in which the air vibrates with sacred resonance. Before we close this reflection, consider once more the invitation extended by the psalmist: "O taste and see that the Lord is good: blessed is the man that trusteth in him" (Psalm 34:8). This tasting and seeing is not a physical act but a spiritual experience—the manifestation of Divine Presence that can be known and sensed in prayer, however humble or grand.Here, dear reader, is the heart of sacred dialogue: the recognition that in every lifted voice, in every whispered thought, and in every silent pause, there breathes a Divine Presence. This presence does not merely listen; it enfolds, it heals, it transforms. It is the eternal companion of the soul's journey—the sacred atmosphere in which the dance of prayer unfolds. May this awareness illumine your own moments of communion, beckoning you deeper into the profound reality that the Divine Presence is not afar but within, around, and among us—majestic in glory, tender in love, eternal in grace.

Prayer as Relationship: The Seeker's Journey

In the quiet spaces between breaths and the rising dawns of new hope, prayer emerges as more than mere words or ritual acts; it becomes the living thread that weaves the seeker's heart to the divine. Prayer as relationship unfolds not as a static moment but as a vibrant, evolving conversation — one that carries the seeker through seasons of doubt and faith, despair and joy, silence and revelation. This journey is uniquely personal yet universally resonant, reflecting the deepest yearnings and the most sacred discoveries of humanity's soul. To understand prayer this way is to enter into a dialogue not only with God but also with oneself, the world, and the very mystery of existence. It is a sacred interchange where voice meets voice, heart meets heart, and presence meets presence. Here, the seeker is not a passive petitioner but an active participant, growing through encounters real and imagined, informed by scripture and shaped by lived experience. Consider the biblical narrative as a sacred map illustrating this intimate journey. The Psalms, for example, pulse with the seeker's voice — cries of anguish, songs of praise, whispers of longing, and declarations of steadfast trust. King David's prayers reveal a man deeply engaged in an ongoing conversation with God, at times bold and boldfaced in his requests, at others melancholy in his doubts, yet always leaning into the covenantal relationship that sustains his soul. This is the invitation: to bring all facets of our humanity into the dialogue with the Divine, trusting that the relationship will deepen as we do. Such intimacy is vividly embodied in the story of Jacob wrestling with God by night (Genesis 32:22–32). The very metaphor of struggle conveys the dynamism of prayer as relationship. Jacob does not receive immediate answers, nor does he emerge unscathed. Instead, he encounters God in a tangible way, wrestling through confusion and fear toward transformation. His new name, Israel, meaning "one who struggles with God," captures the paradox of prayer: it is both battle and embrace, resistance and surrender. For the seeker, this story affirms that prayer is a space where honesty, tension, and persistence lead not only to understanding but also to a new identity. Prayer as a relationship also embraces silence and waiting, aspects often overlooked in hurried spiritual practice. The prophet Habakkuk models this tension in his prayer: "O LORD, how long shall I cry, and thou wilt not hear? even cry out unto thee of violence, and thou wilt not save?" (Habakkuk 1:2). His words ring with frustration and expectation, a dialogue stretched across uncertainty. Yet ultimately, Habakkuk's prayer culminates in a profound declaration of faith: "Though the fig tree shall not blossom... Yet I will rejoice in the LORD" (Habakkuk 3:17–18). This progression maps the seeker's path from complaint to trust, highlighting how prayer as relationship endures through seasons where answers remain hidden. Entering this sacred dialogue invites the seeker into layered storytelling, where biblical voices and personal narratives intertwine. Imagine sitting around an ancient campfire with these figures—David, Jacob, Habakkuk—each sharing their prayers and reflections. Their voices echo through time, resonating with the deepest questions and hopes. "How do I speak when I feel unseen?" "Where is God when I wrestle with fear?" "Can I rejoice without certainty?" These questions do not demand quick solutions but open a space for the seeker's own voice to arise, layered with honesty and yearning. This dialogical encounter blossoms further when scripture itself becomes a conversation partner. Take the Lord's Prayer (Matthew 6:9–13), an archetype of communal and personal prayer. It begins by addressing God as "Our Father," immediately situating prayer in relational and familial terms. The petition for "daily bread" speaks to immediate need, while "forgive us our debts" and "lead us not into temptation" reflect shared ethical awareness and dependence. Through this prayer, the seeker learns that relationship with the Divine includes both intimacy and accountability, provision and guidance. Guided meditations grounded in such scriptural texts encourage seekers to move beyond intellectual understanding toward experiential knowing. For example, a meditation on the Beatitudes frames prayer as oriented toward transformation: "Blessed are the poor in spirit... The meek... The merciful." Each beatitude is an invitation to internalize divine values and open relational channels that shape prayer's texture. As seekers meditate, they engage not only with words but with the realities those words evoke—humility, compassion, justice. Prayer, then, becomes relational formation, where the seeker's heart is shaped in the image of the Divine's compassion. This formation underscores an essential facet of prayer as relationship: it is ongoing. It does not reach a final resolution in a single moment or in a chapter of life but evolves with the seeker's changing understanding and experience. A mother praying by her child's bedside, a youth wrestling with doubt, an elder praising in quiet gratitude—all reveal different facets of this journey. Their prayers may vary in tone, depth, urgency, and content, yet all participate in the same unfolding dialogue. Yet the seeker's journey is not solely inward. Prayer as relationship gently extends outward into the communal and cosmic. When Jesus teaches his disciples how to pray, the intention is collective and inclusive—"Our Father." This plural pronoun reminds all seekers that prayer connects individuals to the larger body of believers and to creation itself. The relationship with the Divine is therefore mirrored in the relationships we hold with one another, inviting accountability, mutual care, and solidarity. Even when prayer feels private or hidden, it participates in this greater web of connection. The woman who silently offers thanks in her heart, the man who cries out from the depths of agony, the child who prays with naïve trust—all are linked within a communal tapestry of faith, hope, and love. Prayer, in this way, reflects and sustains the relational rhythm that holds not only human beings but creation in delicate balance. In the seeker's own experience, these connections may surface as moments of profound insight or quiet assurance—what the mystics call "the cloud of unknowing," where absence becomes presence and silence becomes voice. The King James Bible's archaic but richly poetic language evokes this sense vividly; phrases like "thy rod and thy staff they comfort me" (Psalm 23:4) or "behold, I stand at the door, and knock" (Revelation 3:20) breathe with relational intimacy, blending vulnerability and strength. To enter this sacred relationship is to embrace vulnerability—not as weakness but as openness to the Divine's transformative presence. The seeker's voice, with all its questions, laments, and hopes, finds welcome in this space. The poem-like cadences of scripture invite the heart to shape its language anew, drawing us beyond the superficial to the profound depths where intimate communion dwells. Practically, embracing prayer as relationship means carving intentional moments for dialogue amid life's noise. It requires trust that the Divine listens and responds, though not always as expected or timed by human desire. It calls for perseverance when silence seems unbroken, groundedness when emotions fluctuate, and humility when certainty gives way to mystery. Stories of seekers across time illuminate this lived reality. Saint Teresa of Ávila described prayer as a "friendly conversation with the one who we know loves us," highlighting warmth rather than formality. Similarly, King David's psalms, with their raw honesty, remind us that the Divine does not require polished words but yearnings poured forth in sincerity. Contemporary seekers continue to testify that prayer as relationship nourishes their souls, providing a steady light through shifting shadows. As the journey unfolds, prayer shapes the seeker's identity. Like Jacob's transformation to Israel, each encounter molds character, perspective, and purpose. Prayer moves from asking for change to becoming the change: embodying mercy, extending forgiveness, living in hope. The seeker becomes a partner in divine work, participating in healing, justice, and love. This transformation also reveals a paradox of prayer: though it often begins by addressing God, its ultimate fruit is found in the seeker's life and relationships with others. The relational thread extends outward, weaving individual experience into the broader narrative of God's presence in the world. To assist readers in entering this experience, a series of guided reflections may accompany their journey: Invitation to the Hidden Place: Imagine yourself sitting with the psalmist in a quiet sanctuary. Hear their words echo: "Create in me a clean heart, O God." Speak aloud your own sincerest longing. Let silence receive your words as part of the dialogue . Wrestling at Midnight: Recall Jacob's nighttime struggle—bring your fears, questions, and resistance before the Divine. Feel the tension and release as part of ongoing relationship. What name—what new understanding—might arise from your struggle? Listening in the Silence: Sit in stillness, waiting without demand for response. Embrace the rhythm of breath as a conversation. Notice what feelings or thoughts arise. Trust that this silence is itself a form of communion. Shared Bread, Shared Life: Reflect on the Lord's Prayer. How does this ancient text invite you into shared presence with God and others? What daily bread do you seek—not only physically but spiritually and emotionally? Walking the Beatitudes: Slowly meditate on each beatitude, inviting its qualities to supplant impatience, pride, or fear. How does living these blessings shape your prayer life as relational practice? Together, these meditations help cultivate a posture of openness and intimacy, reinforcing the notion that prayer is an ongoing conversation marked by discovery, surrender, and transformation. Ultimately, the seeker's journey through prayer reveals that relationship with the Divine is both the journey and the destination. It is marked not by perfect knowledge or uninterrupted peace but by the faithful movement toward connection, the courage to keep speaking and listening, and the willingness to be transformed by the encounter. Prayer as relationship is the echo of the Divine's call and the seeker's response—a dialogue that never ceases, inviting every person into the sacred dance of presence and grace. This dialogue transcends the bounds of creed or culture, reaching to the heart of what it means to be human. In every whispered plea, every song of joy, every silent pause, the seeker finds themselves met and known, loved and formed, drawn ever onward toward the Divine mystery that both surpasses and invites our deepest selves. May this understanding inspire the reader to embrace their own prayers as living, breathing conversation; a sacred relationship where questions are welcomed, discoveries cherished, and love continually revealed. The journey is ongoing, the dialogue unfolding—always opening into new horizons of communion with the Divine.

Colors of Hope: The Transformative Power of Prayers

Luminescence in Despair

In the deepest caverns of human suffering, where shadows stretch long and hope seems a distant and flickering ember, prayer emerges not as a mere ritual but as a luminous beacon—an indispensable light that cuts through despair. It is within the sacred pages of the King James Bible that we find the most profound testament to prayer's power, a power that shines brightest not amid triumph, but in the midst of desolation. The prayers of Job, David, and Jonah stand as eternal gold threads, weaving rays of hope through the bleakest valleys of life's trials, offering us lessons on courage, resilience, and divine communion when all seems lost. This subchapter, then, is an intimate journey into those sacred moments where prayer becomes the alchemy that transmutes sorrow into strength, emptiness into renewal, and darkness into a hopeful dawn. The story of Job is perhaps the richest and most poignant portrayal of prayer amid despair. Job's story is not simply that of suffering; it is a vast spiritual confrontation—a raw and honest wrestling with pain, confusion, and the seeming silence of God. From the ashes of his affliction, Job's prayers break forth, not in polished perfection but in profound, unvarnished truth. In Job 3:11, he cries out, "Why did I not perish at birth, and die as I came from the womb?" Here lies the stark reality of human suffering; the prayer is almost a desperate lament, a questioning of existence itself. Yet it is precisely this vulnerable outpouring that transforms his prayers into golden threads of hope. They are threads sown through his spiritual agony, connecting him, however tenuously, to the divine. Job's prayers reflect the remarkable human capacity to hold grief and faith in the same breath. Even when expressing anger or confusion, Job's words remain prayers—an unbroken dialogue with God. They reveal a sacred trust, a faith so deeply rooted that it endures even amid the harshest storms. In Job 1:21, uttered after the loss of all his children and possessions, Job declares, "The Lord gave, and the Lord hath taken away; blessed be the name of the Lord." This paradoxical affirmation is a luminous strand woven through despair, embodying an unfaltering hope that transcends immediate pain. His prayer is a courageous act because it does not deny suffering; rather, it embraces it and persists in faith despite it. In this embrace, prayer serves as a spiritual anchor. The luminescence that arises from Job's dialogue with God is not an erasure of his agony but an invitation to coexist with it amid the divine presence. His story teaches us that prayer, even when steeped in lament and confusion, possesses the power to rekindle faith's fragile flame in dark seasons. It illumines the heart, enabling a resilience born not of denial but of acceptance and trust—a trust that God's justice and love will ultimately prevail beyond human understanding. Similarly, the psalms of David offer a breathtaking panorama of prayer as a courageous defiance of despair. David's life was marked by tumult—betrayals, flight from enemies, personal sin, and profound loss. Yet, in the face of such relentless adversity, his prayers resound with an extraordinary luminescence. The imagery he employs paints prayer as more than petition; it is a vital lifeline, a sacred rebellion against despair's crushing weight. In Psalm 42:11 he asks, "Why art thou cast down, O my soul? and why art thou disquieted within me? hope thou in God: for I shall yet praise him, who is the health of my countenance, and my God." Here, David openly acknowledges his internal darkness, yet his prayer is firmly tethered to hope. The metaphor of hope as a bright light in the shadowed soul transforms prayer into an active, living force. David's prayers illustrate that to pray is to fight despair not with denial but with affirmation—a radical trust in God's presence and deliverance even when all appears lost. His enduring refrain of praise amid hardship reflects a luminous spirit, a vitality that refuses to be quenched. Prayer thus becomes a crucible wherein sorrow is reshaped into spiritual resilience. Within David's prayers, imagery abounds that evokes golden threads stitching possibility into the fabric of suffering. He speaks of God as a rock, a fortress, and a shield (Psalm 18:2), depicting divine protection as a steadfast source of light and strength amid tempestuous nights. The symbolism intertwines prayer with hope, suggesting that to reach out to God is to grasp a thread of golden light that binds the soul to life itself. Jonah's story offers yet another remarkable example of prayer as luminescence amid despair, though his narrative introduces complexity in how prayer transforms human resistance and fear. Jonah's initial flight from God's command reveals a heart burdened by dread and rebellion. Yet, it is within the belly of the great fish where the depth of his despair becomes literal—surrounded by darkness, engulfed by the inevitability of death. Here, Jonah's prayer in Jonah 2:2–9 is startlingly intimate and evocative:"I cried by reason of mine affliction unto the Lord, and he heard me; out of the belly of hell cried I, and thou heardest my voice. For thou hadst cast me into the deep, in the midst of the seas; and the floods compassed me about... I will sacrifice unto thee with the voice of thanksgiving; I will pay that I have vowed. Salvation is of the Lord." Within this prayer, vivid imagery conjures a contrast between profound darkness and the heart's ascending light. The "belly of hell" and "depth of the seas" symbolize the crushing despair surrounding Jonah, yet his words pivot to a declaration of thanksgiving and hope—"Salvation is of the Lord." His prayer is a triumphant beam piercing the shadow, transforming his terrifying confinement into a space of spiritual renewal. Jonah's emergence from the fish is emblematic of prayer's alchemical power—how surrender amid despair births resurgence. His prayer was not merely an escape mechanism but a profound act of inner transformation. It represents the moment when despair's darkness is transmuted into the light of repentance, trust, and renewed purpose. Here, prayer's luminescence is as much a light within as it is a beacon calling outward, proclaiming deliverance to the world. Reflecting upon these scriptural narratives, one perceives a profound theological truth: prayer in despair is not passive submission but dynamic resistance, a courageous assertion of faith's tenacity amid life's shadowed valleys. The golden threads of prayer that weave through Job's lament, David's psalms, and Jonah's supplication form an unbroken chain that binds human hearts to the divine promise. They reveal prayer as the communion that sustains hope when human strength is depleted. This transformative power of prayer has echoes far beyond the biblical text—it resonates profoundly with the human experience across cultures and eras. To pray in despair is to orient one's soul toward the invisible yet palpable radiance of the divine presence, to grasp with trembling hands a thread of light when faced with overwhelming darkness. It is an act of courageous vulnerability, surrender, and yet, paradoxically, potent strength. In personal meditation upon these examples, one discovers that such prayer invites a reimagining of sorrow itself. Sorrow need not be the death knell of faith; instead, prayer illuminates it as a crucible wherein resilience is forged. Through prayer, the believer is drawn into a sacred alchemy, where tears become waters of renewal, loneliness becomes a sacred space for encountering God, and brokenness becomes a pathway to deeper wholeness. The golden threads of prayer are visible as patterns in our own lives. Like Job, we may find ourselves crying out in confusion and anger, questioning the purpose of suffering. Like David, we might stand amid turmoil, choosing to sing praises in the night, reaching toward hope with a steadfast heart. Like Jonah, we may feel swallowed by darkness, yet discover that even there, prayer births resurrection and renewed mission. These parallels bring the ancient scriptures into intimate dialogue with our contemporary experience, affirming prayer's timeless and universal significance. Moreover, prayer's luminescence in despair shapes not only an individual's inner landscape but also ripples outward, inspiring communal hope. When believers gather to lift up prayers born in suffering, they weave collective threads of light that strengthen bonds, encourage perseverance, and remind all that no shadow is impenetrable. The community becomes a tapestry of prayerful hope, where individual laments are transformed into shared songs of faith. Exploring the scriptures with scholarly rigor, the language in these prayers is striking.

The Hebrew words used in Job and the Psalms, the poetic constructions, and the evocative metaphors all point to a profound understanding of the human-divine relationship amid suffering. For instance, the word "hallelujah" (praise the Lord) resounds as a declaration of faith that radiates hope even in darkness. It carries with it the weight of trust that transcends the immediate emotional state, suggesting that praise itself becomes a vehicle of spiritual illumination. Yet, theological reflection on these prayers also invites us to hold space for the realities of unanswered questions. In Job's dialogues, God's responses are often enigmatic, reminding us that prayer does not always yield immediate clarity or deliverance. Instead, prayer may be the means by which one learns to abide in mystery, trusting that divine sovereignty encompasses the depths of human suffering in ways unseen. Prayer becomes a luminous patience, an enduring light that sustains us until understanding dawns. The universal nature of these prayers—echoing across centuries and cultures—affirms that the act of lifting one's voice in anguish and hope is not restricted to one tradition or faith but is a hallmark of spiritual longing worldwide. Prayer's essence as a dialogue between the human and the divine, especially amidst despair, bridges differences and resonates deeply with seekers and believers alike. To live in a world where despair often shadows the human soul, the example of prayer's luminescence in the scriptures offers a vital foundation. It testifies that even the darkest nights hold the potential for dawn, and that prayer is the means by which we can hold on to that promise. The courage to pray amid despair models a faith that neither dismisses pain nor invites its transformation. It is an invitation to weave golden threads of hope into life's fabric, creating a tapestry resilient and radiant. In closing this reflection, one cannot overlook the pastoral implications that flow naturally from these biblical examples. Spiritual leaders and communities are called to nurture spaces where honest prayers of despair are welcomed and honored. Such spaces affirm that to pray in sorrow is a sacred act, not a sign of spiritual failure but a testament to humanity's yearning for light and healing. Encouraging open-hearted prayer serves as a balm and beacon alike, guiding the weary toward renewed strength. Thus, the luminescence found in the prayers of Job, David, and Jonah illuminates a profound theological and existential truth: prayer is not a means to escape despair but a courageous, transformative encounter with it. Like golden threads piercing darkness, prayer mends the torn fabric of the soul with hope, resilience, and divine presence. It rekindles the fading embers of faith and breathes life into weary hearts, affirming that even in despair, the divine light endures and calls us onward.

Healing Through Intercession

Healing Through Intercession. In the vast tapestry of human experience, healing stands as one of the most profound and essential longings. Whether it be the mending of a broken body, the soothing of a troubled mind, or the rekindling of a weary spirit, healing draws us toward the divine in moments of vulnerability and hope. Within the King James Bible, intercessory prayer emerges not only as a means of petitioning for healing but also as a powerful spiritual practice that bridges the physical and the metaphysical, grounding the believer's plea in the assurance of God's compassion and transformative power. This subchapter explores the manifold dimensions of healing through intercession by examining biblical narratives and poetic expressions that illuminate God's role as both healer and comforter. It invites the Seeker to engage with prayer as an instrument of restoration—individually and communally—and encourages openness to the miraculous as the heartbeat of intercession. The biblical witness to healing through intercession is abundant and varied, spanning the poetic laments of the Psalms, the sweeping narratives of prophetic intervention, and the tender moments of Christ's ministry. Intercessory prayer, in its essence, is an outward expression of inward faith. It acknowledges human limitation while appealing to divine sufficiency. In the context of healing, these prayers often carry a twofold purpose: to ask for relief from suffering and to invite transformation into wholeness. The King James Bible's poetic language lends a rhythmic beauty to these prayers, underscoring their power not merely as requests but as acts of hope, trust, and communion with God. Consider, for instance, the Psalms—a treasury of intercessory prayers that vividly portray human frailty alongside divine mercy. Psalm 6, one of the penitential psalms, encapsulates the essence of seeking healing in bodily weakness and spiritual distress: "O LORD, rebuke me not in thine anger, neither chasten me in thy hot displeasure. Have mercy upon me, O LORD; for I am weak: O LORD, heal me; for my bones are vexed." (Psalm 6:1–2) Here, the psalmist lays bare the anguish of suffering, the weariness of a body "vexed," and the yearning for God's healing touch. The poetic repetition of "O LORD" emphasizes dependence and intimate address, evoking a sense of closeness even amid agony. The imagery of chastisement and anger contrasts with the plea for mercy and healing, reminding the Seeker that divine discipline can coexist with compassion. This intercession is not only about physical healing but encompasses the renewal of the entire self, echoing the biblical understanding that God heals the whole person—in body, mind, and spirit. Moving beyond the Psalms, the narratives in the books of Kings and Chronicles highlight the role of intercessory prayer in communal health and restoration. The prophet Elijah's prayer on Mount Carmel, for example, culminated in a dramatic display of divine fire, but underlying this event was his plea for spiritual renewal amidst a nation's apostasy (1 Kings 18). Similarly, King Hezekiah's prayer in the face of death illustrates personal intercession for physical healing: "And Hezekiah turned his face toward the wall, and prayed unto the LORD ... And Isaiah said, Take a lump of figs, and lay it upon the boil, and he shall recover." (Isaiah 38:2, 21) Hezekiah's turning "his face toward the wall" reflects humility and earnestness, a posture of both secrecy and sincerity before God. His prayer is met with tangible intervention, revealing a God who responds to heartfelt intercession with healing. The inclusion of a physical remedy— the figs—combined with the divine word, bridges human agency and divine power. This narrative underscores that healing often involves cooperation between prayer, faith, and practical means. It encourages the

Seeker to engage intercessory prayer with both intention and openness to diverse modes of healing. The New Testament further enriches our understanding of healing through intercession, particularly in the ministry of Jesus Christ and the early church. Christ's healing miracles are inseparable from prayer and faith: the centurion's servant is healed not merely by Jesus' word but through the centurion's remarkable faith (Matthew 8:5–13). Likewise, the woman with the issue of blood is restored by reaching out in faith amidst the crowd (Mark 5:25–34). These stories reveal the multidimensional nature of healing: the external miracle, the internal faith, and the communal witness. Intercession also emerges strongly in the epistles, where believers are encouraged to pray for one another's healing with faith and expectation: "Is any sick among you? let him call for the elders of the church; and let them pray over him, anointing him with oil in the name of the Lord: And the prayer of faith shall save the sick, and the Lord shall raise him up." (James 5:14–15)This passage situates healing within the context of community, emphasizing mutual care and the power of corporate prayer. The anointing with oil is symbolic, representing the outpouring of the Holy Spirit and the tangible presence of God's healing. The "prayer of faith" indicates that intercession is not a mere recitation of words but a vibrant act infused with trust in God's ability to restore. It positions the seeker within a network of spiritual support, underscoring the significance of communal intercession as a vector for healing. Exploring the poetic elements embedded in these prayers enriches the Seeker's appreciation of their depth. Biblical intercessory prayers often employ metaphor, parallelism, and vivid imagery—tools that transform mere requests into sacred dialogue. The metaphor of God as a "rock" and "refuge" appears repeatedly, symbolizing steadfast protection and shelter amidst illness and despair (e. G., Psalm 18:2). Parallelism enhances the rhythm and intensity of the plea, as seen in Psalm 42: "As the hart panteth after the water brooks, so panteth my soul after thee, O God." (Psalm 42:1)This evocative image captures thirst not only for physical sustenance but for spiritual restoration. Such poetic devices invite the Seeker to partake in prayer not just as petition but as embodied yearning, a vibrant movement of the soul toward divine healing. The Divine Presence in these narratives and prayers is both comforter and healer. This dual role is vital to understanding the transformative power of intercession. God is portrayed not only as one who mends the broken body but as the companion who walks alongside the sufferer, offering peace amidst storm. Psalm 23 poignantly exemplifies this, where the "valley of the shadow of death" is traversed with confidence, not because suffering is absent but because the "rod and staff" of the shepherd bring comfort. In the context of healing intercession, recognizing God's presence as comforter helps the Seeker embrace prayer as an act that sustains the soul even before physical healing manifests. The Seeker's contemplation of prayer's role in healing invites reflection on the interplay between divine sovereignty and human agency. Intercessory prayer is not a formulaic transaction; it is an openhearted conversation that trusts in God's wisdom while expressing human need. Prayer becomes a liminal space where the Seeker surrenders control yet remains actively engaged, lifting others up in grace and faith. This dynamic is evident in the communal prayers recorded in the New Testament, wherein believers gather with fervor, united in hope and reliance on God's healing power. Practically, engaging in intercessory prayer for healing demands intentionality and openness. The Seeker is encouraged to approach such prayers with clarity— knowing who and what they are interceding for—while remaining receptive to outcomes beyond their imagining. Healing may come suddenly or gradually; it may be physical restoration or spiritual renewal. Openness to miraculous possibilities invites the Seeker into a posture of wonder, breaking the bounds of expectation and allowing divine surprise. In fostering a practice of healing intercession, several practical principles can guide the Seeker:1. Cultivate an Attitude of Compassionate Presence: Prayer for healing begins with empathy and a heartfelt awareness of the sufferer's pain. The Seeker's prayers are enriched when they imagine entering into the experience of those they intercede for, allowing their own heart to be softened and attuned to God's mercy. 2.

Engage the Community of Faith: Intercession flourishes within the collective body. The gathering of believers praying together amplifies faith and support. Inviting others to join in prayer not only multiplies spiritual strength but fosters bonds of shared hope and love.3. Combine Faith with Action: Biblical healing narratives often weave together prayer with practical steps—such as anointing with oil, laying on of hands, or seeking medical care. The Seeker is encouraged to integrate prayerful petition with tangible acts of care, recognizing that both are expressions of God's love.4. Affirm the Sovereignty of God: While intercessory prayer seeks healing, it also submits to divine will. This posture of surrender doesn't diminish hope but anchors it in God's perfect wisdom and timing. The Seeker learns to pray with persistence and faith, yet without demanding specific outcomes.5. Nurture the Inner Life: Regular personal prayer, meditation on healing scriptures, and reflection on God's promises build spiritual resilience. This inner growth empowers the Seeker to maintain hopeful intercession even amid prolonged trials. In embracing these principles, the Seeker transforms intercessory prayer from a routine recitation into a living ministry of healing and hope. Ultimately, healing through intercession is a sacred dialogue that invites both regard for human vulnerability and trust in divine restoration. The King James Bible's rich texts reveal a God who listens to cries of pain, responds to earnest petitions, and journeys with those who seek wholeness. Whether healing unfolds as a miraculous event or a quiet renewal of strength, prayer remains the conduit of hope—both a balm for the present anguish and a beacon toward future peace. As the reader contemplates this subchapter, may they be encouraged to approach intercessory prayer not only as a request for healing but as an intimate offering of care, a courageous articulation of faith, and a profound participation in the ongoing work of divine restoration. In the sacred act of lifting others up before God, the Seeker discovers not only the power of prayer to heal but the transformative grace that flows through the presence of the Divine—healing the body, refreshing the spirit, and renewing the soul in all its dimensions.

Resilience and Renewal: Stories of Transformation

In the rich tapestry of the King James Bible, prayer emerges not merely as a ritual or routine but as a profound conduit for resilience and renewal, a sacred dialogue through which the inner being undergoes transformation. The subchapter before us embarks on a contemplative journey through some of the Bible's most poignant narratives—stories in which prayer functions as the catalyst for life transfigured. Here, the lives of Hannah, Solomon, and Peter stand as luminous testaments to the power of persistent and faithful prayer to usher in emotional and spiritual metamorphosis. Their stories reveal prayer as a dynamic, living dance, a ballet of hope's colors shifting across the canvas of human experience, as sorrow merges into joy, doubt gives way to wisdom, and failure is transmuted into resilience. Hannah: Prayer as the Seedbed of Hope Amid Desolation The narrative of Hannah, found in the first book of Samuel, is a stirring portrait of anguish turned into abundant blessing through the steadfastness of prayer. Hannah's story begins in the depths of sorrow. She is childless in a culture where barrenness is not only a personal heartbreak but a social stigma, a source of isolation and despair. Yet, it is not her lament alone that moves the story forward; it is the fervent way she lays bare her soul before the Lord. Her prayer in the tabernacle at Shiloh is remarkable for its simplicity and intensity. "Give thy handmaid a man child," she cries, pouring out her heart with tears and a vow—if granted a son, she will dedicate him wholly to the Lord's service. This is no polite petition but an impassioned plea, a moment where every color of hope—from the dark hues of desolation to the bright streaks of faith— blends together. Hannah's prayer is emblematic of a dynamic resilience, a refusal to surrender to despair despite overwhelming odds. What follows offers exquisite insight into how prayer acts upon the soul. Instead of immediate relief, Hannah experiences a deep stillness—a divine exchange where the burden of her sorrow is lifted, replaced by a renewed spirit. She departs the temple no longer weeping but with a calm determination rooted in trust. This emotional shift is pivotal: prayer here functions as a lifeline, enabling her heart to reframe her suffering and anticipate transformation.Hannah's eventual conception and the birth of Samuel bring to light the unfolding of prayer's promise into tangible life. Yet, greater still is the spiritual renewal embedded in this narrative—it is not simply the child who is blessed but the mother herself, who discovers in prayer both solace and the courage to surrender control. Her story is a vibrant illustration that transformational renewal often begins not by changing one's circumstances but by a profound internal metamorphosis wrought through prayerful hope. Solomon: From Innocence to Wisdom through Devoted Supplication The story of Solomon, chronicled in the books of Kings and Chronicles, provides a compelling portrayal of how prayer can birth wisdom and maturity from uncertainty and youthful inexperience. Solomon inherits a vast kingdom, but with it comes daunting responsibility. It is noteworthy that at the onset of his reign, Solomon does not immediately pray for wealth, power, or fame. Instead, he seeks a discerning heart, a mind capable of governing with justice. This prayer, offered in a dream, demonstrates a deep awareness of human limitation and a humble dependence on the divine. "Give therefore thy servant an understanding heart to judge thy people," he begs, "that I may discern between good and bad." Solomon's supplication is not only a request but a spiritual posture, reflecting a soul attuned to the weight of leadership and the necessity of divine guidance.Here again, we witness prayer as a palette of shifting hues—Solomon's initial naiveté blends with a vibrant yearning for wisdom, producing a color of prayer that is as much about self-realization as divine appeal. The subsequent granting of wisdom signifies an inner renewal as much as a blessing; Solomon is transformed from a young, inexperienced prince into a sage king, embodying the fruits of a prayer poured out with sincerity and reverence. Yet, the story does not end in flawless triumph. Solomon's later life is marked by moral and spiritual decline, reminding us that prayer and renewal are ongoing processes subject to the complexities of human nature. Nevertheless, the moment of his heartfelt prayer sets into motion a movement toward wisdom that resonates across generations, underscoring the transformative potential embedded in true, earnest petition. Peter: The Journey from Fear to Faith through Persistent Prayer Turning to the New Testament, the life of Peter captures another vivid narrative of prayer leading to resilience and renewal, a story that follows the trajectory from fear and failure toward courageous faith. Peter, a fisherman by trade and disciple by calling, is no stranger to moments of human frailty—his threefold denial of Christ on the night of His arrest is emblematic of fear's grip and the turmoil within. Yet it is precisely within this context of brokenness that we see prayer functioning as a redemptive force. After the resurrection, Peter's encounter with the risen Christ on the shores of Galilee becomes a pivotal moment that restores and renews. The dialogue—"Lovest thou me?"—is not only a tender restoration but also a call to recommitment, symbolizing the rebirth of Peter's calling through renewed faith. Between these moments of failure and restoration lies a period marked by prayer, reflection, and the gradual building of resilience. The Book of Acts reveals Peter bathed in prayer, empowered by the Holy Spirit to preach boldly and perform miracles. His transformation is radical: from fearful denier to fearless leader of the early church. Prayer here is not a one-time act but a persistent practice, a continuous conversation with God that strengthens and renews the spirit. It is a testament to the tenacity of hope and the healing power that prayer imparts. The emotional and spiritual metamorphosis is palpable—the once timid disciple becomes a pillar of faith, shaped and reshaped by his ongoing relationship with the divine . The Dynamic Dance of Hope's Colors The stories of Hannah, Solomon, and Peter collectively illustrate that prayer is not static; it ebbs and flows like the shades of hope across a wide expanse. In Hannah's story, prayer is the quiet, steady stroke blending sorrow with hope and eventual joy. In Solomon's, prayer is the vivid brush seeking wisdom and balance amidst new responsibilities. In Peter's journey, prayer is the rhythmic dance of grace sustained through failure and redemption. These narratives invite readers to appreciate prayer as an ever-moving process, a spiritual choreography that mirrors life itself. Through trial, supplication, and surrender, prayer shapes the heart, mind, and soul, enabling transformation that ripples outward. The colors of hope do not remain fixed; they shift from deep blues of despair through brilliant golds of divine insight to vibrant reds of passionate faith. Moreover, these biblical experiences affirm that transformation through prayer is accessible to all—believers and seekers alike—because prayer reaches into the core of human experience. It touches on universal impulses: longing, vulnerability, trust, and the desire for renewal. Each story offers a mirror reflecting the potential within every heart to rise anew, no matter the weight of past sorrows or the depths of doubt. Resilience Born of Persistent and Faithful Prayer   At the heart of each transformation lies a consistent element: persistence in prayer despite circumstances that might discourage or dishearten. Hannah's repeated visits to the temple and pouring out of her soul demonstrate steadfastness. Solomon's reflective petition during a moment of uncertainty reveals humility and patience. Peter's continual prayer life amidst his trials marks unwavering dedication. This persistence is not portrayed as a mere act of endurance but as an active engagement with the divine, a faithful refusing to let go of hope even in darkness. It is this quality that breathes life into the human spirit, sparking renewal when all else seems lost. Faithfulness in prayer cultivates a fertile ground for grace to take root. The biblical characters' experiences suggest that renewal is not always immediate or overt; sometimes, it is internal and subtle—an emerging peace, a new understanding, a readiness to act with courage. Yet these internal shifts often lead to external transformations, altering the course of lives and histories. Conclusion: Embracing the Transformative Power of Prayer Through the stories of Hannah, Solomon, and Peter, the king James Bible presents prayer as a powerful force for resilience and renewal—a spiritual wellspring from which the human soul draws strength to endure, hope to persevere, and wisdom to grow. These narratives encourage us to see prayer beyond words spoken or habits observed, inviting a deeper embrace of prayer as a transformative journey. The emotional and spiritual metamorphosis portrayed is a dance of colors—sometimes gentle and subtle, other times bursting forth with radiant intensity—all conveying the living dynamics of hope. In our own lives, whether in moments of quiet despair or overwhelming joy, the example of these biblical figures invites us to bring to prayer our full selves—our fears, desires, doubts, and dreams—trusting that through faithful and persistent communion with the divine, renewal awaits. Prayer becomes not an escape but a path, a sacred journey where transformation is possible, and where hope's palette continues to change and glow, coloring anew the story of our existence.

Praying into Tomorrow: Sustaining Hope

As night yields to dawn, an age-old promise stirs on the horizon: light will break forth again. In the stillness before morning, when shadows cling to the edges of the earth and silence nestles deep in crevices of the soul, prayer stands as the sentinel of hope—an eternal bridge from darkness to day. To pray into tomorrow is to engage with this sacred threshold, wielding hope not as a fragile flicker but as a rising flame, steady and unyielding. It is here, in this liminal space between what was and what shall be, that the true power of prayer reveals itself: the power to sustain hope through all seasons.Hope, like dawn, is not a guaranteed arrival but a patient journey. It is cultivated by the conscious turning of our hearts, the steadfast lifting of our voices, and the quiet resolution to hold fast when the night seems unending. In the King James Bible, prayer is depicted not merely as petition or praise but as a sustained dialogue—a continuous rhythm that resists despair by tethering the human spirit to the divine. To embrace prayer as a habitual practice is to forge a lifeline, a provision to carry us safely into the uncertainties of the coming day. Consider the metaphor of the morning light expanding slowly, reaching gently yet resolutely into every corner where darkness has taken refuge. This gradual illumination mirrors the way hope grows within us: not in sudden eruptions, but in incremental awakenings. Each whispered prayer, each flicker of faith, becomes an actor in this unfolding drama, casting its own ray of brightness into our internal night. Just as the horizon blushes with the promise of a new day, so our prayers are the colors that paint the canvas of tomorrow with possibility. In the Psalms, we find echoes of this enduring hope, woven deftly into verses that have guided countless generations: "I waited patiently for the LORD; and he inclined unto me, and heard my cry." (Psalm 40:1) The psalmist's willingness to wait patiently, sustained by the act of calling out, underscores the vital principle that prayer is a practice of endurance. It invites us to enter into a sacred rhythm of expectation, where the very act of waiting is itself an act of faith. Through prayer, waiting becomes active, a hopeful stance rather than a state of resignation. This active waiting creates a space within us—a sacred pause—where fear diminishes, and courage takes root. Prayer becomes a refuge where we place our uncertainties and worries, and from which courage and hope arise anew. The King James Bible presents instances of persistent prayer that reveal this truth. Consider Hannah, whose earnest prayers for a child transformed her grief into joy, or Nehemiah, whose fervent petitions for the restoration of Jerusalem fortified his resolve. They show us how prayer is not merely about changing circumstances but about transforming the inner bearer of the hope itself. To pray into tomorrow is thus an invitation to incorporate prayer into the fabric of daily life. This means more than occasional moments of adoration or supplication; it requires a deliberate cultivation of a devotional rhythm where prayer becomes as natural and necessary as breathing. Such integration fosters what might be called a spiritual stamina—a fortitude that carries us over trials with a heart anchored in hopeful expectation. Achieving this rhythm often demands intentionality. It may call for specific moments set aside each day—a morning light to kindle our spirits before we step into the busyness of life, or an evening reverence to lay our burdens down at the close of day. These sacred times are not mere rituals, but vital rehearsals in hope, training our hearts to lean continually toward the divine presence, even through the monotony or chaos that life sometimes presents. The imagery evoked by these devotional moments is compelling: as the day unfolds, so does the heart open wider to the possibilities held within prayer's embrace. Each prayer becomes a seed planted in the soil of tomorrow's unknown, nurtured by faith and watered with persistence. Over time, these seeds grow into towering trees of hope whose roots run deep, anchoring us securely against life's tempests. Such spiritual growth, cultivated through unwavering prayer, transforms not only our perspective but also our very being. Moreover, this sustained hope borne from persistent prayer facilitates transformation beyond the self. It instills in us the courage to meet challenges with grace and the generous spirit to foster hope in others. Like the expanding light that cannot be contained within a single room, the hope nurtured through prayer radiates outward, touching communities, families, and even strangers. It becomes a gift that multiplies, a testimony of prayer's expansive power. Within this communal aspect is another profound dimension: prayer as a shared practice that weaves individual hopes into a collective tapestry of faith and expectation. The King James Bible offers ample testimony to this truth, from the congregational prayers of the early church to the intercessions of prophets and leaders who bore the weight of their people's futures. To pray into tomorrow is, therefore, to engage not only in personal hope but in the hope of a world in need—drawing strength from the solidarity of many voices raised as one. In embracing these lessons, readers are invited to reflect on their own journey of hope. What prayers might sustain you as the night fades? How might your daily rhythms of devotion become the steady drumbeat of courage and expectation within your soul? The call is gentle but profound: to allow prayer to shape the very manner in which we meet each new dawn, bringing all its uncertainty into a space consecrated by faith. In practical terms, nurturing hope through prayer can take many forms. It might be the habit of beginning each day with a simple invocation—such as the Lord's Prayer or a personal plea for strength— setting a tone of trust before the demands of the day press in. It could be moments of silent meditation or recitation of scripture that remind us of divine promises, creating a mental ledger of hope to draw upon when discouragement threatens. Even amid sorrow or difficulty, prayer remains an assurance: a beacon lighting the way to a future still shimmering with possibility. Another practice that deeply nourishes this sustaining hope is gratitude expressed through prayer. Recognizing the blessings already present, even amid hardship, reframes our outlook and reinforces the belief that goodness persists. The psalmist's refrain, "this is the day which the LORD hath made; we will rejoice and be glad in it" (Psalm 118:24), exemplifies this posture of thankful expectation. Gratitude and hope are intertwined in the fertile soil of prayer, each nourishing the other as they grow within the soul. As prayer becomes a daily sanctuary and hope its enduring melody, the ordinary moments of life take on a new radiance. Challenges cease to be mere obstacles and become invitations to deeper faith. Waiting no longer feels like empty time but a sacred space where preparation for future blessings occurs. Our hearts become tuned to discern the subtle hand of grace amid the noise, the gentle unfolding of dawn amid the lingering darkness. Ultimately, praying into tomorrow is an act of trust—trust in a divine presence that hears, loves, and sustains. It transcends temporal concerns, holding fast to a vision of the eternal, a hope that is not confined by circumstance but deeply rooted in the spiritual truth that light follows darkness. This truth has carried believers across centuries, from the earliest voices recorded in scripture to the prayers whispered in quiet moments today. In this shared human experience, prayer serves as both anchor and sail. It grounds us in the reality of divine care while propelling us forward into the unknown with confidence. The metaphor of dawn expanding into day beautifully captures this duality—the stillness before the sun rises and the dynamic brightness that follows—reminding us that hope is both a place of rest and a call to journey. Therefore, as this chapter closes, the invitation stands clear: let prayer be the lens through which you view tomorrow, allowing its light to penetrate fears and doubts, illuminating your path with steadfast hope. Embrace the lessons found in the sacred stories of prayer's enduring power. Integrate them into your daily devotional rhythms so that courage may deepen and hopeful expectation bloom like the morning sun breaking across the landscape of your life. May your prayers be the colors that paint your tomorrows with promise—a vibrant tapestry woven from faith, patience, and love. As you continue to pray into tomorrow, may you find strength in the breaking dawn, and may hope expand endlessly within your heart, transforming your life and the lives of those you touch.

Gary E. Risenhoover

Voices Through the Wilderness: Lamentation and Faith

The Sacred Cry: Exploring Lament

In the boundless landscape of biblical prayer, the sacred cry of lament occupies a solemn and profound place. Unlike prayers of praise or supplication, lament folds the soul into the rawest depths of human experience, where sorrow and anguish break the surface like waves crashing against the shores of hope. These voices, captured so vividly in the Psalms, the book of Lamentations, and the prophetic writings, offer an unvarnished invitation to wrestle with suffering—not to deny it, sugarcoat it, or bypass pain, but to step fully into its shadowed realm and call upon God with unfiltered honesty. In this space, grief is neither a sign of weak faith nor a detour from the spiritual path; it is an essential dimension of the faith journey, a sacred dialogue that acknowledges the brokenness of the world and the heart's cry for divine presence. The Psalms, a treasury of ancient prayers, contain numerous laments that articulate the collective and individual sufferings of God's people. Within their verses, we encounter a spectrum of grief—desperation mingled with hope, accusation coupled with trust, despair interwoven with expectation. These are not merely poetic expressions of sadness but urgent pleas for deliverance, reflections on injustice, and proclamations of faith amidst trials. The Psalms show us that lament is not a retreat from God but a reaching out—sometimes trembling, sometimes fierce— toward a God who listens, who is both just and merciful. Consider Psalm 13, where David begins with a plaintive question: "How long, O LORD? wilt thou forget me forever? how long wilt thou hide thy face from me?" The psalm unfolds with intimate transparency—feeling forgotten, abandoned, overwhelmed by enemies and sorrow. Yet amidst this dark night, the psalmist chooses a posture of patient hope: "But I have trusted in thy mercy; my heart shall rejoice in thy salvation." This psalm illustrates the dual cadence of lament: an unflinching expression of suffering alongside a resolute trust in God's eventual intervention.Lamentations, the book mournfully named for its genre, stands as a somber monument to communal grief. Written likely in the aftermath of Jerusalem's destruction and the exile, its five chapters are a poetic dirge that chronicles the devastation and desolation experienced by a people torn from homeland and hope. The writer's voice carries a unique weight—historical calamity fused with theological reflection—turning personal sorrow into universal lament. The images are haunting: "The roads to Zion mourn, for none come to the solemn feasts; all her gates are desolate." The text wrestles with the paradox of divine justice and mercy, questioning why God's wrath was unleashed while still clinging to a fragile hope of restoration. The power of Lamentations lies not only in its vivid portrayal of loss but in its invitation to grieve openly before God. Where silence might isolate and stoicism might numb, lament breathes life into anguish. It becomes a sacred language that validates pain as worthy of expression—and in doing so, creates space for healing. The lamenting community embodies both the weight of absence and the stubborn persistence of faith, echoing the embodied experience of suffering that transcends epochs. Prophetic literature further enriches this tapestry of lament, often blending sorrow with calls for repentance, justice, and the promise of renewal. Prophets such as Jeremiah, Ezekiel, and Habakkuk declare laments that voice the pain of a nation under judgment, the perplexities of divine silence, and the yearning for God's intervention. Jeremiah, called the "weeping prophet," articulated a lament so deep that it reverberated through generations: "O that my head were waters, and mine eyes a fountain of tears, that I might weep day and night... for the slain of the daughter of my people." His lament reveals not only personal sorrow but also communal anguish, making it an act of empathy and spiritual solidarity. In Habakkuk, the dialogue with God opens the window onto the struggle with divine justice: "How long, O LORD, must I call for help, but you do not listen? Or cry out to you, 'Violence!' but you do not save?" This candid questioning captures the tension many believers face in times of crisis—trusting God while grappling with the reality of suffering and silence. The prophetic laments do not shy away from demanding answers; instead, they model a faith that is honest, unguarded, and deeply relational. As we attend to these sacred cries, we must recognize that lament prayer refuses to gloss over pain or rush toward platitudes. It is the language of wilderness—where answers are scarce, where the soul is laid bare, and where God's presence may seem distant or hidden. Yet it is precisely in this wilderness that lament becomes an act of spiritual courage. To lament is to risk vulnerability before God, to pour out the woes of the heart without guarantee of immediate relief. It is to acknowledge that faith encompasses seasons of silence, confusion, and sorrow alongside moments of joy and praise. The emotional textures of lament are rich and varied. The indigo depths and muted silver tones evoke a complex spectrum—from the heavy weight of despair to the flickering glimmers of hope. Psalm 42 offers a vivid example: "As the hart panteth after the water brooks, so panteth my soul after thee, O God... deep calleth unto deep at the noise of thy waterspouts." Here, the psalmist's thirst for God amid desolation conveys a profound tension— deep sorrow encountering the possibility of divine refreshment. It is a lament that holds within it the seeds of renewal, bathed in both shadow and light. To lament is also to situate personal pain within the larger community of faith. Biblical laments often move between "I" and "we," underscoring that sorrow is shared and that healing requires communal acknowledgment and support. The Psalter, the prophets, and Lamentations collectively model a faith community that embraces lament as a vital expression of life. This collective voice encourages believers across generations to recognize lament not as failure but as integrity in prayer—a refusal to hide wounds from God. In contemporary spiritual experience, lament remains deeply relevant. In times of personal loss, social injustice, or global crisis, lament invites believers and seekers to bring their pain honestly before the divine. It speaks against cultural tendencies toward superficial positivity or emotional avoidance, reminding us that authentic spirituality embraces the full spectrum of human emotion. Lament protects and nourishes the soul by giving sanctioned space to express grief, fear, anger, and disorientation. Moreover, lament challenges theological notions that equate faith with unbroken optimism. It complicates simplistic images of God as a problem-solver who eradicates all distress on command. Instead, biblical lament reveals a God who welcomes raw prayers, who listens to cries, and who ultimately brings hope amid brokenness. The act of lament becomes a transformative spiritual exercise—inviting vulnerability, persistence, and an openness to God's mysterious working even when immediate answers remain elusive. The procession of mournful prayers captured in the Scriptures offers a mirror to our own moments of wilderness. They teach that faith is not immunity to suffering but engagement with it in God's presence. They affirm that lament is not a spiritual detour but an integral pilgrimage of the soul. To engage in lament is, in fact, to echo the divine-human dialogue where longing, protest, and trust coexist. It is to give voice to the sacred cry that reverberates through time—a cry that declares, "I am in pain, I am in loss, and yet I call upon you, O God." Through this exploration of biblical lament, readers are invited into a profound spiritual posture. Far from being a sign of despair, lament is a courageous act of faithfulness—a raw, unguarded expression of the human heart that beckons God's presence into the wilderness. It teaches us to honor our grief, to embrace the complexity of emotions, and to hold fast to the hope that even in deepest sorrow, prayer remains a vital thread connecting frailty with the divine. The sacred cry of lament thus emerges as a powerful testament to the enduring resilience of faith—the voice that neither fears darkness nor silences pain but speaks truth into the vast mystery of God's abiding love.

Faith Tested: Wilderness as Spiritual Crucible

The wilderness has long been a potent symbol in the biblical narrative—a place both physical and metaphorical where faith is confronted, challenged, and ultimately honed. Within its vast expanse of barrenness and solitude, the stories of Elijah and the Israelites vividly illustrate how the Divine Presence can seem both hidden and unmistakably near, serving as a crucible in which the soul's mettle is tested and strengthened. Through their journeys, we encounter the raw intersection of human vulnerability and divine fidelity, a dynamic that resonates as profoundly today as it did millennia ago. This subchapter seeks to inhabit the wilderness alongside these biblical figures, to enter their struggle and hopeful endurance, and by doing so, to illuminate the intimate dance of absence and communion that defines faith's most arduous seasons. To embark upon this reflection, it is essential to appreciate what the wilderness represents in biblical imagination. More than mere geography—the deserts, barren lands, and wilderness regions that physically challenged ancient Israelites and prophets—the wilderness is a liminal space. It lies outside the ordered and settled world, a realm of uncertainty where the comforts of civilization recede and the familiar supports of social and spiritual life are stripped away. In the wilderness, one confronts the essentials: hunger and thirst, exposure and solitude, fear and longing. But beyond these tangible hardships, the wilderness embodies spiritual trial and transformation. It is where surface faith is peeled back, where inner crises unfold, and where the soul is pressed to redefine its trust in God. Here, doubt and despair may wander close like shadowy companions, yet so too may intuition and revelation emerge like shafts of light breaking through storm clouds. The story of the Israelites in the wilderness journey after their exodus from Egypt epitomizes this duality. Departing from bondage and crossing the Red Sea, the people find themselves in a vast desert wilderness—a place both threatening and formative. As they traverse this desolate landscape for forty years, their faith undergoes a relentless testing. Food and water are scarce, the promise of the Promised Land seems at best distant and at times unreachable, and their leadership, hope, and identity are repeatedly strained. Yet amid the hardships, the Divine Presence is paradoxically evident. God reveals Himself in pillars of cloud and fire, in manna from heaven, and in the giving of the Law at Mount Sinai. These moments of divine intervention punctuate a narrative that is otherwise marked by human frailty and complaint. The wilderness, then, becomes a spiritual crucible—both metaphorically and literally—where the Israelites confront the painful reality that faith is not a one-time declaration but a continuous act of endurance and surrender. Their lamentations, cries, and moments of rebellion are transparently recorded, granting us insight into the authentic struggle of maintaining hope amid prolonged trial. These scriptures do not sanitize or diminish the difficulty of the wilderness experience; on the contrary, they portray faith as tested not in comfort but in hardship, and divine companionship as experienced not only in light but also amidst shadows. Elijah's narrative presents a similarly profound encounter with wilderness as both place and spiritual discipline. After the dramatic confrontation with the prophets of Baal on Mount Carmel, Elijah flees into the wilderness, worn by fear, isolation, and despair. The desert landscape that he crosses physically mirrors his inner turmoil, where he believes himself alone and hunted, the future bleak, and God absent. Yet, it is precisely within this arid seclusion that God's presence becomes manifest, albeit in unexpected forms. The biblical text describes God's communication to Elijah not in tumult or spectacle but in a "still small voice." This subtle yet profound manifestation captures the essence of wilderness experience—the interplay between apparent divine silence and hidden divine companionship. Elijah's encounter challenges any notion that God's presence must always be dramatic or unmistakable; sometimes it is found precisely in the quiet spaces, in the shadows where hope lingers even when light seems distant. This paradox invites readers to reconsider their own moments of spiritual dryness or isolation not as signs of abandonment, but as fertile grounds for encountering God's gentler, patient, and sustaining presence. Wilderness testing, therefore, is not merely about survival or endurance in the physical sense; it is about spiritual refinement. Like ore purified by fire, faith is distilled by trial. The obscurity of wilderness strips away false securities, forces frank self-examination, and demands a reorientation toward the Divine that is grounded not in certainty of outcome but in steadfastness of relationship. The narratives of Elijah and the Israelites expose this process in raw and relatable terms—faith that struggles, questions, and laments is faith that is alive, dynamic, and ultimately fruitful. For contemporary readers, these wilderness stories invite profound reflection on the nature of their own faith journeys. Times of life that feel barren, lonely, or confusing echo these biblical themes. The wilderness, whether external circumstance or internal state of being, becomes a sacred metaphor for those seasons when prayer is difficult, answers are unclear, and God's presence seems veiled. Yet, just as Elijah and the Israelites found, these are also crucibles where faith is shaped into deeper resilience and purity. In embracing this perspective, readers are invited not to dismiss their wilderness experiences but to enter them with intentionality and hope. The biblical wilderness does not represent final abandonment but an essential passage—a testing ground from which new life and clarity emerge. Prayer in the wilderness, then, becomes an act of persistence and honesty, a wrestling with shadows that acknowledges darkness without surrendering to it, a reaching for light that may appear faint but is unyielding in its promise. The Divine presence in the wilderness is complex, portrayed through contrasts of absence and nearness, silence and voice, despair and hope. For the Israelites, God is both the provider of manna and the fire that consumes the rebellious. For Elijah, God is both hidden in the whirlwind and revealed in the whisper. This dialectical presence echoes universal human experience of the divine as a mystery that both eludes and envelops us, revealing itself fully only through patient waiting and sustained faith. Furthermore, wilderness as a spiritual crucible teaches that faith is not a static possession but a dynamic journey. The tests faced by Elijah and the Israelites are not punitive but formative, shaping character, deepening trust, and expanding the capacity to hope. Their wilderness journeys are marked by cycles of lamentation and renewal, despair and courage, separation and reunion, reflecting the oscillating rhythms of the spiritual life. These stories encourage readers to honor their own cycles of struggle and hope, to recognize that lamentation is itself a form of prayer—a voice lifted from the wilderness inviting divine response. Ultimately, the wilderness invites transformation through encounter. For the Israelites, the wilderness journey led to the Promised Land, a new identity, and covenantal relationship with God. For Elijah, the wilderness encounter preceded a renewed mission and deeper understanding of God's ways. In both cases, the wilderness is not an endpoint but a passage—an in-between space where faith is tested, purified, and enlarged. To embrace the wilderness then, as both metaphor and reality, is to accept the paradox that faith's most profound growth often arises in seasons of apparent desolation. It is an invitation to hold on in the shadows, to listen for the still small voice amid the silence, and to trust that beneath the surface of despair there lies a divine pattern of hope and restoration. In conclusion, the wilderness as spiritual crucible in the stories of Elijah and the Israelites powerfully conveys the universal experience of faith under trial. It reveals the contours of a faith that does not escape struggle but is refined through it, and a divine presence that is both hidden and revealed in the midst of human vulnerability. For all readers, regardless of religious tradition, these narratives offer a profound and compassionate framework for understanding their own moments of darkness and hope, inviting them into a deeper awareness of prayer as the courageous voice of faith wrestling with the mystery of God in the midst of the wilderness.

Transforming Grief into Praise

In the rich tapestry of scripture, the journey from grief to praise stands as one of the most profound transformations witnessed within the landscape of prayer. This metamorphosis is not merely a change in emotional tone but a divine movement within the soul, where the cries of lament serve as essential intrusions upon the barriers of silence and despair. It is here, often within the shadowed valley of sorrow, that the deepest encounter with faith begins to take shape, crafting a sacred narrative that moves from brokenness to beauty. This cyclical nature of prayer—where despair gives way to hope, and sorrow to joy—is intricately woven throughout the King James Bible, inviting believers and seekers alike to dwell within the paradox of lamentation and thanksgiving. From the very outset, the Bible does not shy away from the rawness of human pain. The Psalms, for instance, echo with voices drenched in distress that cry out to God with unabashed honesty. Take Psalm 42, where the psalmist laments, "Why art thou cast down, O my soul? and why art thou disquieted within me?" This poignant question is an invitation into the tumultuous depths of internal struggle. Yet, the trajectory of this lament does not end in desolation; it turns toward hope with the refrain, "Hope thou in God: for I shall yet praise him, who is the health of my countenance, and my God." The psalmist's heart moves from anguish to anticipation of divine restoration, illustrating that lament is neither the terminus of faith nor the absence of praise. Instead, it is the raw material from which new songs of gratitude and trust emerge. This movement from grief to praise reveals an essential rhythm within sacred prayer—a rhythm that recognizes the sacredness of expressing sorrow but refuses to dwell there indefinitely. It acknowledges that faith is not a negation of pain but a steadfast tether that holds through it. In the biblical narrative, sorrowful prayers enact a vivid dialogue wherein the supplicant wrestles with the divine presence, questioning, accusing, and yearning. Yet the ultimate posture of this dialogue is one of trust, surrender, and renewed affirmation of God's sovereignty and mercy. This cyclical dynamic redefines prayer, not simply as petition or praise, but as a sacred journey through wilderness and wonder, where the heart repeatedly reorients itself toward divine light even amid darkness. Examining the story of Hannah in 1 Samuel provides a compelling portrait of transforming grief through prayer. Hannah's barrenness is a source of deep shame and anguish, a trial narrated with raw emotional intensity. In her desperate petition to the Lord, she pours out her soul "in bitterness of soul," yet with a vow of faithfulness should her prayers be answered. The articulation of her pain does not conceal her hope; rather, it is the very crucible from which praise will later spring. When God grants her request and she gives birth to Samuel, her prayer shifts seamlessly into a song of thanksgiving—the famous "Song of Hannah" in 1 Samuel 2. This prayer encapsulates the essence of lament turned praise, celebrating divine intervention that exalts the lowly and fulfills the promises of deliverance. Hannah's story is an archetype affirming that grief expressed transparently before God is not wasted, but a prelude to thanksgiving and renewed covenant relationship. The Psalms offer innumerable other examples where lament gives way to exaltation. Psalm 30 opens with the psalmist declaring, "I will exalt thee, O Lord; for thou hast lifted me up," immediately followed by an acknowledgment of having been "cast down to the pit." The tension between these states highlights the transformative power of prayer: from the depths of despair, the faithful voice rises in praise because of God's intervention. This shift is not simply emotional relief but an act of faithful recognition—that God's presence can penetrate even the darkest moments and bring restoration. The psalmist's journey embodies a sacred movement, one that allows vulnerability to coalesce into trust, vulnerability that becomes the foundation of praise. Exploring the poetic imagery within these prayers further enriches our understanding of this transformation. Grief is often depicted as a consuming fire, a tempest, or a deep shadow—images that evoke the intensity of sorrow and isolation. Yet praise emerges as light piercing darkness, as the dawn after a night, or as a spring of water refreshed by divine blessing. This interplay of imagery conveys the dynamic tension inherent in the spiritual experience, a tension that invites the soul into trust despite confusion and loss. The very act of naming one's grief before God becomes a sacred ritual that prepares the heart for the ensuing shift to praise. The movement is organic and cyclical, a continual return from wilderness wandering to sanctuary song. The prophet Habakkuk provides a striking example of this progression. In Habakkuk 3, the prophet shifts from a deep existential lament about the injustices he witnesses to a concluding affirmation of trust: "Though the fig tree shall not blossom, neither shall fruit be in the vines... yet I will rejoice in the Lord, I will joy in the God of my salvation." Habakkuk's prayer does not deny the persistence of sorrow, but transcends it by resting in the assurance of God's ultimate justice and presence. His words model a mature faith that allows lament and praise to coexist, not as contradictory states but as mutually enriching expressions of spiritual resilience. This cyclical pattern of prayer reflects an important theological truth: lament is not the antithesis of faith but one of its profound expressions. It acknowledges the reality of human suffering while holding fast to hope in divine goodness. The act of lament becomes a precursor to praise because it strips away false pretenses and brings the supplicant into an authentic encounter with God. This encounter fosters a faith grounded less in superficial optimism and more in the enduring relationship between human frailty and divine steadfastness. Moreover, the notion of transforming grief into praise challenges modern stereotypes about spirituality that valorize only joy and thankfulness while minimizing sorrow. The biblical witness validates the full spectrum of human emotion as legitimate within prayer. It teaches that honest lamentation is itself an act of worship, a courageous declaration that God is worthy of our truth, even when that truth includes doubt, anger, and pain. The movement toward praise is not an escape from these emotions but their transformation through divine grace. This grace does not obliterate grief but transfigures it into a source of praise that resonates with deeper understanding and gratitude.Literary analysis further shows that the structure of many biblical prayers mirrors this transformative process. They often begin with complaint or petition, progress through confession and confrontation, and conclude with expressions of trust and praise. This progression models for believers a spiritual discipline of allowing grief to lead into renewal. The cyclical nature insists that this process repeats throughout the spiritual journey, reflecting the ebb and flow of human experience. Such rhythms invite prayer not as a one-time event but as a continuous sacred practice of moving with the tides of life—embracing lament and celebrating restoration. The New Testament also embodies this theme, particularly in the words of Jesus and the prayers attributed to him. In the Garden of Gethsemane, Jesus expresses a profound lament: "O my Father, if it be possible, let this cup pass from me." His anguish is palpable, a moment of raw human vulnerability. Yet this moment is immediately followed by the prayer of surrender: "Nevertheless not as I will, but as thou wilt." Here, Jesus models the divine-human spirit of lament transforming into obedience and trust. The path through grief to praise is shown as a dynamic process of surrendering human will to divine purpose, illuminating the universal call to embrace lament as part of faith's maturation. This theme also resonates in the epistles, where believers are encouraged to "rejoice in hope, be patient in tribulation, be constant in prayer" (Romans 12:12). The injunction to be "patient in tribulation" validates the reality of suffering within the life of faith, while urging the community toward a hopeful perseverance that results in eventual praise. The interweaving of sorrow and rejoicing in these early Christian writings reflects a continuity with the Old Testament tradition of lament and renewal, underscoring the cyclical nature of prayer as a hallmark of authentic spirituality. Beyond the biblical texts themselves, the experience of transforming grief into praise finds expression in the communal prayers and hymns of the faith tradition. The Book of Common Prayer and many hymnals contain litanies that begin with lament and end in doxology, reflecting centuries of worship shaped by the rhythms of sorrow and joy. These liturgical forms provide believers with structured opportunities to bring their darkest emotions into the presence of God, knowing that such prayers have historically moved toward the affirmation of divine grace. The communal dimension of this movement extends the personal cycle of prayer into the shared life of the faith community, reinforcing that lament and praise are integral to spiritual identity. It is also important to note that transforming grief into praise does not imply forgetting or dismissing sorrow. Rather, it calls for the integration of pain into a larger narrative of hope. The psalmist in Psalm 126 declares, "They that sow in tears shall reap in joy." This agricultural metaphor encapsulates the productivity of lament in spiritual life. Tears are not wasted; they prepare the soil of the soul for the seeds of praise to grow. This image reassures believers that their suffering is not meaningless but formative, contributing to spiritual fruitfulness. It reminds us that praise arising from pain is deeply authentic and richly textured, embodying a faith that has been tested and refined by sorrow. In practical terms, this transformation invites a posture of openness before God, where no feeling is too heavy or raw to be brought into prayer. It supports the practice of naming grief explicitly rather than suppressing it, trusting that the act of prayer itself initiates healing. This is a hopeful message for all who struggle with the weight of loss or despair, affirming that sacred dialogue includes the full range of human experience and that such openness can lead to renewal. Prayer, then, becomes not only a means of petition but a transformative process, where each lament is a step toward rediscovering the joy rooted in divine presence. Finally, this subchapter calls upon readers to recognize that the cycle of grief to praise is not solely an individual journey but a communal and intergenerational one. The prayers of lament recorded in scripture have echoed through centuries, finding expression in countless lives and cultures. By entering into this ancient rhythm, believers today join a vast chorus of voices who have found in sorrow a path to praise. This shared journey enriches the spiritual imagination and strengthens the resilient spirit that sustains faith through every wilderness. In sum, the transformation of grief into praise is central to understanding the depth and universality of prayer as depicted in the King James Bible. Through scriptural patterns, poetic imagery, and lived faith, lament reveals itself as the fertile ground from which praise springs. This cyclical movement underscores the resilient spirit that inhabits sacred dialogue—a spirit that embraces sorrow, trusts in divine faithfulness, and rejoices in the renewal wrought by God's healing touch. As such, it offers a timeless invitation to all who seek to navigate the complexities of human suffering with a heart open to divine grace and an enduring song of thanksgiving.

The Universal Language: Prayer Beyond Boundaries

Prayer Across Cultures: A Global Tapestry

Prayer Across Cultures: A Global TapestryPrayer, in its many forms and expressions, is one of the most profound and universal elements of human spiritual life. While rooted deeply in the King James Bible and the Christian tradition, prayer extends far beyond any single religious framework, permeating the religious and cultural landscapes of the entire world. Across continents, languages, and belief systems, prayer reveals itself as a universal human practice, a spiritual pulse that connects the individual with the unseen, the sacred, and the transcendent. This subchapter embarks on a journey through this global tapestry of prayer, mapping its reach beyond biblical text and Christian practice. By exploring diverse faith traditions, it uncovers the common emotions, hopes, and rhythms that underlie these many voices, showing that beneath outward differences lies a shared yearning—a longing for communion, peace, guidance, and transformation. From the whispered chants of monasteries nestled in the mountains of Tibet to the rhythmic invocations of Islamic worshippers facing Mecca, from the silent meditations of Jewish mystics to the spirited shouts of Pentecostal congregations in Africa, the vast array of prayer forms testifies to prayer's limitless capacity to embrace human experience. This variety, enriched by culture and history, reflects the infinite ways humans seek dialogue with the divine. Yet, in all this diversity, there flows a connecting current of intention and feeling—an affirmation that prayer is a bridge, a place where the temporal and eternal meet. To appreciate this full spectrum, we begin by considering the essential nature and role of prayer across different religious traditions, noting the similarities and diverse expressions. As we move from one culture to another, the common threads that unite these practices come into focus: the universal human need to express vulnerability, gratitude, supplication, and adoration; the profound desire to find meaning amidst life's uncertainties; and the intuitive understanding that some form of sacred connection offers comfort and strength. Among the oldest known human prayers are found in indigenous traditions, where prayer is often inseparable from the natural world. In the animist worldviews of many indigenous communities—from North America's Native American tribes to the Aboriginal peoples of Australia—prayer is a dialogue with the spirits inherent in nature itself. Here, prayer may take the form of songs, dances, or offerings, each an expression of respect and communion with mountains, rivers, animals, and ancestors. This intimate relationship between prayer and the earth reveals a deep recognition of interdependence and reverence for life's interconnectedness, a sense that the sacred course through every element of existence. Such prayers often seek healing, protection, or guidance but also express gratitude—for rain to nourish the crops or for the balance of the seasons. They remind us that prayer can be not only words but also acts, gestures, and presence, embodying a broader spiritual consciousness. Moving from indigenous spirituality to the great world religions, it becomes clear that prayer is both a personal and communal anchor. In Hinduism, prayer takes shape as "puja" and mantra recitation. Devotees may offer flowers, incense, and light to deities such as Vishnu, Shiva, or Kali, while chanting specific verses believed to carry spiritual power. The repetition of mantras—sacred sound formulas like "Om" or the "Gayatri Mantra"—is intended to sharpen concentration and connect the devotee to the cosmic source. Hindu prayer reflects a vibrant interplay between the personal self (atman) and the universal (Brahman), acknowledging the mystery of the divine within and beyond. Despite its complex rituals and polytheistic elements, underlying it all is a recognition of prayer as a means to transcend individuality and realize unity with the divine essence. This deep longing for transcendence resonates with Christian prayer's themes of surrender and communion with God. Similarly, in Buddhism, particularly in its Mahayana and Vajrayana expressions, prayer often takes the form of chanting sutras, prostrations, and meditation on sacred images such as the Buddha or bodhisattvas. While traditional Buddhist thought emphasizes meditation and mindfulness over petitionary prayer, the practice of devotional prayer remains significant, especially in East Asian contexts. Prayers may include wishes for enlightenment, liberation from suffering, or compassion for all beings. The universal human desire for peace and release from suffering is thus expressed through prayers that focus on wisdom and loving-kindness, echoing the biblical themes of mercy and hope. The use of prayer beads or mala helps practitioners cultivate mindfulness and count repetitions, underlining prayer's role as both a spiritual discipline and a heartfelt devotion. In the Abrahamic traditions beyond Christianity, the Jewish and Islamic worlds also articulate rich and diverse prayer practices that have both shaped and been shaped by history and culture. Jewish prayer, centered on the Siddur—the Jewish prayer book—includes daily prayers like the Shema and the Amidah, each invoking God's unity, justice, and mercy. Prayer in Judaism is both a commandment and a covenantal act, a way to connect with the God of Abraham, Isaac, and Jacob. Its communal nature is strongly emphasized; synagogue services and group prayers reinforce belonging and identity. Yet Jewish prayer also opens a space for personal lament and yearning, as found in the Psalms, which have heavily influenced Christian prayer as well. The rich tradition of chanting and melodic recitation imbues Jewish prayer with a musical and emotional depth that invites both mindfulness and fervor. Islamic prayer, or Salat, exemplifies one of the most structured and universally observed expressions of prayer. Muslims perform five daily prayers at prescribed times, involving movements such as standing, bowing, and prostrating, directly facing the Kaaba in Mecca. These physical and verbal acts of prayer combine discipline with devotion and create a rhythm that governs daily life for millions of believers worldwide. The recitation of the Qur'an within prayer makes it a direct encounter with the sacred word, and the repeated declarations of faith—"There is no god but Allah, and Muhammad is His messenger"—serve as affirmations of identity and submission to the divine will. Beyond the five obligatory prayers, Muslims also express personal supplications (du'a) with intimate, spontaneous words, showing prayer's accessibility and emotional range. Shifting focus to East Asia, the Confucian and Taoist traditions offer further insights into the cultural forms of prayer. While Confucianism is often seen less as a religion than a philosophy emphasizing ethics and social harmony, it nevertheless incorporates prayer-like rituals, especially ancestor veneration. Ritual offerings and respectful speech directed toward deceased family members serve as prayers of remembrance and gratitude, affirming the ongoing relationship between the living and the sacred past. Such practices illustrate how prayer can extend beyond direct address to a deity, becoming a means of honoring continuity and seeking blessings through lineage and tradition. Taoism, with its emphasis on the Tao—the ineffable way—infuses prayer with an attitude of harmony rather than direct petition. Prayers may be improvised, poetic, or involve offerings at temples dedicated to various spirits or immortals who intercede with cosmic forces. The prayerful act in Taoism suggests a flow with nature and the universe, a surrender to the mystery beyond human control. This dimension reflects back on Christian mysticism's themes of surrender and union with God, reminding us that prayer often transcends linguistic boundaries and enters the realm of existential encounter. In the indigenous religions of Africa, prayer life is vibrant, dynamic, and community-centered. Whether in the Yoruba religion, the Zulu traditions, or other local spiritual systems, prayer blends song, dance, drumming, and invocation. Here, prayer connects to ancestors, nature spirits, and the supreme creator god, forming a spiritual ecosystem that nourishes identity and social cohesion. The call-and-response patterns found in many African prayers engage the entire community and elicit shared emotion. This communal and bodily expression echoes New Testament descriptions of early Christian worship and Pentecostal exuberance, highlighting again that prayer is as much embodied as it is verbal. In the contemporary world, new forms of prayer also emerge, shaped by globalization, interfaith encounters, and technological change. Meditation and contemplative practices derived from Buddhism and Hinduism find places in secular wellness, while interfaith prayer gatherings showcase humanity's collective yearning for peace and understanding across boundaries. Yet even amid these innovations, the familiar human themes endure: the desire to be heard, to surrender fear and doubt, and to affirm hope. Underlying the surface variety, prayer's linguistic cadences reveal patterns that suggest a shared human instinct. Repetition—be it in mantras, psalms, or litany—functions to deepen concentration and bring the individual into a state of sacred awareness. Silence, too, is a universal feature, providing space for reflection and receptivity. Invocation—the calling upon a higher power by name— serves to personalize and focus the spiritual encounter. These elements, though expressed differently in diverse traditions, testify to prayer as a universal language of the heart. Moreover, the emotions coursing through prayers across cultures are strikingly similar. Gratitude offers a common refrain—the recognition that life itself is a gift. Supplication reveals human vulnerability and trust, whether asking for healing, guidance, or deliverance from trials. Praise and adoration celebrate the goodness and greatness of the divine, embodying wonder and awe. Confession and lament articulate the struggle with sin, pain, or loss, offering catharsis and hope for renewal. Each of these emotional expressions illustrates prayer's role as a vessel for the full spectrum of human experience. This interconnectedness between prayer practices worldwide enriches our understanding of prayer as more than religious obligation; it is a vital human impulse to seek meaning and relationship beyond oneself. Such a perspective invites readers of the King James Bible—and believers and seekers of all backgrounds alike—to embrace prayer as both a personal discipline and a shared human heritage. Studying prayer across cultures encourages humility and openness, breaking down barriers of misunderstanding and tribalism. It reveals that, in spite of doctrinal differences and ritual specificity, the act of raising one's voice or folding one's hands in prayer affirms a universal truth: humanity is woven together by the sacred threads of hope, longing, and devotion. And through this global tapestry, prayer continues to be a living and dynamic force, echoing the divine in the hearts of all who seek. In conclusion, the exploration of prayer across cultures presents a radiant mosaic—each piece distinct, each tradition with its own history and expression, yet all united by the pulse of the human spirit reaching out to the sacred. The King James Bible's depiction of prayer thus stands within a larger, vibrant world of faith, and its teachings gain new depth when illuminated by this global chorus. It is this shared pulse, the universal language of prayer, that invites us to listen deeply, to enter into solidarity, and to find in prayer a transformative pathway that transcends boundaries and brings humanity closer to the divine.

Interfaith Dialogues and Shared Yearnings

In a world increasingly interconnected yet marked by profound diversity, prayer emerges not merely as a private act of devotion but as a bridge spanning faith traditions, cultures, and worldviews. Interfaith dialogues—spaces where people of varied religious backgrounds come together to share, reflect, and learn—highlight prayer's unique capacity to foster connection beyond doctrinal boundaries. Through these encounters, prayer reveals itself as a universal language, rich with both convergence and distinction, a profound expression of humanity's yearning for the sacred. At the heart of this dynamic lies a subtle but powerful truth: while religious traditions articulate their beliefs and hopes in distinctive terms, the fundamental impulses underlying prayer—the desire for communion, peace, guidance, healing, and transcendence—resonate across all. It is precisely in these shared yearnings, voiced in diverse modes and expressions, that interfaith dialogue flourishes, inviting a recognition of common ground amid difference. The King James Bible, with its majestic and poetic rendering of biblical prayers, occupies a distinctive role in this conversation. Its elegant cadence and evocative imagery invite not only Christians but seekers of many paths to listen closely, to enter into the depths of contemplation that prayer invites. The King James text's lyrical beauty thus becomes a vibrant participant in the universal dialogue of prayer, offering a lens through which the full spectrum of human supplication and praise can be appreciated. Prayer as a Universal Dialogue Interfaith encounters often revolve around testimony—sharing of beliefs, stories, and rituals—but prayer adds an additional, sometimes subtle dimension: it is at once personal and communal, transcending theological particulars while embodying them. When adherents of different traditions pray side by side, in celebration or in crisis, what emerges often surprises and enlightens participants. The rhythms of prayer, its cadences, the turning of the heart toward the sacred, find expressions that, while unique in form, are recognizably kin in spirit. Consider the African-American spirituals sung in Christian worship alongside the melodic chants of Buddhism, the vibrant recitations of Hindu mantras paired with the contemplative silence of Quaker meetings. Though varied in methods and words, each channel conveys a yearning for peace, a call for healing, a reaching toward divine presence. Interfaith settings reveal how these threads interweave, forming a rich tapestry whose beauty emerges through contrast and harmony alike. This experience is not a mere academic exercise: it touches something deeply human. The participants come to understand that prayer is not a proprietary possession of any one tradition but a shared human resource for nourishment, courage, and transformation. In this way, prayer becomes a dialogue not only among people but among the sacred stories and spiritual frameworks they embody. The King James Bible's Poetic Voice in Interfaith Contexts The King James Bible, first published in 1611, remains among the most influential and widely-read English translations of Scripture. Its distinctive style—marked by rhythmic cadences, archaic but evocative language, and an interwoven poetic structure—imbues biblical prayers with a grandeur that transcends temporal and cultural boundaries. Even among those who do not claim the Christian faith, the King James text often resonates as literature, as spiritual poetry, inviting reflection on themes common to many religious traditions. For example, the penitential tone of the Psalms, the humble supplications of Daniel, the visionary prayers of Isaiah—all rendered with majestic phraseology—express human vulnerability, hope, and the search for divine consolation. An interfaith gathering that includes readings from the King James Psalter alongside prayers from other traditions invites participants to hear echoes of their own aspirations and struggles in these ancient verses. The universality of such themes facilitates respectful listening and shared spiritual experience. Moreover, the King James Bible exemplifies how language itself can function as a bridge. Its influence on English literature and thought means that its echoes permeate the ways many speak about prayer, morality, and the sacred. Interfaith dialogues, therefore, can find themselves navigating and appreciating this shared cultural and linguistic legacy, even as they honor differences in theology. Shared Yearnings: The Consonance in Diversity Across faith traditions, the content of prayers often circles the same essential themes: the pursuit of peace, the appeal for justice, the plea for healing, the desire for wisdom, and ultimately, surrender to the divine will. While the form and vocabulary may differ—be it the chanting of Om, the recitation of the Lord's Prayer, the intonations of the Islamic Salah, or the silent meditation of the Buddhist practitioner—the underlying yearning remains constant. Interfaith dialogues that include prayerful practices underscore this consonance. Participants find that even when theological explanations diverge—conceptions of God as triune, monotheistic, pantheistic, or non-theistic—they stand face to face with the shared human experience of awe and dependency before forces beyond themselves. This realization fosters a deepened respect for the "other," not as someone alien, but as a fellow traveler seeking connection and meaning. Instances of such dialogues abound in contemporary settings: interfaith peace vigils, multi-religious prayer breakfasts, or spiritual retreats that invite representatives from diverse faiths to share prayers and reflections. These moments often reveal how prayer can soften boundaries, creating spaces where differences coexist without conflict, where the sacred energies of various traditions blend and enrich one another rather than clash. Respectful Differences: Navigating Distinctiveness with Grace While emphasizing harmony and shared yearning, interfaith dialogues acknowledge that prayer also articulates important differences: in how the divine is perceived, in the rituals and structures surrounding prayer, and in the ethical imperatives arising therefrom. This acknowledgment does not diminish the possibility of shared spiritual experience; rather, it situates it within a context of honest recognition and respect. For example, some prayers focus on petition and expression of gratitude toward a personal God, others on silent communion with an impersonal ultimate reality. Some traditions expect prayer to invoke miraculous intervention, others view it primarily as a means of aligning the seeker's mind and will with divine principles. Understanding these nuances enriches the dialogue, moving it beyond superficial similarity toward a grasp of prayer's multifaceted nature. The King James Bible, too, offers space for such complexity. It contains prayers of lament, joy, and petition; prayers exposing human doubt and anger alongside those of unwavering faith. Its texts reflect a wrestling with the divine that resonates with other traditions that embrace candid honesty in their spiritual expressions. Interfaith encounters can thus draw on these biblical prayers to model openness and vulnerability in prayer— qualities essential to authentic dialogue. Contemporary Expressions: Prayer as a Bridge in Practice In real-world contexts, prayer often serves as a medium for healing communal pain and fostering reconciliation. Interfaith groups have found in shared prayer the capacity to move beyond historical grievances and conflicts to a place where empathy and hope take root. For instance, in regions marked by sectarian violence, joint prayer vigils explicitly call for peace by drawing upon the sacred languages and symbols of multiple faiths. These gatherings illustrate how prayer functions as a living, dynamic process: it is not static doctrine but active engagement with present realities. Prayer, when shared across faiths, challenges participants to recognize each other's dignity, to listen deeply, and to act compassionately in the world. The King James Bible's prayers, read aloud or contemplated alongside other traditions' sacred words, offer a resonant voice calling toward justice, mercy, and humility. Furthermore, prayer's immediacy makes it accessible. It need not depend on theological agreement to be meaningful; it invites each person to bring their own experience of yearning and surrender. This inclusivity enables interfaith encounters to move beyond intellectual debate into spaces of shared spiritual practice—where words give way to silence or chant, where diverse symbols interlace into a mosaic of devotion. The Poetic Power of the King James Bible in Interfaith Reflection The literary and spiritual qualities of the King James Bible enhance its role in interfaith contexts. Its rhythms mirror the natural cadences of human speech and breath, encouraging meditation and introspection. The vivid imagery— for example, "the valley of the shadow of death," "the pillars of the earth," or "wings like the dove"—transcends cultural specificity, evoking universal human experiences of fear, stability, and longing. In interfaith prayer services or study groups, the King James Bible's poetic passages often invite not only Christian participants but those from other traditions to ponder truths that cross boundaries: the calls for mercy and justice, the laments over suffering, the hope for redemption. This participation is not about conversion but about entering a spiritual dialogue that enriches all voices involved. Moreover, the Bible's emphasis on prayer as an ongoing conversation with the divine—sometimes confident, sometimes pleading, sometimes questioning—mirrors the openness necessary in interfaith relations. The King James translations preserve this raw honesty, providing a textual space that welcomes complexity and ambiguity rather than demanding facile certainty. Challenges and Opportunities in Interfaith Prayer Dialogues Despite its promise, interfaith prayer encounters also pose challenges. They require sensitivity to avoid appropriation or dilution of sacred traditions. Participants must approach others' prayers with reverence and a willingness to listen without judgment. Language differences, theological disparities, and ritual distinctiveness can complicate joint prayer experiences.Nonetheless, these challenges underscore the opportunities inherent in such dialogues. They invite mutual learning about the plurality of ways human beings relate to the sacred. In doing so, they foster humility, broaden understanding, and promote peace. The King James Bible, widely studied and admired, offers a stable and poetic anchor amid these complexities. Its prayers, contextualized thoughtfully within interfaith settings, can illuminate shared human experiences and ethical imperatives that resonate well beyond denominational lines. Toward a Shared Spiritual Future The spiritual landscape of the 21st century is marked by both fragmentation and renewed desire for connection. Interfaith dialogues around prayer symbolize a hopeful pathway forward—a recognition that while faith traditions differ, the language of the heart—the prayer—speaks to universal realities. By embracing the King James Bible's rich poetic tradition alongside the prayers of other faiths, communities can nurture authentic encounters rooted in respect and openness. These shared moments of prayer do not erase difference but allow it to coexist within a broader harmony, reflecting the multifaceted human search for meaning and the divine. Ultimately, "Interfaith Dialogues and Shared Yearnings" presents prayer as a living testimony to the interconnectedness of humanity's spiritual heritage. Amid the echoes of diverse sacred voices, the King James Bible's prayers remain vibrant threads, inviting all to join a universal conversation—one heart, many prayers, a common hope.

The Cosmic Language of Prayer

In the vast tapestry of human experience, prayer emerges not merely as a petition or a ritualistic utterance but as a profound cosmic language— one that transcends the confines of spoken tongues, dogmatic traditions, and cultural boundaries. This language, ineffable yet intimate, weaves together silent spaces and articulated yearnings into a dynamic symphony of spiritual communion. As the King James Bible frequently intimates, prayer is less a human initiative and more a responsive dance within the boundless presence of the Divine, an invitation to join in a cosmic dialogue that echoes through all creation. To envision prayer as a cosmic language invites us to expand beyond the conventional image of it as a secluded act of individual devotion. Instead, we are called to perceive it as a fundamental and universal expression shaped by an energetic landscape in which every whispered hope or thunderous cry participates in a larger symphony. In this metropolitan interplay, the Divine Presence functions much like the ever-expanding universe itself—limitless, mysterious, and alive. The King James Bible, with its rich poetic cadence and resonant metaphors, lays a foundation for this vision, offering glimpses into the interplay of the seen and unseen, the temporal and eternal, the finite human soul and the infinite divine. At its core, the metaphor of prayer as a cosmic language suggests that prayer is a mode of communication that transcends verbal articulation, one that operates through frequencies of intention, vibration, and resonance. It is a language of the heart, rooted in surrender and trust, yet simultaneously bursting forth in fervent desire and hope. It is both silent and vocal, a conversation stretching from the depths of the human spirit upward to the heights of divine eternity. This duality resides at the heart of many biblical prayers—those spoken aloud and those held in the silent chambers of the soul, both equally valid and potent. Consider the imagery in Psalm 19:1, "The heavens declare the glory of God; and the firmament sheweth his handywork." Here, the heavens themselves are depicted as speaking in a language beyond words, one that all creation understands. The Psalmist frames the cosmos as a living testament, continually proclaiming divine greatness. Within this celestial proclamation lies the essence of prayer as a cosmic language: it is not confined to earthly utterance but is embodied in the very fabric of creation. Humanity's prayers, then, become threads intricately woven into this cosmic narrative, each adding its distinct vibrancy to the greater spiritual mosaic. Expanding this perspective reveals prayer as an interface not only between the human and the divine but also between the individual and the collective, between the temporal and the eternal. It is a living dialogue in which the petitioner's voice merges with countless others, heard simultaneously in the tranquil stillness of midnight vigils and the collective hymns of ancient congregations. This universal language dissolves the walls erected by sectarian divisions and invites a recognition of spiritual kinship across all people. The King James Bible, though rooted in a particular religious tradition, offers an abundant wellspring of prayers and poetic affirmations that carry this transcendent dimension, serving as archetypes and templates pointing toward the unified cosmic dance of souls reaching upward and outward in longing and thanksgiving. To comprehend prayer as a cosmic language is also to engage with the interplay of silence and sound, presence and absence, movement and rest. The space between words—the silent pauses, the breath held in expectant stillness—becomes as vital as the words themselves. These silences can be understood as the "space" in which the divine interacts with human consciousness, a sacred pause receptive to the Spirit's promptings. The King James Bible reflects this dynamic tension through passages that emphasize waiting on the Lord (Psalm 27:14) or the stillness wherein God's powerful voice is not found in the wind or earthquake but in the "still small voice" (1 Kings 19:12). Such descriptions elevate silent receptivity and attentiveness as integral components of the cosmic dance of prayer. In this energetic landscape, prayer is not merely an act of asking or proclaiming; it is actively co-creative. The individual who prays engages in a mysterious reciprocity where surrender and assertion intertwine. The cosmic language of prayer evokes an image of waves upon the ocean—each prayer a ripple that merges into the greater currents of divine interaction, influencing and being influenced in turn. This dynamic is echoed within the King James Bible's portrayals of intercession, where the prayers of the faithful can change the course of events (as in the story of Abraham interceding for Sodom, Genesis 18) or bring about transformation in both the supplicant and the world. Moreover, this cosmic language of prayer connects deeply with the timeless human yearning to touch something beyond oneself, to find meaning in the midst of mystery, and to align with a reality that transcends the visible. Prayer, in this sense, becomes a universal code—a language that all hearts can speak and understand, irrespective of creed or culture. It is the rhythm underlying all spiritual traditions and practices, a foundational impulse echoing through monastic chants, indigenous invocations, contemplative meditation, and spontaneous cries of despair or joy. This universal character of prayer is powerfully captured in the Sermon on the Mount's teaching about the nature of God and prayer: "Your Father which is in heaven... knoweth what things ye have need of, before ye ask him" (Matthew 6:32-8). This suggests that prayer is less about informing God and more about tuning human consciousness to a divine frequency already present, about aligning with a cosmic reality that precedes and enfolds human petition. Prayer, therefore, becomes a means of attuning oneself to the Divine Presence that pervades the entire universe, connecting all beings through an invisible but palpable web of spiritual energy. As we meditate on this concept, it becomes evident that engaging with the cosmic language of prayer involves a fundamental transformation in awareness. Instead of viewing prayer as a transactional exchange—where one asks and receives—it is an invitation to participate in an ancient, living dialogue that transcends time and space. Each prayer, whether whispered beneath breath or shouted in collective fervor, resonates within this vast network of sacred connection. One is invited to imagine one's voice joining myriad others—those of patriarchs and prophets, sinners and saints, seekers and skeptics—creating a chorus of spiritual longing and praise that vibrates across the cosmos. Such an expansive vision of prayer naturally fosters humility and wonder. It reminds the supplicant that their small utterance holds significance far beyond its immediate context, contributing to the unfolding drama of divine-human encounter. Simultaneously, it underscores that the Divine Presence is not confined to one place or tradition but moves fluidly through all creation, responding to and encompassing the breadth of human experience. The cosmic language of prayer is thus a celebration of both individual intimacy and shared belonging within a universal spiritual family. This idea also challenges modern assumptions about communication and spirituality. In a world saturated with language barriers, noise pollution, and fragmented community, the metaphor of prayer as a cosmic language offers an alternative framework—one that invites listening beyond words and speaking beyond phrases, tuning into the spiritual vibrations that unite all existence. It suggests that prayer can be both deeply personal and universally accessible, that the sacred is not locked away in ancient texts or hidden temples but is alive here and now, ready to receive even the quietest murmurings of the soul. Biblical narratives reinforce this concept repeatedly. The experience of Moses at the burning bush (Exodus 3) reveals the interplay of presence and voice where God speaks not through human language alone but through a manifest sign, a fire enveloping a bush yet unconsumed—a symbol of a divine mystery communicating beyond ordinary speech. Similarly, the Psalms are replete with cries and laments that transcend mere words, often encompassing a fuller range of emotional and spiritual vibration. When David declares, "Make a joyful noise unto the Lord, all ye lands" (Psalm 100:1), the text suggests that prayer touches every level of being—from primal sound to soaring song, from heartfelt silence to exuberant praise. Furthermore, the incarnation of Christ itself can be understood within this cosmic language framework. Jesus, as the Word made flesh, embodies the perfect union of divine communication and human reception, bridging the chasm between heaven and earth. His prayers recorded in the Gospel—often laden with deep intimacy and universal yearning—exemplify the dynamic rhythm of this cosmic dance. Whether in solitary solitude or public supplication, Jesus models a prayerful life attuned to the Divine Presence, inviting all to join in this boundless, universal communion. From a theological standpoint, the cosmic language of prayer aligns with the biblical notion of the Spirit moving across the waters in creation (Genesis 1:2), hovering over the deep with a mysterious creative energy. This Spirit continues to inspire, intercede, and unite across God's diverse family. Saint Paul's reference to the Spirit helping in our weakness, interceding "with groanings which cannot be uttered" (Romans 8:26), poignantly illustrates this cosmic communication beyond human speech, underscoring that prayer is not limited to our conscious words but participates in a cosmic dialogue facilitated by divine love. Individuals from varying faith traditions and spiritual perspectives can also find resonance with this metaphor. For instance, the idea that prayer is a signal within a universal frequency mirrors concepts found in mystical Christianity, Sufism, Kabbalah, and even certain forms of modern contemplative practice. This universality bridges divides, offering a shared sacred language rooted not in doctrinal specifics but in the common experience of reaching beyond the self toward the Divine Mystery. In practical spiritual terms, embracing the cosmic language of prayer invites practitioners to cultivate awareness of the spaces between words—the vital silences and lingering pauses where communion deepens. It encourages an expansive listening, attuned to the subtle pulses of the heart and the gentle stirrings of the Spirit. Prayer becomes less about producing a specific outcome and more about entering into rhythm with the divine cadence pervading the cosmos. This cosmic vision also has profound implications for how believers relate to one another and to the world. Recognizing prayer as a universal language invites respect for the diverse forms through which others connect with the sacred, fostering humility and openness. It counters spiritual insularity by affirming that at the heart of all authentic prayer lies a shared human impulse—a longing for connection, for meaning, for transformation—that transcends labels and divisions. The Kingdom of Heaven proclaimed in the Gospels may be visualized as this vast dynamic web of spiritual interaction, where all prayers, silent or spoken, mingle and pulse with the Divine Presence. This "kingdom" is not confined to an earthly location or a future time but is accessible now, experienced in moments of genuine communion and reverence. When Jesus taught the Lord's Prayer, his words encapsulated this universal aspiration, a framework for connecting with God as our Father and aligning our will with a cosmic order characterized by justice, mercy, and peace. Indeed, the act of praying within this cosmic language may itself transform the individual, awakening a sense of their place within the grand design. It fosters a spirituality grounded in interconnectedness, where personal desires and collective needs meet in a shared encounter with the sacred. Each prayer, therefore, contributes not only to personal growth but to the healing and harmonizing of the broader spiritual cosmos, resonating with the biblical promise that "if two of you shall agree on earth as touching any thing that they shall ask, it shall be done for them of my Father which is in heaven" (Matthew 18:19). In summary, the metaphor of prayer as a cosmic language accessible to all offers a transformative lens through which to view and engage in the spiritual practice of prayer. It highlights the dynamic interplay of silent spaces and voiced petitions, embracing a boundless Divine Presence that transcends particular religions and traditions. This perspective invites readers to imagine their prayers as threads within a vast, living tapestry of spiritual communion—a cosmic dance where every voice, every silence, every longing contributes to the unfolding mystery of divine-human relationship. By embracing this vision, seekers and believers alike can find both solace and empowerment, recognizing that prayer is not a solitary act confined to narrow borders but a universal expression of the human spirit reaching outward toward the Divine. The King James Bible, with its majestic language and timeless insights, offers rich guidance and inspiration, reminding us that prayer is, in essence, the language of the cosmos itself—a sacred conversation unfolding in infinite space and eternal time.

Invitation to the Seeker: Embracing Prayer's Universality

In the quiet spaces between heartbeats, when the world's clamor softens and a gentle stillness takes hold, there lies an invitation—a call not bound by creed, culture, or conviction but reaching across the tapestry of human experience. This invitation is to the seeker, the one whose soul stirs with questions and whose spirit longs for connection beyond mere words. Prayer, in its essence, is such an invitation: an open door extending to all who hunger for meaning, solace, or communion with a presence greater than themselves. As the concluding reflection of this chapter, we turn our gaze toward this seeker—the embodiment of openness and curiosity—and extend to every reader an embrace of prayer as a universal language, a vessel of hope, and a bridge of spiritual kinship. The seeker stands at the crossroads of wonder and yearning, a figure both ancient and timeless. Across the pages of the King James Bible, while the faithful are vividly portrayed in their steadfast expressions of devotion, the seeker's stance is no less honored. Figures like the psalmist David who cries out in anguish and doubt, Job who wrestles with suffering and silence, and even the wise king Solomon who yearns for understanding, all reflect aspects of the seeker's journey. They remind us that prayer is not limited to the confident or the learned but is the rightful solace of anyone who seeks to pour out the depths of their heart—be it in hope, confusion, grief, or joy. This openness—the willingness to approach the divine mystery without pretense or certainty—is at the heart of prayer's universality. Consider, for a moment, the simple but profound words from the Book of Psalms, "O God, thou art my God; early will I seek thee: my soul thirsteth for thee, my flesh longeth for thee in a dry and thirsty land, where no water is." (Psalm 63:1) These verses capture the essence of spiritual yearning that transcends specific doctrine. The thirst, the longing, the early seeking—all speak to a condition common to every human heart. To thirst for connection, to long for meaning or peace, is a universal impulse. Prayer becomes the language of that thirst, spoken in silence, spoken aloud, or whispered in the depths of one's being. Imagining a seeker's voice, unbound by tradition yet saturated with sincerity, invites us to reconsider the boundaries often imposed around prayer. Too often, theological or cultural frameworks restrict prayer's scope, relegating it to ritualistic compliance or exclusive divine access. Yet the biblical record, especially in the King James Bible, reveals a far wider and more inclusive vision. It unfolds prayer as an act of relationship rather than mere recitation; as a reaching out to the divine that invites reciprocal presence and transformation. This transformative power is available not only to a chosen few but to all who dare to embrace it. One cannot explore this universal invitation without reflecting on the power of storytelling.

Stories, after all, are the vessels through which experience is shared and wisdom transmitted. The King James Bible is replete with stories that dance between the sacred and the human, offering portraits of prayer as deeply personal yet profoundly communal. The story of Hannah, the barren woman who poured out her soul in silent anguish and emerged with hope restored, illustrates prayer as a cry from the depths that touches the heart of God. Her story is a mirror for countless seekers who know despair but still turn toward the divine with trembling hope. Likewise, the narrative of the prodigal son invites the seeker into a dynamic of return, reconciliation, and renewed belonging. This story, while centered in the Christian tradition, resonates universally because it speaks to the sacred possibility embodied in every seeking heart. Prayer becomes not just an address to the divine but a journey inward and outward—toward forgiveness, healing, and acceptance. Scriptural echoes reverberate throughout these stories, gently reminding us that prayer is woven into the fabric of human existence. It is the sigh of the oppressed, the song of the grateful, the confession of the penitent, and the praise of the joyful. These threads, found in the biblical narrative, illustrate prayer's multifaceted nature—tender and bold, individual and collective, simple and profound. For the seeker, such echoes offer encouragement: your experience, your words, your silence—all have a place in the sacred language of prayer. Meditations on these themes deepen the invitation. Imagine sitting beside a quiet stream, watching the water flow with steady persistence despite the rocks and bends. Such is the flow of prayer in the life of the seeker—sometimes clear and focused, sometimes murky and uncertain, always moving toward a source beyond itself. This metaphor illustrates prayer's endurance and adaptability. It is not a static gift but a living, breathing practice that unfolds uniquely in each human soul. The seeker is invited to take up this prayer—not as a task or obligation but as a sacred act of engagement with the divine and the self. Through meditation, contemplation, or spontaneous utterance, prayer offers a sanctuary for the heart's expressions. It is a place where the seeker can lay down burdens, find clarity amidst confusion, and nurture an emerging sense of spiritual kinship with others whom they may never meet yet whose prayers ripple across time and space. This kinship is perhaps the most extraordinary aspect of prayer's universality. When we pray—regardless of our words, forms, or beliefs—we join an unbroken chain of human longing. Consider the profound connection evoked by the Lord's Prayer, recited by millions across centuries: "Our Father which art in heaven... Give us this day our daily bread." These words transcend denominational walls, touching a core of human dependency and trust. They articulate a shared human condition—a recognition that all life depends upon divine providence and mercy. The seeker, by embracing prayer, also embraces this community of seekers and believers across time. From the psalmist's ancient cries to the whispered prayers of saints and sinners alike, there is a communion beyond physical boundaries. This communion offers solace, solidarity, and strength. It is a reminder that the seeker is never truly alone in their search. Moreover, prayer's universality is evident in its capacity to bring hope. Hope is the seed sown in the soil of uncertainty—sometimes fragile, sometimes fierce. The King James Bible contains countless prayers of hope that inspire the seeker. Consider the words of Isaiah: "They that wait upon the Lord shall renew their strength; they shall mount up with wings as eagles." (Isaiah 40:31) To wait upon the Lord is to pray—to surrender one's fears, to trust beyond sight, and to receive renewed strength. This promise of hope, carried by the act of prayer, transcends all boundaries of culture, language, and faith tradition. For the seeker hesitant or unsure, this reflection offers reassurance: prayer does not demand perfection or polished language. "Behold, I stand at the door and knock," declares the Revelation narrator (Revelation 3:20), a call suggesting that the divine is ever-present, ever-patient, inviting the simplest act of openness. Prayer begins with the invitation, not the mastery of form. It begins with a heart willing to listen and speak, to offer and to receive. In embracing prayer's universality, the seeker also embraces freedom—the freedom to make prayer their own. While the King James Bible provides a treasury of language and imagery, it is not a straitjacket but a muse that inspires countless forms of prayer.

This freedom affirms the seeker's unique spiritual expression. Whether through silent meditation, spoken word, song, or ritual, prayer is a profoundly personal act that reflects the seeker's context, culture, and inner life. Thus, the seeker steps onto a path that is both ancient and ever-new. This path—paved with prayers, stories, and meditations—invites continual discovery. It reveals prayer as a universal sanctuary where all who seek can find a home. It offers a courage to confront loneliness, despair, and doubt; a grace to receive comfort, clarity, and peace; and a connection to the divine mystery that animates all creation. To the reader who identifies as the seeker, the invitation is simple yet profound: approach prayer without fear or hesitation. Let your voice, whatever its form, mingle with the chorus of humanity's prayers. Let your heart's questions and longings find expression in this universal language. Embrace prayer as a sacred vessel—an enduring testimony to the unquenchable human spirit reaching toward the divine. In this embracing lies a promise: the promise of transformation—not in some distant, ethereal realm but here and now. Prayer molds the seeker's spirit, opening eyes to grace, softening hearts to compassion, and igniting a flame of hope that endures through life's deepest trials. It is a bridge spanning the worlds within and without, a line of light connecting the individual to the universal. And so, the seeker journeys forward, stepping beyond tradition's walls and cultural divides, drawn by the call of a voice unseen yet deeply known. This journey is itself a prayer—a movement toward union, understanding, and love. It is a gift offered to all who choose to accept it. May every seeker who reads these words feel the gentle touch of invitation, hear the whispered welcome of the eternal, and discover in prayer the universal thread that unites all humankind in hope, grace, and divine kinship.

Gary E. Risenhoover

Temples of Silence: The Stillness Within Prayer

The Sacred Pause: Silence as Prayerful Space

In the tapestry of human expression, few threads weave as profoundly through the fabric of spirituality as silence. Within the sacred tradition of prayer, silence is not an empty void, a mere pause between spoken words, but rather the essential container within which dialogue with the divine breathes and unfolds. It is a sanctuary, both vast and intimate, where the restless clamors of the mind subside and a stillness deeper than understanding arises. This stillness is a temple—an inner sanctuary built not of stone or wood but of presence, openness, and waiting. In this space, prayer transcends the limitations of language and becomes a living encounter with the mystery of being itself. The King James Bible, whose majestic cadence has inspired generations, holds within its verses evocative instances of silence used as a canvas for divine encounter. These moments reveal that silence is not merely the absence of speech, but the fullness of readiness—a precious pause pregnant with expectation. From the quiet before creation to the hushed reverence of the psalmist, and the silent wrestling of the soul in the wilderness, biblical silence beckons us to enter a sacred pause where prayer is not just said but is felt in the very core of our being. Consider the very beginning of the sacred narrative: "And the earth was without form, and void; and darkness was upon the face of the deep. And the Spirit of God moved upon the face of the waters" (Genesis 1:2). Before the divine word commanded light to shine, there was a profound stillness enveloping the void. This silence, pregnant with potential, is the primordial prayer of creation itself—a contemplative waiting that invites the breath of God. Here, silence is not emptiness; it is the womb of all that is to come, an unspoken communion between the divine and the formless. In the life of the patriarchs and prophets, moments of silent anticipation punctuate their journeys. Moses approaches the burning bush, not rushing with words but standing in silent awe as God calls him by name. Elijah, weary and hunted, finds God not in the roaring wind, the earthquake, or the fire, but in "a still small voice" (1 Kings 19:12). The psalms often echo the reverent pause of silence, "Be still, and know that I am God" (Psalm 46:10), directing the soul to rest from its striving and enter into a prayerful stillness where divine presence may be known beyond the reach of speech. Silence in these biblical moments functions as a threshold; it prepares the heart to receive, to be transformed, and to listen deeply. It is both an act of trust—yielding control, stepping into the unknown—and a space of profound openness. This paradox of silence is awe-inspiring: it is both absence and presence, void and fullness. In silence, the heart becomes a sacred chamber that vibrates with unseen colors and textures, shimmering faintly like light filtering through stained glass—a subtle dance beyond words. Such biblical silences find their echo and expansion in the rich traditions of modern contemplative practice, where quietude is cultivated intentionally as prayerful space. The Christian mystical tradition, drawing from these scriptural wells, has long embraced silence as the language of a deeper communion with God. The Desert Fathers and Mothers wandered far into the wilderness, seeking not voices nor visions, but the silence where God's presence might be encountered face-to-face. Through practices like centering prayer, the Jesus Prayer, and meditative reading (lectio divina), practitioners enter the sacred pause to listen, not with the ears of the flesh, but of the spirit. This deliberate silence is often described as a temple in itself. Imagine, if you will, an inner sanctuary where the cacophony of daily life is stilled, where the mind's river slows to a gentle pool. In this temple, the air is dense yet light; sounds dissolve into an ocean of quietude; shadows and light interweave softly upon the walls of consciousness. Here, prayer transcends its verbal form; it becomes a dance of presence, a silent resonance vibrating between the soul and God, where nothing more is needed but to be. The colors in this sanctuary are not painted with pigments but with sensations—warmth, peace, longing, and awe—that shimmer beneath the surface of experience. It is in this sacred pause that prayer finds its most profound expression. Spoken words can be clumsy, fragmented, even shields against vulnerability. Silence strips away these barriers and reveals the soul in its nakedness and truth. To enter silence in prayer is to surrender the urge to control, to fix, to persuade, and instead to receive—to hold one's heart open like a chalice, ready to be filled with grace. This surrender is itself a prayer: a profound yes to the divine mystery, a humble acknowledgment of human limitation and divine transcendence. Moreover, silence as prayerful space invites a transformation not only in relation to God but in relation to self. It cultivates a sacred attentiveness, a listening that reorients the soul from the turmoil of ego and desire toward the calm of non-desiring presence. Here, the self becomes less a commander and more a witness—aware, receptive, and at peace. This internal stillness ripples outward, infusing daily life with a grace that steadies the spirit, deepens compassion, and fortifies hope amid adversity. The paradox of silence never ceases to astonish. In the absence of spoken word, a fullness emerges—a richness of spiritual sensation that fills the empty space with unarticulated love and longing. Silence holds all the questions that cannot be answered by words and all the answers that cannot be fully expressed. It contains grief and joy side by side, despair and hope intertwined. It is a sanctuary into which all of life's complexities enter and are held gently, without hurry or judgment. To appreciate silence as a prayerful space, it is helpful to consider the contrast with our contemporary world, often characterized by relentless noise and distraction. Incessant chatter, media stimuli, and the unending activity of the mind pull us from inner presence. Yet, the biblical witness and the spiritual disciplines remind us that beneath this noise lies the eternal silence—a deep wellspring of peace accessible through intention and grace. Cultivating this silence is an act of spiritual courage and love: courage to face the interior desert, love that opens the heart to divine encounter beyond words. In practice, entering the sacred pause begins with awareness—recognizing the restless currents of thought and emotion, then gently guiding attention inward. This inward journey is not about forcing the mind into blankness but rather about making space for what is: a presence, a breath, a stillness beneath the surface. As the soul settles, prayer evolves from saying into being. Words may vanish, replaced by breaths that echo with gratitude, awe, and surrender. Within this silence, time itself seems to bend. Moments stretch and deepen, holding a weightless infinity that contrasts starkly with the urgency of worldly hours. This suspension of time invites a perspective beyond temporal concerns, connecting the worshipper to the eternal rhythm of creation. Silent prayer becomes a dance with eternity, discrete moments that touch the infinite and then return to daily life transformed, as if carrying a secret light beneath the skin. This light is the fruit of the sacred pause—a luminous awareness that God is not distant but immanent, not far but near, residing in the stillness where words fail. It is a presence that eludes definition yet fills every nook of the inner sanctuary, infusing it with peace that surpasses understanding. This peace is not absence of trial, but a sustaining strength amid trial, a calm anchor in the storms of life. The sacred pause also invites a communal dimension. Though silence is often associated with solitude, its power resonates deeply in shared prayer and worship. Across millennia, communities have gathered in silent prayer—monastic orders, Quaker meetings, and countless worship services—discovering that collective silence holds a unique sacredness. In such moments, individuals align their stillness, creating a living temple of silent hearts united in waiting and longing. This silent congregation becomes a harbinger of peace, a counterpoint to the noise of division and discord, an embodiment of hope. Returning to the biblical image, we see that the sacred pause is the space where promises are heard and faith is forged. When Anna, the prophetess, 'spake of him to all them that looked for redemption in Jerusalem' (Luke 2:38), it was after years of silent waiting in the temple courts. When the disciples waited on the day of Pentecost, they 'were all with one accord in one place'—a unified silence before the rushing wind of the Spirit (Acts 2:1-4). These narratives remind us that silence is not absence of action but preparation for divine revelation and empowerment. In the present age, amidst the busyness and clamor, embracing the sacred pause is both an act of ancient wisdom and contemporary necessity. It calls us to reclaim a lost conversation—with God, with ourselves, and with the world—spoken not in words but in the language of stillness. Through silence, prayer becomes less about petition and more about presence; less about telling God what we want and more about listening to what God wishes to reveal. To enter this sacred pause is to rediscover prayer's original and eternal form: a silent encounter marked by love and waiting, by surrender and hope. In it, the barriers between the human and the divine soften, and a profound intimacy emerges—a meeting of heart with Heart, soul with Soul. This temple of silence within prayer is a refuge and a wellspring, where the noise of the world is stilled and the shimmer of sacred presence illuminates the depths. Ultimately, silence as prayerful space invites a transformation of our seeing and being. It turns our attention away from the outer sphere of action and accomplishment to the inner realm of listening and becoming. It recalls us to the place where words fall away and the soul is naked in the presence of the divine—a place not of loneliness but of profound communion. Here, in this sacred temple of silence, prayer breathes most deeply, echoing the eternal rhythms of heaven and earth, a silent song that embraces all who enter.

Listening Beyond Speech

In the quiet spaces between words and thoughts lies a profound dimension of prayer that often escapes our hurried grasp. While prayer is commonly understood as an act of speaking—to petition, praise, confess, or give thanks—there is an equally vital and transformative aspect to prayer that invites us to become still, to listen deeply beyond speech. This listening is not a passive pause or an empty interval; rather, it is an active, intentional encounter with the Divine Presence—a presence that does not thunder but whispers; does not demand but invites; does not overwhelm but enfolds. It is in this fertile stillness, in this sacred silence, that prayer reveals itself as a dialogue, a communion, and a shared space where the human heart meets the Divine heart. The King James Bible abounds with subtle intimations of this silent listening, though often it is overshadowed by the more prominent prayers of speech and petition. Yet tucked within psalms, prophets' lamentations, and the wisdom literature are clues that prayer is as much about receiving as it is about speaking. The biblical narrative invites us to a kind of hearing that transcends the words themselves—a listening "with the ear of the heart," as some mystics have described it, tuning our spirits to the divine frequency that humbles, heals, and transforms. To enter into this listening beyond speech requires a deliberate cultivation of silence—an inner temple where the soul can become attentive and receptive. Here, silence is not simply the absence of noise but a presence in itself; a living essence that carries the fragrance of grace and beckons the restless spirit to rest. The psalmist's exhortation, "Be still, and know that I am God" (Psalm 46:10), encapsulates this invitation. This stillness is neither inert nor vacant; it is a dynamic posture of openness—like a carefully tuned instrument ready to receive the Divine melody.Listening in this profound sense involves more than passive hearing; it is a posture of surrender and attentiveness to the divine whisper. The Divine Presence, as suggested throughout Scripture, does not often come as overpowering force or spectacular manifestation but rather as a still, small voice beneath the roar of chaos (1 Kings 19:11-13). Elijah's encounter with God on Mount Horeb demonstrates this truth powerfully: after earthquakes, fire, and wind, it was the gentle whisper that revealed God's nearness. This subtlety teaches us that the sacred is often felt in what is barely perceived—in the gentle stirrings of the heart and the quiet urgings of conscience. In this dimension, prayer ceases to be a monologue and becomes a dialogic exchange. It is not merely about voicing needs or desires but about creating space for divine response and encounter. When we open ourselves to this sacred dialogue, the barriers between speaking and listening blur, and prayer becomes an intimate dance—two hearts communicating beyond words. This transforms prayer into a relational reality that transcends time and space, uniting the finite human soul with the infinite Divine Spirit. To nurture this capacity for listening beyond speech invites us to reflect on the nature of the heart as both source and receiver. King David, the archetypal psalmist, often portrayed his soul as a vessel longing for God—"My soul waiteth for the Lord more than they that watch for the morning" (Psalm 130:6). This waiting is active, a patient expectation shaped by trust and attentiveness rather than anxious clamor. Such waiting can be cultivated through practices of stillness and meditation, grounding the seeker in the present moment and enabling them to receive insights, comfort, or guidance that arise from the depths of prayerful receptivity. Yet our age presents challenges. We live amidst relentless noise—external and internal—that can drown out this sacred stillness. The ceaseless bustle of modern life, the endless hum of digital chatter, and the turmoil within the mind all conspire to scatter the spirit, making it difficult to center in silence. And yet, precisely in this fractured landscape, the need to develop a capacity for listening beyond speech becomes more urgent. The invitation to stillness is a radical act of resistance against distraction and fragmentation. It is a reclaiming of the innate human ability to attune to the Divine Presence hidden beneath the surface of everyday clamor. To engage more fully with this mystery, consider first what it means to listen inwardly—not just to the literal sounds or thoughts within, but to the unfolding sacredness beneath the surface. Many spiritual teachers have emphasized the importance of "listening with the heart" or "listening without an agenda"—a posture of humble openness and quiet expectation. This kind of listening is not about trying to control or command the experience but rather about cultivating a receptive space where the divine can move freely. One can think here of prayer not as a transaction but as a relationship akin to that of a child and a parent, a lover and beloved, or close friends. When a child speaks, they pour out their heart, but they also listen for the response with wide-eyed trust. When silence follows, the child waits, often sensing the presence of love even when no words are spoken. Similarly, in prayer, the Divine Presence may not immediately answer in a way we expect; the response may take the form of peace, a shift in perspective, a feeling of being known and held, or simply the mysterious awareness of companionship in solitude. King Solomon's reflections in Ecclesiastes underscore the ambivalence of human striving and knowing. "For in much wisdom is much grief: and he that increaseth knowledge increaseth sorrow" (Ecclesiastes 1:18). Sometimes the deepest answers elude the intellect; they reside in the realm of the heart's silent knowing. The silence within prayer is therefore not a void but a sacred space where wisdom beyond words unfolds. Inside this silence, the Divine Presence stirs, calling the seeker to deeper trust and surrender. The practice of listening beyond speech requires intentionality and discipline. In the biblical context, the prophets often demonstrated this through periods of fasting, solitude, and waiting upon God. These practices foster a deliberate withdrawal from distractions and create fertile ground for encounter. Elijah's retreat to the wilderness, Jesus's time in the desert, and David's moments of solitary lament are illustrative of a pattern in Scripture—moving away from external noise to find communion in quiet. Modern readers, too, can adopt practices that cultivate such listening. Simple disciplines—setting aside time for silent contemplation, focusing on breathing, inviting the mind to settle—can facilitate a gentle inner stillness. Prayer in this sense becomes less about "doing" and more about "being"—being present, being vulnerable, being open to the subtle promptings of the Spirit. Yet, this is not always easy. The mind resists silence, often filling it with restless thoughts or anxious questioning. To listen beyond speech takes patience and persistence, a willingness to remain even when nothing seems to happen. It is a faith exercise, trusting that the silence itself is charged with presence and meaning. The Psalmist's experience reflects this paradox: "I waited patiently for the Lord; and he inclined unto me, and heard my cry" (Psalm 40:1). Patient waiting in silence becomes a way of hearing—an active receptivity that enables the sacred whisper to be discerned. As this listening deepens, it can transform not only our prayer life but our entire way of relating to the world. When we learn to hear with the heart, the sacred presence is no longer confined to formal prayer moments but permeates all of life's rhythms. The divine whisper may be found in the rustling leaves, in the compassion of a friend, in the quiet kindness of a stranger, or in the stillness of a morning sunrise. Prayer becomes a continuous interplay of speech and silence, of speaking and listening, of offering and receiving. This leads us to a profound realization: prayer, at its core, is more about relationship than mechanics. It transcends formulas or practices. It is the unfolding of a sacred dialogue wherein both human and Divine speak and listen, call and respond, invite and abide. The Divine Presence, as an ambient essence, never forces its way into consciousness but gently invites us to engage—through silence, through breath, through the tender stirrings of the spirit. To better understand this dynamic, reflect upon the dialogue between Jesus and his disciples. He spoke often of the Father, yet he also modeled prayer as moments of withdrawal and silent communion—prayers in the garden of Gethsemane where anguish and surrender intertwine. These moments show that the deepest prayers are sometimes those without words; the cries of the heart laid bare before the quiet of God's presence. Moreover, the Apostle Paul's exhortations hint at this ongoing listening posture: "Pray without ceasing" (1 Thessalonians 5:17). This exhortation may sound like ceaseless verbal petitioning, but it is better understood as cultivating a continual openness—an awareness of and responsiveness to the divine breath that sustains all life. Prayer as ceaseless listening is a state of being, a habit of heart, where every moment can be an encounter with the sacred. Successful listening beyond speech also involves trust in the unseen and unknown. We must accept that the Divine response will not always match our desires or timelines. This humility is echoed in the prayer of Jesus: "Not my will, but thine, be done" (Luke 22:42). In the surrender of will and expectation, the heart opens to divine wisdom and guidance that surpass human understanding. Silence in prayer becomes a holy space where we learn to live with mystery and paradox, comforted by the trust that the Divine presence is always near—even when silent. This trust allows us to embrace the "dark night of the soul" moments when prayer feels empty, when silence feels deafening. Mystics throughout the centuries have testified to the paradox that sometimes the deepest divine encounter happens precisely in the absence of words, in the felt sense of abandonment that clears the way for new life. This period of spiritual silence and desolation is not to be feared but welcomed as a passage toward deeper union and transformation.Listening beyond speech, therefore, is an invitation into a sacred rhythm—a dance of descent into stillness and ascent into divine awareness. It is a practice of attuning the entire self—the mind, heart, body, and spirit—to the subtleties of divine presence. This practice nurtures a spiritual sensitivity that over time grows more profound, allowing the practitioner to notice the divine messages hidden in the everyday and to respond with faith and grace. The King James Bible, with its majestic language and spiritual depth, is particularly suited to evoke this contemplative posture. The cadences and rhythms of its verses can act as a balm to the weary soul, quieting the mind and opening the heart. Verses like "Be still, and know that I am God" and the many Psalms of longing and trust become invitations to enter into the temple of one's own soul, where the Divine Presence waits not with thunder but with whisper. In practical terms, encouraging a posture of listening beyond speech in personal prayer might begin by setting aside intentional time for silence—beginning with a few minutes that gradually lengthen as comfort with stillness grows. Using scriptural passages as gentle guides rather than demands, one might enter into wordless meditation, allowing phrases like "wait on the Lord" or "the Lord is my shepherd" to settle in the heart without rush or analysis. This mode shifts focus from speaking at God to being with God, cultivating a fertile ground for inner transformation. Communal worship can also nurture listening beyond speech, especially through practices such as contemplative silence, reflective readings, or the singing of simple chants that focus the spirit inward. In these moments, the community collectively embodies a temple of silence where the sacred ambient presence is felt and shared. This collective stillness strengthens individual prayer by reminding each person that they are not alone in the silence but part of a larger spiritual body. Ultimately, learning to listen beyond speech reorients prayer from a strategy of influence or control to a humble reception of grace. It reminds us that prayer is not about telling

God what to do but about opening ourselves to be shaped by the divine will and love. It also reveals that silence is not emptiness but fullness—a sacred presence that undergirds and sustains all life and all prayer, known and unknown. This shift from vocalization to receptivity does not diminish the value of spoken prayer but deepens it, enriching it with an awareness that prayer is as much about being heard as it is about hearing. This reciprocal dimension honors the human spirit's capacity to commune with the divine mystery in ways that transcend language and reach into the core of being. In the stillness where words fall away, we come to stand in the presence of a love that enfolds us without condition or demand, a presence that listens with infinite patience and responds not with words but with transformation. In that space, prayer becomes a sacred conversation, a mutual dwelling, a meeting of hearts where silence itself speaks volumes. To embrace listening beyond speech is to embark on a journey inward, toward the deepest self and outward toward the Divine mystery—an invitation to dwell in the temple of silence and to discover the eternal and gentle whisper of God's presence flowing through our very breath and being. Through this listening, prayer becomes not only a practice but a way of life, an abiding attunement to the divine harmony that sings softly beneath the noise of the world.

Meditations on Breath and Being

In the vast tapestry of prayer as reflected within the King James Bible, there exists a subtle yet profound thread weaving through the practice that often escapes immediate notice: the rhythm of breath. Breath is the quiet pulse beneath the spoken word and the silent pause that frames the divine encounter. It is both the bridge and the boundary—the living pulse by which prayer moves from mere utterance into the realm of sacred stillness. To meditate on breath is to engage in the most primal of spiritual acts, for breath carries within it the essence of life, the presence of the divine, and the invitation to deeper being. This meditation invites us to lean into the breath's rhythm as a vital conduit between our human expression and the silent communion with God. From the very beginning of Genesis to the poignant passages of the Psalms, breath symbolizes more than physical respiration—it is the divine spark, the life-giving spirit. "And the LORD God formed man of the dust of the ground, and breathed into his nostrils the breath of life; and man became a living soul" (Genesis 2:7). This foundational moment establishes breath as not only the sustainer of temporal life but as the incarnation of God's communication, the spark that animates the soul. Every inhalation is a renewing of this divine gift; every exhalation is a surrender back into the mystery. As Psalm 150 exhorts, "Let every thing that hath breath praise the LORD," breath itself becomes a sacred instrument of worship, a continuous hymn flowing through the body and spirit. Breath, then, holds prayer's vitality. It is the unseen movement that animates words, the silent context from which speech emerges and into which it returns. When prayer rises into audible form, it does so borne upon the waves of inhalation drawn deeply from the well of stillness. Upon completion, the prayer recedes quietly on the exhalation, allowing space for reflection, receptivity, and communion. The rhythm of breath reflects the very nature of prayer as a dynamic exchange—a dance between speaking and listening, between human longing and divine response. To recognize this rhythm is to reconnect prayer with the embodied presence of the individual praying. In a fast-paced world awash with distractions and noise, the simple awareness of one's breath can anchor the restless heart to a place of stillness and receptivity. This embodied awareness fosters an integration of the soul's utterance with the body's sacred temple, producing a prayer that extends beyond words into a living experience of presence. The Psalms repeatedly evoke this interplay between breath and being. Consider Psalm 46:10, "Be still, and know that I am God." Here, stillness is not a passive absence of activity but an active spiritual posture, often accessed through rhythmic breath and quiet attentiveness. In the act of breathing deeply and slowly, the mind can loosen its grip on anxious thoughts and hurry, settling instead into the profound truth of God's steady presence. Such stillness becomes a temple within, a sacred sanctuary where prayer becomes less about the quantity of words and more about the quality of surrender and communion. To meditate on breath as divine communication is to acknowledge the Mystery that dwells within all existence. Breath is a liminal force, inseparably tied to life's fragility and God's sustaining power. In many biblical prayers, one senses an intuitive awareness of this sacred dynamic—where lamentation, praise, supplication, and silence intermingle fluidly within the human spirit, carried always on the breath that God first gave. Practically speaking, cultivating breath awareness opens a powerful portal for grounded devotional practice. It invites the praying person to slow their pace, to witness their interior landscape with gentleness and curiosity, and to invite divine presence into the body as well as the mind. When breath and prayer unite, the soul engages in a holistic act—transcending mere thought and joining the spirit in sacred embodiment. The following practical exercises are offered as pathways into this embodied presence: 1. Conscious Breathing Preparation Find a quiet place where you can sit comfortably, spine erect but relaxed. Close your eyes gently. Begin with a few moments of noticing breath—not trying to change it, just observing the natural inhalation and exhalation. Feel the coolness of the air entering your nostrils and the warmth as it leaves. Sense the rise and fall of your chest or abdomen. Let each breath ground you in the present moment. 2. Breath-Rooted Invocation Begin your prayer by synchronizing it with breath. Inhale deeply and silently say, "LORD," drawing the name inward with your breath. Exhale fully and silently say, "have mercy." Repeat this simple invocation for several minutes, allowing the breath to carry the prayer steadily and unhurriedly. Feel your heart opening with each cycle, surrendering tensions and inviting peace. 3. Silent Centering with Breath After any spoken or sung prayer, allow the body to settle. Return to the quiet rhythm of breathing. With each exhale, release any lingering distractions or worries. With each inhale, receive a word or image slowly arising from your heart or mind—perhaps "peace," "love," or simply the awareness of God's presence. Let this word or image become the focus, gently returning to it with each breath when the mind wanders.

4. Breath and Scripture Alignment Choose a passage of scripture that resonates deeply—perhaps Psalm 23 or Isaiah 40:31. Read it slowly aloud or silently, and then read it again, this time aligning each phrase with a breath. Inhale deeply as you prepare to speak, and exhale as you pronounce the words, letting breath and scripture unite as a living prayer. Return to silence, feeling the scripture's meaning settle within your being alongside your breath. 5. Exhalation of Surrender At the conclusion of prayer time, use the breath consciously to release. Inhale deeply, gathering all your intentions, fears, hopes. Exhale with a palpable act of surrender— letting go, trusting in God's loving provision. Repeat this several times, experiencing a deepening of peace and a lightening of heart. These exercises are not meant as rigid prescriptions but as invitations to explore the living interplay between breath, prayer, and divine presence. Within the King James Bible's timeless language, the encounter with God often happens not in clamor or multitude of words, but in the quiet depths of the soul's breathing. Across different biblical narratives, the metaphor and reality of breath speak consistently to this holy relationship. When the prophet Ezekiel receives God's spirit, it is breath that revives the dry bones (Ezekiel 37:9-10), symbolizing resurrection and renewal. When the Psalmist expresses deep longing, breath becomes a metaphor for the soul's yearning, as in Psalm 42:1, "As the hart panteth after the water brooks, so panteth my soul after thee, O God." Here the breath expresses not only life's physical needs but the soul's profound spiritual thirst. In the New Testament, breath and spirit intertwine as Jesus breathes on the disciples and imparts the Holy Ghost (John 20:22), reinforcing breath as the bearer of divine life and mission. The breath also symbolizes the hidden continuity between human frailty and divine eternity. While words can fragment and fade, breath flows endlessly in cycles, mirroring the eternal breath of God that sustains all things. This continuity reminds the believer and seeker alike that prayer is not a series of isolated moments but a life lived in rhythm with the divine pulse. To meditate on breath is to rediscover prayer in its most elemental form. It dissolves the boundary between speaker and listener, between human and divine, allowing prayer

to become a sacred dance of presence where word and silence harmonize. In this temple of silence within, breath does more than sustain—breath reveals the living God who breathes life into every heart and invites all creation into intimacy. As you cultivate this practice of breath awareness in your devotional life, you may find that prayer deepens beyond requests or recitations into a tender landscape of mutual indwelling. Breath becomes prayer become breath—continuous, intimate, transformative. Here, in the stillness between inhales and exhales, the soul discovers the temple where God's whisper is found waiting, the divine echo of all prayer's yearning. May this meditation on breath awaken within you the sacred vitality of prayer's embodied presence, a bridge that carries your spirit into the quiet heart of God. With each conscious breath, may you step more fully into the divine conversation, where silence speaks volumes and being becomes prayer itself.

Hands Raised in Reverence: Ritual and Practice in Prayer

Textures and Symbols of Sacred Gesture

Throughout the vast tapestry of prayer woven within the pages of the King James Bible, one thread remains constant and compelling: the physical expression of the heart's communication with the Divine. While prayer is often understood primarily as an internal dialogue—a conversation of the soul with God—it flows naturally into outward gestures that manifest the inner posture of reverence, supplication, and surrender. These sacred gestures, rich in symbolism and sensory texture, form a language beyond words, inviting both the person praying and the observer to encounter the sacred through movement, touch, and presence. This subchapter delves into the varied expressions accompanying prayer as depicted and implied in the biblical text, reflecting on their spiritual significance and the tangible textures that render prayer a holistic act of worship and connection. From the earliest chapters of Scripture, physical gestures in prayer communicate attitudes of humility, anticipation, praise, and devotion. The folded hands we so often observe in Christian tradition, the lifting of palms heavenward, the act of kneeling, and the profound posture of prostration all carry distinct meanings that resonate deeply with the biblical narrative. They are not merely ritualistic acts but invitations to engage the whole person—body, mind, and spirit—in the sacred dialogue with God. Consider the image of hands folded—a gesture so familiar that it has become almost synonymous with prayer itself. While the Bible does not prescribe folding hands as a universal posture, the symbolism embedded in this quiet clasping is compelling. Hands folded in front of the heart suggest a shutting away of worldly distractions, an enclosing of oneself into an intimate space of communication with God. This gesture echoes the psalmist's cry for attentiveness and focus: "Hear my prayer, O God; give ear to the words of my mouth" (Psalm 54:2). The physical act of folding hands can quiet the restlessness of the limbs, offering a tactile reminder to bow the mind and spirit. Yet prayer, in its biblical richness, embraces many forms beyond folded hands. Perhaps the most vivid and recurring image is that of raised palms, an open and upward gesture of supplication and surrender. Psalm 63:4 proclaims, "So will I bless thee while I live: I will lift up my hands in thy name." This lifting of hands signifies an openness to receive, a reaching toward the divine, and a declaration of reliance upon God's power and grace. It is a gesture of vulnerability and trust; the hands, empty and exposed, say, "I have nothing but you." The tactile sensation of palms turned skyward, sometimes outstretched fully or gently raised, carries with it a profound invitation into the presence of God, where the barriers between human and divine are bridged. Kneeling as a posture of prayer, frequently referenced in the Old and New Testaments, conveys a layered symbolism of respect, submission, and earnest petition. In 2 Chronicles 7:3, we read, "And when all the children of Israel saw how the fire came down, and the glory of the Lord upon the house, they bowed themselves on the pavement, and worshipped, and praised the Lord... and kneeled down upon the pavement with their faces to the ground." The act of lowering the body toward the earth grounds the worshiper in humility, a physical sign of yielding to a greater authority. Kneeling envelops the prayer with a rhythm—descending into the earth, bowing the head, folding the hands or resting them on the knees—each movement a sacred choreography that shapes the spiritual posture of the supplicant. Extending even further in gestures of deep reverence and submission is the practice of prostration, a total laying down of the body in face-down surrender. The act of prostrating oneself before God is depicted throughout Scripture, particularly in moments of awe, repentance, or adoration. Daniel offers a prime example: "And when he prayed, he was in his chamber with his windows open toward

Jerusalem, and he kneeled upon his knees three times a day, and prayed, and gave thanks before his God..." (Daniel 6:10). Although this passage emphasizes kneeling, other passages describe Israelites falling on their faces—prostrating—as a gesture of profound worship (see Exodus 34:8). The texture of this gesture is humbling and visceral: the body surrendered fully to the ground, the face close to the earth, a tactile connection with creation that simultaneously signifies reverence to the Creator. The sensory world that envelops these gestures adds an additional layer of sacredness to the act of prayer. The feel of hands—warm, sometimes trembling in anticipation or steady in resolve—the gentle rub of palms together, or the slight pressure as fingers entwine all forge a physical intimacy with the moment. Through our tactile senses, prayer becomes not an abstract concept but a living encounter. The smell of incense, described subtly in the tabernacle worship and temple rituals, engages the olfactory senses, creating an atmosphere thick with symbolism and sanctity. In Psalm 141:2, David prays, "Let my prayer be set forth before thee as incense; and the lifting up of my hands as the evening sacrifice." Incense smoke rising upward parallels the trajectory of lifted hands—both visible signs of prayers ascending to God. The aromatic texture of incense, delicate yet pervasive, envelops the worship space and the body in a subtle embrace, inviting the senses into the worshipful presence. Chant and song, often intertwined with gestures of prayer, possess their own rhythm—a tempo that shapes the flow and focus of the worshiper's heart. The Psalms, which are replete with lyrical prayers and praises, suggest that sound undergirds sacred movement. The cadence of a psalm or a prayer chanted aloud establishes a tempo that can quicken or slow the heartbeat, marking time in sacred intervals. The body moves in harmony with this rhythm: hands raised slowly with the rise of a melodic phrase, lips moving in synchrony with sacred words, knees bending with the flow of reverence. This dance of sound and gesture enacts a choreography of prayer that engages the entire being. In examining the biblical roots of these gestures, it becomes evident that they are more than mere actions; they are physical manifestations of profound spiritual states. The variety of postures reminds us that prayer encompasses a spectrum of experiences—joy and longing, grief and praise, confession and hope. The gestures shape and reflect these experiences, offering a language accessible to all, beyond words and intellect alone. Moreover, the use of different postures and gestures in prayer also acknowledges the complexity of human relationship with God. Raised hands may express a confident boldness, as in Paul's encouragement in 1 Timothy 2:8: "I will therefore that men pray every where, lifting up holy hands, without wrath and doubting." Kneeling, as seen in Hannah's fervent prayer for a child (1 Samuel 1:9), communicates an urgent humility, a deep need felt in the core of the soul. Prostration, as the ultimate physical surrender, corresponds with awe before the holy, as when Moses bowed low in the presence of God on Mount Sinai (Exodus 34:8). Each texture and symbol combines to create an embodied spirituality, one that invites the worshiper into a fuller engagement with the divine mystery. As the outward gesture flows from the inner attitude, so too does the sacred posture prompt the heart to deeper devotion. The tactile and sensorial elements—the warmth of hands clasped in prayer, the incense drifting through the air, the echo of sacred chants—envelop the worshiper and remind the praying person that prayer is a whole-person act. It pulses with life, connecting skin, breath, voice, and spirit. This embodied expression also roots prayer in the biblical community's shared memory and identity. In the tabernacle, the temple, and synagogues, gestures formed part of a collective language of worship that united generations of God's people. The recurring posture of lifted hands or bowed knees forms a bridge across time, linking ancient worshipers with contemporary seekers. When a believer today lifts hands or kneels in prayer, they step into a living tradition that echoes through the corridors of biblical history, affirming a shared spiritual heritage. Importantly, these gestures invite not only physical engagement but also vulnerability and openness. To fold one's hands, to lift palms, to bend the knees—each act exposes the worshiper to God's presence in a way that words alone cannot. The body becomes a vessel for spiritual expression, revealing inner truths and inviting divine transformation. The submission implicit in kneeling or prostration speaks to the surrender necessary for profound prayer, a letting go of control and an acknowledgment of God's sovereignty. Even for readers unfamiliar or distant from these particular traditions, encountering the textures and symbols of sacred gesture offers a rich invitation. Engaging the body as a partner in prayer opens new pathways for experience, allowing the prayerful soul to express feelings that may elude verbal articulation. The tactile rhythms—the press of palms together, the coolness of kneeling on stone, the gentle cascade of incense smoke—become touchstones of divine encounter. Throughout the King James Bible, the integration of gesture and prayer forms part of a holistic spirituality that marries word, movement, and heart. Scriptural imagery reveals how God relates to the entire human being, not merely the mind or the voice. The divine honors the sacred dance of body and spirit in prayer, welcoming each gesture as honesty worn in the skin and flesh. Thus, the textures and symbols of sacred gesture are intrinsic to the prayer experience—physical expressions that elevate the soul and shape the spiritual posture. They serve not as mere formalities but as earnest acts that bridge heaven and earth. Whether traditional or spontaneously embraced, these gestures invite every believer and seeker to partake in a tangible, sensory encounter with the divine presence. The rich choreography of prayerful reverence unfolds through these movements, textures, and symbols, speaking a universal language of humility, hope, and surrender that transcends time and culture. In this way, prayer emerges not solely as a silent, internal thought, but as a full-bodied dialogue marked by touches, postures, and sacred rhythms—a living echo of the divine call and human response, reverberating through the ages and inviting each generation to listen anew.

Rituals of Time and Space

The experience of prayer is never confined solely to the ephemeral moment of spoken words or silent meditation; rather, it is inextricably woven into the fabric of time and space, consecrated by ritual and rhythm. Within the King James Bible's embrace of prayer, one discerns a profound awareness that the sacred is made manifest not only through the content of supplication or praise but through the very cadence and setting in which those spiritual dialogues unfold. This intertwining of divine encounter with cycles of time and sanctified places forms a vital dimension of the believer's prayer life, inviting the soul into a sacred dance — an ordered interplay where structure meets spontaneity, and the temporal converges with the eternal. The Sacredness of Time: Cycles, Seasons, and Sacred Hours Time, in the biblical worldview, is far from being a mere quantitative continuum or a sequence of arbitrary moments. Instead, it is a living canvas for God's unfolding purposes, marked by cycles that reflect the divine order. The King James Bible reveals manifold instances where prayer is embedded rhythmically within these sacred cycles, inviting the faithful to attune themselves to the sacred heartbeat of creation and covenant. Central among these temporal rhythms are the appointed times — set hours of prayer and worship ordained to create regular opportunities to commune with God. The Psalms, a treasury of prayer, frequently allude to these sacred hours: "Evening, and morning, and at noon, will I pray, and cry aloud: and he shall hear my voice" (Psalm 55:17). This triadic pattern of devotion punctuates the day with intentional pauses, anchoring prayer within the natural flow of daily life. It reflects an understanding that God's presence is continuous, yet human attentiveness requires reminders, a ritualized calling back. In the morning, prayer often dawns with a sense of renewal and consecration. The rising sun becomes a living symbol of divine faithfulness, as in Lamentations 3:22-23, where the steadfast love of the Lord is renewed every morning. Morning prayers open the soul to the day's challenges and blessings, initiating a rhythm of dependence and surrender. Evening prayers, conversely, serve as moments of reflection and closure, opportunities to offer thanksgiving and seek peace amid the unfolding night. Such diurnal cycles honor the movement of time while embedding prayer within natural markers that transcend human invention. Beyond daily hours, larger sacred seasons shape the spiritual rhythm. The ancient biblical calendar was marked by festivals and holy convocations, each accompanied by prescribed prayers, offerings, and rituals. The Feast of Pentecost, the Day of Atonement, and the Passover functioned as spiritual focal points around which the community's life turned. Their prayers and ceremonies sanctified entire periods, providing communal resonance to personal devotion. These seasons invited believers to remember foundational events — deliverance, forgiveness, covenant — while simultaneously looking forward in hope and anticipation. The cyclical return of sacred time thus cultivates a continual reorientation toward God's purposes. The King James Bible, while focusing on prayer's spiritual content, unmistakably underscores this embedding of petition and praise within cosmic and calendrical cycles. Such liturgical structuring is not intended to cage the spirit but to guide it, much like the measured steps of a dance form a frame within which freedom and creativity flourish. The ritual rhythms of sacred time channel the soul's longing, harmonizing individual devotion with the divine temporal order. Sanctified Spaces: Inner Sanctuaries and Sacred Places Equally significant as the rhythms of time is the consecration of space in which prayer takes place. Sacred spaces, whether physical or internal, serve as crucibles where the temporal and eternal meet. These environments help the believer to transcend mundane distractions and enter more deeply into the presence of the Divine. The biblical narrative is replete with instances where particular places become hallowed by prayer and divine encounter. The tabernacle and later the temple were the quintessential sacred spaces in Israelite worship — carefully constructed and ritually purified, these sites were regarded as earthly homes of God's presence. Prayer offered within these walls was suffused with a sense of awe and reverence, as the holy of holies symbolized the heart of divine mystery. David's Psalms often express longing for the courts of the Lord's house (Psalm 84), revealing how sacred architecture inspires and shapes the worshipper's heart. Yet the sacred space illuminated in scripture is not limited to grand edifices. Fields, mountains, gardens, and even solitary wilderness spots become sanctuaries of intimacy with God. Jacob's vision at Bethel, Moses atop Mount Sinai, and Jesus praying in the garden of Gethsemane demonstrate that the Divine can be approached in varied and often simple locales. These places become consecrated through prayer and presence, revealing that sacred space is not fixed solely to physical sites but occurs wherever heart and spirit open to communion. Most profoundly, the King James Bible invites the individual into the awareness of an inner sanctuary — a sacred space within the human soul where God's presence dwells. The Apostle Paul's exhortation to "pray without ceasing" (1 Thessalonians 5:17) points beyond external timing and setting, beckoning believers into a continual awareness of communion. Prayer thus becomes an inward act of positioning the heart as God's dwelling place, where the outer rhythms of time and place intersect and converge with inner sanctity. In this light, the physical act of "lifting up holy hands" as described in 1 Timothy 2:8 transcends mere gesture, embodying a bodily orientation that aligns the physical self with an inner prayerful posture. The body and soul together become a temple, a space sanctified by intentionality and faith. This fusion of inner and outer sanctuaries engenders a holistic worship, where the material and spiritual are united in reverence. Ritual as a Bridge Between Structure and Spontaneity The embedding of prayer within sacred time and space rituals delicately balances the need for order with the vitality of personal expression. A common misconception is that ritual constrains and empties prayer of freshness, but the King James Bible reveals a richer dynamic where ritual provides a context, a container within which the spontaneity of the Spirit can flourish. Fixed prayers, repeated invocation, and liturgical seasons offer a scaffold that supports the soul when inside chaos or fatigue. They train the heart to return, again and again, to the Divine presence, creating a discipline that nurtures perseverance and growth. The Psalter itself is structured with patterns of praise, lament, thanksgiving, and supplication, marked by refrains and recurring themes that bring coherence to varied human experience. This repetition is not monotonous; rather, it deepens familiarity and invites reflection, allowing meaning to mature like a steady drumbeat beneath a melody. Yet within this ordered framework, the Bible also celebrates moments of unbidden lament, ecstatic praise, and raw confession — cries of the soul that defy neatness but are embraced within the ritual space. King David's prayers oscillate between carefully composed worship and spontaneous outpouring, affirming the human ability to inhabit both order and freedom. Ritual thus is not the end but the soil in which spontaneous prayer takes root and blossoms. Moreover, sanctifying time and space in regular, communal contexts models the integration of personal and collective prayer. The assembly in the temple or the gathering for appointed prayer times forges a shared rhythm, weaving individual hearts into the fabric of the faith community. This dialogue between private devotion and public worship deepens the experience of God's immanence and transcendence, hinting at the universal scope of prayer as a human expression. Practical Expressions: The Daily Rhythms of Prayer The spiritual ideals explored in Scripture manifest in a variety of devotional practices that integrate time and space. Early morning prayers, often accompanied by turning toward the east, align with biblical symbolism of facing the rising sun — a tangible orientation linking physical direction with spiritual hope. Evening prayers, sometimes performed with bowed head or folded hands, prepare the soul to release control and entrust the night to God's watchfulness. The Psalms themselves were used in daily and weekly patterns of prayer in both the first-century Jewish and early Christian traditions, establishing a rhythm of praise and reflection intended to sanctify any moment. The mother of King Hezekiah praying by the pool of Siloam, Daniel praying thrice daily facing Jerusalem, and Jesus withdrawing to solitary places all showcase how time and place become intentional frameworks for dialogue with God. In more contemplative traditions, the "hours" of prayer — such as Matins, Lauds, Vespers — embody the biblical calling to pray without ceasing by segmenting the day into punctuated spiritual moments. These souvenirs of sacred time provide stability amidst the whirlwind of life, reminding believers that each hour, no matter how mundane, bears the potential for divine encounter. Physical spaces, too, become extensions of spiritual sanctuary. Simple home altars, corners dedicated to meditation, or natural retreats serve as modern sanctuaries reminiscent of biblical sacred places. Such spaces invite the worshipper to step out of ordinary routine and enter a sphere where time slows, and the soul is stilled. Here the body remembers, and the spirit awakens, as if touched by the ancient holiness once reserved for the temple precincts. Transforming the Ordinary: The Alchemy of Ritual A subtle but profound truth threaded through biblical prayer is the capacity of ritualized time and sacred space to transform the ordinary into the extraordinary. Repetition, when imbued with faith, becomes a kind of spiritual alchemy that elevates simple acts into encounters with the divine. Washing hands before prayer, lighting lamps, lifting hands, bowing, or prostrating — these ritual gestures transcend their physicality to become acts of consecration. The sanctification of time also renders every day an opportunity for renewal. By breaking the temporal flow into sacred intervals, believers are invited to live within an ongoing cycle of blessing and petition, surrender and praise, hope and trust. The reoccurrence of these moments reiterates that spiritual life is not a one-time event but an ever-renewing journey. Wherever ritual is present within prayer, it embodies an essential link between heaven and earth, between human limitations and divine infinitude. It grounds the intangible yearnings of the spirit in a tangible form, creating pathways through which God's invisible presence can be accessed and cherished. Conclusion: The Soul's Sacred Dance To pray is to engage fully in the soul's sacred dance, choreographed by rituals of time and sanctified spaces. The King James Bible invites the believer into this rhythm, not as a rigid duty but as an embrace of life's sacred order. Within the patterns of morning and evening, within spaces hallowed by tradition or quiet solitude, prayer becomes both a discipline and delight — a harmonizing of the soul's restless desire with the steady pulse of divine presence. Rituals of time and space offer a sacred architecture within which the human spirit may find peace, passion, and purpose. They open a threshold, a liminal zone where heaven's eternal pulse touches earth's temporal drum, and where the soul learns to move freely — with reverence and joy — in the presence of the Divine. In this way, the echoes of ancient prayers continue to resonate today, inviting every seeker and believer alike to find their place within the sacred dance, lifted upon the wings of ritual, aligned in time, and sanctified in space. Prayer, then, becomes not merely a human act but a divine encounter, made manifest through the holy ordering of life itself.

The Dance of Community and Solitude

In the sacred rhythm of human spirituality, prayer unfolds as a dance—sometimes performed in the swirling embrace of community, sometimes in the quiet stillness of solitude. These two modes of engaging with the divine, seemingly opposite in outward form, are in truth deeply intertwined, their interplay revealing the multifaceted essence of prayer itself. The corporate gathering and the solitary moment are like colors blending on an artist's palette—each vibrant and distinct, yet enriched and deepened when they meet. Together, they compose a living tapestry of worship and encounter that reflects the profound complexity of the human soul's longing for connection, both with others and with God. When believers come together in prayer, there is an unmistakable power in their unified voices, raised in harmony and lifted in reverence. The corporate assembly creates a sacred space where individual faiths converge and resonate, weaving a communal fabric that transcends personal stories and reaches toward collective yearning. These gatherings crystallize the biblical vision of the body of believers, a living organism bound by shared hope and mutual support, where the act of calling upon the divine becomes a communal symphony. Contrastingly, the solitary moment of prayer invites a more intimate encounter—an unveiling of the soul's depths in a confidential whisper or a silent breath. In solitude, the seeker steps away from the chorus to listen for the divine voice speaking directly to the heart. Here, prayer becomes a tender dialogue, an unguarded communing that allows for vulnerability, reflection, and a personal reckoning with the sacred. The absence of human accompaniment often magnifies the presence of the divine, its echoes filling the quietude with profound solace and insight. The dance between these two states—the communal and the solitary—is an essential rhythm for the spiritual journey. Neither is superior nor sufficient alone; rather, they complement and sustain one another in a sacred balance. The communal gathering offers affirmation, encouragement, and the tangible sense of belonging, while solitude supplies depth, authenticity, and the opportunity for inner transformation. Just as sunrise needs sunset, so too does prayer thrive in the harmony of these contrasting expressions. In ancient biblical times, this dynamic is vividly portrayed through ritual and narrative. The psalms sing of both jubilant multitudes praising in harmony and personal laments of solitary distress. The assembly of Israel in the tabernacle and later the temple stand as monumental symbols of collective devotion, yet the prophet Elijah's solitary encounter on Mount Horeb embodies the power of quiet, personal communion. The dance is scripted into the text itself, reminding readers that prayer's true embodiment encompasses the breadth of human experience—together and alone. The Communal Tapestry: Prayer as Shared Expression There is a sacred electricity that sparks when voices lift together in praise or petition. The act of corporate prayer roots deeply in the human need for connection and mutual recognition. In its very essence, the corporate setting transforms prayer from a solitary act into a shared journey, creating unity from diversity. Each individual voice is like a thread woven into a tapestry; alone, it holds meaning, but together it reveals a magnificent design. Consider the scene of worship seen in the early chapters of the Book of Acts, where "they continued stedfastly in the apostles' doctrine and fellowship, and in breaking of bread, and in prayers" (Acts 2:42). Here, prayer is not merely a private exercise but a foundation for communal identity. The early Christians found in their gathered prayers both a wellspring of courage and a source of communal encouragement. They were emboldened to face conflicts, to sustain hope in persecution, and to serve one another in tangible ways. Their prayers mirrored their shared life, a rhythm of dependence and intercession that moved beyond individual needs toward a collective embrace of God's presence. The Psalms, too, evoke this wide spectrum of communal prayer—sometimes expressed with triumphant exultation, at other times spoken from the depths of communal mourning. Psalm 133 opens with a joyful affirmation: "Behold, how good and how pleasant it is for brethren to dwell together in unity!" This verse encapsulates the power of the gathered assembly. The image of brothers dwelling together resonates with the warmth of shared faith and common purpose. To dwell together in unity is to participate in a spiritual sweetness, like fresh oil poured upon the head, runneth down upon the beard, even Aaron's beard (Psalm 133:2). Here, the communal prayer is presented as not simply a duty but a delight—a fragrant blessing that enlivens the spirit and strengthens relational bonds. In corporate prayer, there is also the visible act of ritual itself: hands raised, voices lifted, incense burning, hymns chanted, scriptures read aloud. These shared symbols become touchstones, precious anchors that link one worshipper to another and to generations past. The external gestures echo the internal disposition, shaping hearts toward reverence and focus. When a congregation moves in unison—kneeling, standing, bowing—it embodies a collective humility and submission before the divine. Such synchrony cultivates empathy and solidarity, allowing the individual to transcend isolation and partake in a living community of faith. Moreover, corporate prayer often assumes the form of intercession—for one another, for leaders, for the sick, for the oppressed. This intercessory dimension embodies the tangible expression of love and burden-bearing within a community. When Christians or seekers gather to uplift the needs of others before God, they participate in a profound mutual care that extends beyond spoken words. There is a spiritual solidarity that emerges from joining together in intercession: a shared hope that no prayer is offered in vain, and that collective faith can move mountains. This mutual intercession is a powerful reminder that the spiritual vitality of the community relies upon the prayer of its members, each offering their unique voice for the good of all. It is important to note that corporate prayer also teaches discipline and rhythm. Collective gatherings occur within appointed times and places—Sabbath assemblies, daily prayers, festivals. These patterns become sacred markers, transforming time and space. The repetition and regularity of communal prayer shape character and foster perseverance in faith. They remind believers that prayer is not merely an occasional act but a continuous presence, a lifeline tethering the people to God through the seasons of joy and trial. The Solitary Sanctuary: Prayer as Intimate Encounter In contrast to the external vibrancy of communal prayer, the silent sanctuary of solitude offers a refuge for the soul. It is within these private moments, removed from the crowds and divided duties, that one encounters prayer stripped to its essence—a direct communion between the individual and the Infinite. Solitary prayer moves beyond formality and spectacle, touching the tender possibility of authenticity and vulnerability. The biblical narrative affords many luminous examples of solitary prayer, where prophets, kings, and ordinary individuals seek the face of God alone. David's psalms often reflect a lonely wrestling with despair, shame, and hope. Psalm 42 echoes the cry of a soul longing like a deer panting for water (Psalm 42:1), an image that powerfully conveys the inner thirst felt in moments of isolation. Such poetry invites the seeker into a quiet wilderness of the heart, a place where one can pour out sorrows and plead for mercy with no one watching, no audience but God. Solitude in prayer also fosters deep listening. It creates space for silence, which, though often filled with inner noise, holds a holy potential for encounter. In the stillness, one may better discern the subtle promptings of the Spirit, the whisper of wisdom, or the warmth of consolation. Jesus himself modeled this sacred rhythm, withdrawing from the crowds to pray alone in the garden, seeking strength and surrender (Luke 5:16; Matthew 26:39). These moments of solitude affirm that divine intimacy often blossoms in quietness beyond the reach of public declarations. Furthermore, solitary prayer nurtures honesty and rawness that cannot always be expressed within the crowd. In individual lament, confession, or gratitude, the heart faces its true reflection, acknowledging brokenness, desperation, or joy without pretense. There is a sacred courage in this personal vulnerability—allowing one's soul to be laid bare before God without shame or fear. Such moments can catalyze transformation, healing hidden wounds and fostering resilience. Despite its deeply private nature, solitary prayer is never an isolated departure from communal faith. The individual's private sacrifice of prayer contributes unseen vectors to the larger spiritual community. It is as if the solitary petitioner becomes a hidden root feeding the visible branches of the faith family. Many mystics throughout history have spoken of this paradox: by withdrawing into solitary communion, one deepens their capacity to serve, love, and uphold the community. Physical settings, too, shape the texture of solitary prayer. A quiet corner, a mountain stillness, a predawn dawn— these spaces hold their own sacred resonance. Like sacred vessels, they invite the spirit to come deeper into itself. The solitude of prayer affords a tactile intimacy as well—kneeling on worn earth, feeling the coolness of stone, folding hands in habitual posture—every element grounding the encounter. Sensory presence in solitude heightens awareness, making the divine encounter tangible and real, even in absence of others. The Interweaving of Community and Solitude: Poetic Imagery of Prayer's Colors If corporate prayer is a vibrant tapestry, and solitary prayer a lucid pool, then together they form a living canvas where hues intermingle in dynamic dialogue. Imagine two threads—one bright and energetic, the other calm and reflective—woven seamlessly. This interweaving is not merely conceptual but lived in the cyclical rhythms of faith life. Community offers the glory of audacious hope and shared strength; solitude offers the sanctuary of personal truth and quiet surrender. Together, they resemble the ancient metaphor of fire and ash—flames create illumination and warmth visible to all, yet ashes hold the smoldering heart within, waiting to rekindle. Prayer blends these polarities as a dance of light and shadow, echoing the complexity of human yearning. The dance may be imagined through the imagery of colors. Corporate prayer is like the bright gold of sunrise flooding a gathering sky, filling the horizon with hues of joy and expectation. Its energy pulses like vibrant reds of a beating heart, synchronized breaths of a multitude. Solitary prayer, in contrast, is the deep indigo twilight curling softly over one's spirit—a time for reflection, mystery, and the whispering depth of the soul. Between these extremes lie infinite shades: the gentle lavender of dawn's first quiet moments, the rich burgundy of evening's closing meditations, and the pure white light of transparency and peace. The sacred dance between these expressions reveals prayer's inclusive nature. It is not a rigid formula bound to one mode but a fluid spectrum where human experience finds fitting expression. Just as the King James Bible itself weaves majestic presences of public declarations and heartfelt private cries, so too does prayer encompass vast emotional and relational landscapes. Jesus' own practice thus becomes model and mystery. We witness him walking among crowds, healing, teaching, and raising his voice in communal worship; then again, we see him slipping away to isolated heights, praying with lifted eyes and bowed head. His life enacts the sacred flow between the gathering of the people and the silent surrender before the Father. By following this model, prayer becomes a dance, responsive to the rhythms of life and soul—the external call of community and the internal drawing of solitude. The interplay between community and solitude also reflects theological truths. The nature of God as both immanently close and transcendently vast invites worship that is at once shared and profoundly personal. Believers, created in the image of this relational God, reflect divine communion in their own prayer lives by embodying both connection and interiority. The community gathers as an echo of the divine fellowship of the Trinity; the solitary heart enters the mystery of God's presence in intimate reception. This duality offers a shelter from extremes. Community without solitude can devolve into superficiality, losing depth in the clamor of the crowd. Solitude without community risks isolation, breeding spiritual dryness or even despair. Together, they form a resilient wholeness, supporting an authentic and sustained prayer life. The Rhythm of Movement: Practical Ways the Dance Unfolds For believers and seekers today, engaging this dance means embracing both public and private dimensions of prayer with intention. Many traditions offer structured moments for communal prayer—church services, prayer meetings, group devotions—where the shared experience nurtures faith and fellowship. Participating faithfully in these gatherings strengthens bonds and cultivates spiritual momentum. Equally important is cultivating regular solitary prayer—daily moments carved out for silence, meditation, and personal petition. Spiritual disciplines such as lectio divina, contemplative stillness, or journaling prayer provide practical frameworks for deepening the solitary encounter. These practices invite the seeker into the rich interior world where prayer becomes a heartfelt conversation, undistracted and sincere. Both forms of prayer can also be integrated creatively. One might commence a solitary prayer with meditations drawn from communal readings; or, after corporate worship, retreat to a personal setting for reflection on images or words encountered. This fluidity honors the dynamic nature of prayer as a living relationship, not a constrained ritual. Most importantly, the dance invites recognition of the sacred posture within each form: lifting hands and voices in collective praise, and bending the head in private reverence. Through this interplay, prayer becomes a multi-hued expression of human longing and divine grace—ever reaching outward and inward, ever meeting God and one another. Conclusion In the delicate dance between community and solitude, prayer reveals its profound richness. The communal gathering paints the sky with brilliant colors of shared faith, hope, and worship, while the solitary moment dips into the deep wells of intimate divine encounter. These two expressions, far from opposing forces, are essential partners in the spiritual journey, each nourishing and enriching the other. Their intertwined beauty calls every believer and seeker to step into the dance, embracing the fullness of prayer as a sacred dialogue of connection and solitude, collective voice and silent heart. Through this dance, prayer becomes a vivid reflection of our humanity—complex, relational, and ultimately destined to rest in the mystery of the divine. Whether in the chorus of many or the hush of one, the soul's voice rises as an echo of the eternal; in both spaces, the whispers and shouts of prayer reveal us as creatures knit into the vast and holy tapestry of God's love.

Inviting Participation: Practical Guides for Ritual Prayer

In the rich tapestry of spiritual practice woven throughout the ages, ritual prayer stands as a vibrant thread—dynamic yet rooted, intimate yet universal. As we draw this exploration of ritual and practice in prayer to a close, the essential invitation is clear: prayer is not merely an act to be observed or an ancient custom to be admired from afar, but a living, breathing dialogue that beckons each person to participate actively. Whether new to prayer or seasoned in spiritual disciplines, believers and seekers alike find in ritual prayer a profound means to enter into communion with the divine. This subchapter offers practical guidance, meditative prompts, and exercises designed to help readers discover, adopt, and adapt prayer rituals that touch their hearts and nourish their spirits.### Embracing Ritual Prayer in Personal PracticeRitual prayer is fundamentally about intention and presence. It is a practice that transcends formula, inviting the practitioner into a sacred space—physical, mental, and spiritual—where meaningful communication with God or the transcendent can unfold. The King James Bible, with its majestic language and deep spiritual resonance, conveys ritual prayers that are both structured and flexible, allowing for personal engagement and adaptation. By drawing upon these traditions and infusing them with contemporary awareness, readers can cultivate prayer rituals that reflect their unique faith journeys and contexts. The steps toward integrating ritual prayer into daily life begin with openness and experimentation. It is not necessary to replicate ancient rites precisely, but important to honor their essence: moments set apart, repeated rhythms, intentional posture, and focused words or silence. These outward expressions serve as conduits that help quiet the mind, steady the heart, and foster a receptive spirit.### Creating a Sacred Space Before engaging in ritual prayer, it is helpful to establish a space—whether a physical corner in your home, a quiet outdoor spot, or a particular time of day—that signals to your senses and soul the commencement of something sacred. This space need not be elaborate; simplicity and consistency are often more effective. Lighting a candle, arranging a small altar with meaningful objects, or simply sitting in a comfortable chair can mark the transition from ordinary busyness to prayerful focus. Consider these suggestions:- Natural Elements: Incorporate elements of nature such as a sprig of greenery, a stone, or water in a vessel. These tactile items can root your awareness in creation and God's handiwork.- Visual Aids: A carefully chosen image or scripture verse displayed nearby can serve as a focal point for meditation and invocation.- Scent: Aromatic incense, essential oils, or fresh flowers may invoke a sensory experience that helps calm and center you. As you spend time in this space, allow yourself to feel that boundaries between the mundane and the sacred begin to blur, making room for transcendent connection.### Postures of Prayer: The Body's Role in RitualRitual prayer engages the whole person—mind, heart, and body. Posture is not incidental; it communicates our attitude and can facilitate deeper spiritual engagement. The King James Bible references varying postures for prayer: kneeling, standing, bowing the head, lifting hands, and even lying prostrate on the ground. Each of these positions expresses reverence, submission, longing, or praise. As you develop your personal ritual, try experimenting with different postures to discover what most naturally fosters your prayerful state:- Kneeling: Symbolizes humility and dependence on God. Take time to gently lower your body and feel the ground beneath you.- Standing: Conveys readiness, honor, and strength in coming before the divine.- Hands Raised: Opens the heart and spirit; an ancient gesture of invitation and surrender.- Bow of the Head or Prostration: Demonstrates awe and deep respect, acknowledging the greatness of God.- Seated with Eyes Closed: Offers stillness and inward contemplation, useful for meditative prayer.Notice any changes in your awareness or emotional state as you try these postures. Allow the physical embodiment of prayer to deepen your connection beyond words alone.### Structure and Rhythm: Drawing from Biblical Patterns. Many biblical prayers follow patterns that can guide personal practice, providing stability while allowing room for spontaneous expression.

Familiarity with these structures can ease the introduction of ritual prayer into one's life. A common biblical pattern includes several elements:- Addressing God: Begin by calling upon the Divine by name or title. This grounds your prayer in relationship.- Praise and Thanksgiving: Acknowledge God's nature and blessings received.- Confession: Openly admit shortcomings or failures, seeking mercy.- Petition: Present needs, desires, or intercessions with honesty.- Commitment or Affirmation: Close with trust or resolve to follow God's will. This flow creates a balanced engagement with the divine, moving from reverence to relational honesty. Familiar examples include the Lord's Prayer (Matthew 6:9-13) and the Psalms, which balance lament, praise, and petition.#### Practical Exercise: Composing a Personal Prayer CycleTake a moment to create your own prayer cycle based on the biblical pattern:1. Address God with a name or phrase that resonates deeply—"Heavenly Father," "Creator," "Lord of Mercy," or another.2. Offer one or two sentences of praise or thanksgiving drawn from your life experience.3. Speak a brief confession of struggle or need for forgiveness.4. Present a heartfelt petition or intercession.5. Close with an affirmation or statement of trust, such as "I rest in Your care," or "Thy will be done."Practice this cycle silently or aloud, adjusting the wording as feels authentic to you.### Centering Prayer: Embracing Stillness Within Ritual. While many associate ritual prayer with spoken words or set formulas, silence holds a sacred place in biblical tradition. Psalm 46:10 famously counsels, "Be still, and know that I am God." Incorporating contemplative silence into ritual prayer opens space for the Spirit to speak, for healing presence to be felt, and for soul-deep peace to grow.#### Meditative Prompt: The Breath as PrayerBegin by sitting comfortably with eyes closed. Breathe deeply and naturally, centering your attention on the breath's rhythm. On the inhalation, silently say or think the word "Come." On the exhalation, say or think "Lord." Repeat for several minutes, letting this sacred two-word prayer anchor your mind. Afterward, remain in silence for as long as feels comfortable, simply resting in the awareness of God's presence. This form of centering prayer disarms the busy mind and invites a restorative communion beyond words.### The Power of Repetition: Mantras, Psalms, and Sacred WordsRepetition is a hallmark of many prayer traditions, echoed in the biblical psalms and other scriptures where phrases repeated build intensity and focus. In the King James Bible, Psalm 136 exemplifies this beautifully, ending every verse with the refrain, "for his mercy endureth forever."Choosing a phrase, verse, or word to repeat during your prayer can center your thoughts and open deeper spiritual focus. This practice can be especially grounding in times of stress or distraction.#### Exercise: Select Your Sacred RefrainReflect quietly on a word or phrase that calls to your spirit. It might be "Peace," "Grace," "Abide with me," or a short scripture verse like "The Lord is my shepherd." Repeat this phrase slowly and rhythmically aloud or in the heart during prayer.Notice how the repetition shifts your awareness, softens mental clutter, and draws you into divine presence.### Incorporating Physical Symbols and ActsPhysical symbols and acts in prayer rituals serve as anchors for spiritual intention and expressions of belief. The Bible references multiple symbolic actions such as laying on of hands, anointing with oil, washing hands, or opening sacred scrolls. These gestures bridge the inward and outward dimensions of prayer.#### Suggestion: Adapt a Symbolic Act in Your RitualConsider integrating one or more simple symbolic acts into your prayer, such as:- Anointing with oil: Lightly anoint your forehead or hands with blessed oil or simply with clean water, accompanied by a silent prayer for blessing and healing.- Lighting a candle: Symbolizes Christ as the light or the presence of the Spirit; light a candle at the start of your prayer session as a visual focus.- Writing a prayer note: Compose a short prayer or intention on paper and place it in a special place, releasing your words symbolically.- Touching Scripture: Hold or trace your finger over a meaningful verse as you pray for deeper connection to God's word. Experiment with these actions as ways to engage your senses and ground your spiritual focus in physical expression.### Prayer Journaling: Reflection and GrowthDocumenting your prayer experiences can enrich your spiritual journey. Prayer journaling creates a dialogue not only with God but also with yourself, providing a space to record insights, express emotions, and track changes over time. Try setting aside a journal or notebook solely for prayer notes. After praying, take a few moments to write down:- Thoughts and feelings stirred during prayer- Words or images that arose unexpectedly- Gratitudes or answered prayers- Challenges or doubts encounteredOver weeks or months, review your entries to notice patterns, growth, and new directions in your prayer life.### Group Ritual Prayer: Building Community ConnectionRitual prayer is not restricted to solitary practice. Throughout biblical history, prayer gathered people together, creating bonds of faith and mutual support. The early church, as depicted in Acts, frequently prayed in community, sharing burdens and praises. If you feel led, consider inviting others to join you in ritual prayer regularly. This might take the form of:- Sharing a structured prayer cycle, each person leading an element.- Reading psalms or scripture aloud in turn.- Quietly praying in a circle or with hands raised.- Offering intercessions aloud for each other's needs. Group prayer amplifies communal faith and can provide encouragement as well as divine encounter.### Adapting Rituals for Modern Contexts and Diverse TraditionsYour personal or communal prayer ritual need not be bound strictly to the forms found in the King James Bible or any one tradition. The sacred invitation extends to adapting rituals in ways that resonate with your spiritual inclinations, cultural background, and contemporary life demands. For example:- Incorporate music or chanting that inspires your heart.- Use technology to set reminders or play recorded prayers.- Praying while walking or engaging in other gentle movement.- Applying Scripture-based affirmations during daily activities. The key is integrity—allowing the ritual to foster genuine connection, presence, and transformation rather than becoming rote or mechanical.### Sample Routine: A Morning Ritual of Prayer and MeditationTo bring these practices together, here is a sample morning ritual incorporating biblical motifs, posture, and meditative prompts. Feel free to adjust as needed:1. Prepare your sacred space: Light a candle or open a window for fresh air.2. Adopt prayer posture: Kneel or sit with hands open in front of you.3. Begin with

Scripture: Read a short passage aloud, such as Psalm 23 or Philippians 4:6-7.4. Praise and thanksgiving: Speak words of gratitude aloud or silently.5. Centering prayer: Practice the breath prayer "Come, Lord" for five minutes.6. Petition: Present your requests and intercessions.7. Repetition and meditation: Slowly repeat a sacred word or verse.8. Symbolic act: Anoint your hands with water or oil.9. Close with commitment: Affirm your trust and intention for the day.10. Journal briefly: Write one insight or intention. This ritual takes approximately 15–20 minutes but can be adapted to fit shorter or longer time frames.### Meditative Prompts to Deepen EngagementBelow are several prompts to assist you in entering a reflective prayerful state, usable alone or woven into ritual prayer:- Reflect on a moment of God's faithfulness in your life. How does recalling this sustain your hope?- Consider a personal struggle or doubt. What would it mean to surrender this fully in prayer?- Imagine yourself as a character in a biblical psalm or prayer—what feelings or needs emerge?- Contemplate the phrase "thy will be done." What fears or hopes arise as you pray this?- Invite the presence of the Holy Spirit or divine light, and silently ask for guidance and peace. Return to these prompts regularly as doors into deeper prayer dialogue.### Overcoming Barriers: Practical AdviceFor many, establishing new prayer rituals can encounter obstacles such as time constraints, distractions, or feelings of inadequacy. Here are practical tips to navigate these challenges:- Set realistic goals: Start with brief periods (even two or three minutes) and gradually build.- Create reminders: Use alarms, notes, or visual cues in your environment.- Minimize distractions: Choose a quiet time, turn off devices, and communicate boundaries to others.- Release perfectionism: Allow your prayer to be simple, honest, and as it is—not as you think it "should" be.- Seek accountability: Partner with a prayer buddy or join a prayer group for encouragement. Remember, the heart of ritual prayer is relationship, not ritual itself.### A Final InvitationPrayer rituals are gifts passed across generations and cultures, each adapted by those who cherish them. They hold the power to transform ordinary moments into sacred encounters, to shape character, and to direct the soul towards hope, peace, and purpose. By inviting participation through practical steps and meditative invitations, this journey into prayer ritual becomes yours—to embrace, shape, and enrich. May you find in your hands raised in reverence the echo of divine invitation, the solace of heartfelt expression, and the renewal that only intimate connection with the sacred can bring. Whether spoken or silent, still or jubilant, structured or free, your prayer ritual is a sacred dance of the human spirit with the divine mystery—timeless, profound, and deeply personal. Step forward now with these tools and insights. Allow ritual prayer to take root in your life as a wellspring of grace, guidance, and transformation. The ancient words live still, inviting your voice. The eternal God waits—not afar, but near—welcoming your prayerful heart into the embrace of unending love.

The Prayerful Heart: Embodying Faith's Whisper

The Heart as Spiritual Drum

There is a rhythm to prayer that transcends words—a pulse, steady and unyielding, that echoes from the very core of our being. This pulse arises not merely in the mind or spirit alone, but in the chest, where the heart rests as a sacred drum beating its soulful cadence. To understand the heart as a spiritual drum is to delve into the intimate dance between body and spirit, where prayer becomes more than a ritual or spoken invocation. It becomes a living, breathing experience, shaped by emotions that ripple through the heart's chambers like resonant vibrations in a timeless melody. The King James Bible, with its majestic language and profound imagery, often invites us into such bodily and emotional communion with God. Throughout Scripture, the heart is symbolically and literally presented as the wellspring of life, the seat of desires, fears, hopes, and sorrows. When the Psalmist declares, "Deep calleth unto deep at the noise of thy waterspouts" (Psalm 42:7), it is an invitation to listen beyond surface words—to the depths of the heart's cry, where divine longing and human need converge like a sacred drumbeat sounding through the corridors of time. Prayer, then, becomes an embodied act— a silent echo or a vocal release that resonates through the sacred drum of the heart. The chest, gently rising and falling with breath, becomes the vessel wherein emotions are transformed into spiritual sound. Each beat carries with it the raw textures of human experience: love glimmers as a tender vibration, longing pulses as an urgent rhythm, penitence mourns with a slow, heavy stroke. These emotional hues color prayer's cadence and give it its profound power to connect the temporal with the eternal.

To imagine the heart as a spiritual drum is to enter a sacred realm where the physical and metaphysical entwine. This perspective compels us to recognize that prayer is not merely a transaction of spoken words or mental petitions, but a visceral expression of faith's whisper. It is a dance of breath and beat, silence and sound, a sacred oscillation where the deepest yearnings of the soul find their voice in the pulsation of life itself. Consider the figure of King David, the psalmist whose prayers are among the most evocative in the Bible. His heart's rhythm is unmistakable, a tempest of emotion through which he pours his joys and fears before God. In Psalm 51, after his grievous sin, David cries, "Create in me a clean heart, O God; and renew a right spirit within me." The gravity of his penitence is carried not solely in the meaning of the words but in the heavy beating of the contrite heart, echoing repentance and hope for divine renewal. The heart drums out a sorrowful yet hopeful cadence, revealing that prayer, layered with emotion, transforms both the supplicant and the divine encounter. This relational heartbeat of prayer speaks to a universal human experience. Across faiths and cultures, the rhythmic beating of the chest—our most intimate drum—accompanies moments of profound connection, whether in mourning, celebration, or supplication. The pulse of the heart becomes a shared language, resonating beyond doctrinal divisions as an expression of the deepest longings of the human spirit for transcendence and communion. Emotion is the vivid color that stains the melody of prayer. Love infuses it with warmth and tenderness, reminding us that prayer is, at its heart, an act of relationship. Biblical prayers often reveal love not only for God but also for neighbors, creation, and the self. The Song of Solomon, though poetic and romantic, offers a glimpse into how desire and affectionate longing can embody divine love, inspiring prayers that vibrate with intimacy and devotion.Longing, another profound emotional undercurrent, pulses strongly in many biblical prayers. It drives the seeker forward with restless energy, a heartbeat that will not be stilled until fulfillment is found. The penitent's cry in Lamentations or the yearning expressed in Psalms such as Psalm 63 — "My soul thirsteth for thee, my flesh longeth for thee in a dry and thirsty land" — demonstrate how desire moves prayer beyond mere asking into the realm of deep spiritual hunger. This longing transforms the heart into a sacred drum demanding the attention of heaven. Penitence, too, marks its own measured tempo. It beats in slow, deliberate rhythms, drawing attention to the weight of wrongdoing and the hope for forgiveness. The biblical tradition is rich with such expressions—broken hearts and contrite spirits that find their deepest voice not in fear or despair, but in the steady drumbeat of confession and grace. These rhythms remind us that prayer's power lies not only in exaltation but also in vulnerability and surrender. Attuning oneself to the heart as a spiritual drum requires cultivating awareness of these emotional currents flowing beneath the litany of words. It asks us to listen inwardly, to the subtle rise and fall of breath and pulse, to the nuanced vibrations of affection, sorrow, hope, and yearning. This attunement is an invitation to embody prayer fully, allowing the body and soul to be instruments of sacred expression. In doing so, prayer is no longer external and detached; it becomes an intimate, ongoing dialogue with the divine, stirred by the very rhythm of life. In practical terms, attuning to this embodied experience might begin simply by placing a hand over the chest and feeling the heartbeat during prayer or silent meditation. This simple act partners the physical sensation of life with spiritual intention, grounding the prayer in the immediacy of the present moment. Breathing deeply, one can notice how the heart's pulse aligns with feelings awakened by sacred words or personal petitions. Such mindfulness transforms prayer into a sacred art where body, mind, and spirit play in harmonious rhythm. The effectiveness of prayer as spiritual drumbeat is also evidenced in communal worship, where congregants' hearts seem to beat as one, creating a powerful resonance of shared faith. The communal heartbeat amplifies the individual pulse, weaving many rhythms into a complex, yet unified pattern of devotion. This collective drumming calls heaven and earth into sacred dialogue, reminding us that our solo prayers partake in a larger symphony rooted in the heartbeats of all creation. Moreover, the heart as a spiritual drum challenges modern notions that often separate emotion from faith or treat prayer as an intellectual exercise alone. Instead, it calls for a holistic spirituality attentive to the body's wisdom, the language of emotions, and the rhythms of life. It affirms that prayer engages the whole person: soul, mind, body, and heart. The King James Bible, with its poetic grandeur, provides abundant imagery affirming this embodied spirituality. The word "heart" appears over 800 times, denoting not only the seat of intellect or will but also the emotional, visceral core. Passages such as Proverbs 4:23— "Keep thy heart with all diligence; for out of it are the issues of life"—invite an understanding that the heart's condition determines the flow and quality of life itself. When we consider prayer in this light, the heart's steady drumbeat is a lifeline to divine presence. Prayer, then, is not only a practice of beseeching or praising but also a rhythmic beating that carries the essence of our relationship with God. The pulsing heart becomes a sacred drum that transforms invisible emotions into audible, felt, and lived prayers that echo beyond the individual into the infinite. This metaphor also opens a door to creativity in prayer. Just as drummers create rhythms that move people emotionally and spiritually, so too can the prayerful heart create varying tempos and patterns corresponding to the shifting landscape of human experience. A fast, urgent beating might embody cries for help or intercession; a slow, meditative rhythm might reflect thanksgiving and peace. Silence between beats, too, holds meaning—the pregnant pause where faith listens, waits, and trusts. In embracing this imagery, believers and seekers alike can find freedom to express prayer in ways that honor their authentic emotional reality. No prayer is too raw, no emotion too intense or subdued to find a place in the drumbeat of the heart's sacred conversation with God. This holistic view liberates prayer from rigid forms, inviting a deeper encounter where feelings become part of the language of the soul's yearning. Modern spiritual teachers and therapists have often emphasized the importance of embodied prayer and meditation, recognizing that the body holds memories and emotions that can be accessed and released through mindful practice. The heart as a spiritual drum speaks to this wisdom, holding the rhythms of past joys and pains and the anticipation of future hope. When the heart beats in prayer, it touches all times at once, echoing ancient calls and present needs in continuous, sacred sound. This perspective also invites an understanding of prayer as a transforming force. Just as the beating drum energizes the dancer or warrior, so too can the pulsing heart in prayer empower the believer to face life's challenges with renewed courage and hope. The visceral rhythm grounds faith in the reality of lived experience, encompassing suffering and rejoicing, doubt and trust, despair and faith. Through the King James Bible's majestic and often poetic phrasing, we glimpse the beauty of this deeply embodied spirituality. The Psalms, in particular, are filled with metaphors of heart and breath that invite readers into the sacred interplay of body and spirit. The psalmist's cry "My heart is sore pained" (Psalm 38:8) reveals that prayer is not a detached intellectual act but a living experience of the heart's vulnerability. In this vulnerability, faith whispers its most authentic truths. Ultimately, by envisioning the heart as a spiritual drum, we are invited into a prayerful rhythm that transcends time, culture, and tradition—a universal beat that connects our humanity with the divine. It is the pulse that invites us to listen deeply, to feel profoundly, and to join in the eternal song of creation where every beat is itself a prayer. To nurture this rhythm, the reader is encouraged to cultivate moments of quiet stillness, listening inward to the drumbeat of their own heart as they pray. Attending to breath, emotion, and bodily sensation awakens a fuller awareness of prayer's living presence. Whether through contemplative silence, spoken liturgy, or spontaneous cries, the heart's drum can become a sacred instrument playing the music of faith's whisper. In a world often disconnected from the body's wisdom and silenced by external noise, reclaiming the heart as a spiritual drum is an act of radical invitation—to trust the intimate language of emotions and the sacred rhythms that pulse within. Prayer then becomes less about words said perfectly and more about the faith-filled drumbeat of a heart longing, loving, waiting, and surrendering. Through these pulsations, the divine speaks, and we, in turn, answer with the timeless rhythm of our prayerful hearts. This drumbeat is the ever-present echo of God's nearness, inviting us into continual communion where faith becomes a whisper felt deeply within, resonating outward to touch the world.

Emotional Intercession and Compassion

In the vast tapestry of prayer woven throughout the King James Bible, few threads shine as brightly as those of emotional intercession and compassion. These prayers overflow with the heart's deepest desires, reaching beyond personal petitions to encompass the hopes, sufferings, and restoration of others. They reveal the prayerful heart not merely as an isolated vessel for individual communication with the divine but as a living conduit, bridging personal faith with communal experience. This sacred exchange enriches both the spiritual and emotional dimensions of life, underscoring prayer's profound role in shaping empathy, connection, and transformation. To begin with, we must understand emotional intercession not simply as the act of asking on another's behalf but as a dynamic, heartfelt engagement that intertwines the supplicant's spirit with those for whom they pray. Compassion, a key motif throughout Scripture, is the soil from which such intercession grows. The biblical narrative presents compassion not as mere sentimentality but as an actionable, spirit-driven force—a call from the marrow of the heart that compels one to stand in the gap for others. It is in this place, between the desolation of human suffering and the hope of divine mercy, that prayerful compassion pulses vividly. Take, for example, the prayer of Abraham in Genesis 18. Upon hearing God's intention to judge Sodom and Gomorrah, Abraham does not recoil in fear or resignation; instead, he intercedes passionately for the city. His prayer is a dialogue steeped in respect, humility, and profound concern for the innocent lives at stake. Abraham pleads, negotiating with God, "Peradventure there be fifty righteous within the city: wilt thou also destroy and not spare the place for fifty righteous that are therein?" (Genesis 18:24). As the conversation progresses, Abraham's heart reveals a tender mercifulness that moves beyond self-interest—his intercession is motivated by both justice and love for others. Here, prayer becomes an active engagement of the heart's compassion, wielding spiritual agency for communal salvation. This pattern of deeply felt intercession continues throughout the Psalms, which serve as a rich reservoir of emotional prayer. Figures like King David frequently pour out fervent supplications not only for personal deliverance but for the well-being of others or the community. Psalm 35 presents a vivid example of this intercessory spirit: David prays, "Plead my cause, O Lord, with them that strive with me: fight against them that fight against me." Yet within this petition, there is a yearning not merely for personal vindication but for justice that echoes beyond himself. In Psalm 44, the communal aspect is explicit: "O God, we have heard with our ears, our fathers have told us, what work thou didst in their days, in the times of old. How thou didst drive out the heathen with thy hand, and plantedst them." David's heart, burdened by national distress and seeking God's mercy, exemplifies the heart as a spiritual meeting place where individual and communal anguish merge. Moving forward into the prophetic books, the emotional intensity of intercession and compassion reaches new heights. Jeremiah, the "weeping prophet," embodies a raw, vulnerable spirit that refuses to remain passive in the face of his people's downfall. His prayers, suffused with lamentation and heartfelt pleading, demonstrate the weight of the intercessor's burden. In Jeremiah 14, he implores God, "O Lord, though our iniquities testify against us, do thou it for thy name's sake: for our backslidings are many; we have sinned against thee." This prayer reveals layers of emotional complexity: confession, sorrow, hope, and an aching desire to restore the covenant relationship on behalf of his community. Jeremiah's personal grief becomes the channel through which the collective brokenness is laid before God, illustrating how emotional intercession knits individual empathetic pain into the fabric of communal prayer. Within the New Testament, the example of Jesus Christ himself offers the most profound illustration of compassion-filled intercession. His prayers, as recorded in the King James Bible, embody complete submission to the will of the

Father, yet they also reveal his boundless care for humanity's salvation and suffering. At the Garden of Gethsemane, before his arrest, Jesus prays with intense emotional fervor: "O my Father, if it be possible, let this cup pass from me: nevertheless not as I will, but as thou wilt" (Matthew 26:39). This prayer captures the tension between human vulnerability and divine surrender, an expression of raw emotional intercession on a deeply personal level. Moreover, Jesus's intercessory love extends outward in his High Priestly Prayer (John 17), where he prays not for himself but for his disciples and all who will believe through their word. His compassionate intercession includes petitions for their protection, unity, sanctification, and ultimate glory: "Holy Father, keep through thine own name those whom thou hast given me" (John 17:11). This prayer is a timeless model of compassionate intercession, exemplifying how the heart of the believer is called to embody love by standing in solidarity with others before God. Parallel to Jesus's example, the apostolic prayers recorded in the epistles abound with emotional intercession that reveals the maturity and depth of early Christian prayer life. Paul, in particular, frequently expresses a heart brimming with compassion as he prays for the churches and individuals he has mentored. Consider the prayer in Ephesians 3:14-19, where Paul petitions: "That he would grant you, according to the riches of his glory, to be strengthened with might by his Spirit in the inner man... that ye might be filled with all the fulness of God." This prayer radiates pastoral care and deep-hearted concern for believers' spiritual growth and wholeness. Paul's intercession is not abstract or doctrinal alone; it reflects his invested love and emotional connection with his spiritual children. Across these biblical examples, several key features of emotional intercession and compassion emerge that enrich both the spiritual and emotional life of the believer. First, the heart's role as a conduit is paramount. It functions as the intersection where individual faith encounters the suffering and needs of others, generating a prayerful engagement that transcends selfishness. It is within this "betwixt and between" space that prayers become more than words; they become spiritual embraces that hold the broken and the vulnerable.

Second, the affective dimension of these prayers exposes the interplay between vulnerability and strength. Prayers often articulate raw feelings—fear, sorrow, longing, and pleading—yet they are undergirded by confidence in God's faithfulness. This dynamic tension enriches the believer's emotional intelligence by legitimizing the expression of authentic emotion in the encounter with the divine. It models a holistic spirituality that embraces the full spectrum of human feeling while anchoring hope securely in God. Third, these prayers affirm the indispensability of empathy in spiritual practice. Intercessory prayer requires the capacity to enter imaginatively and emotionally into another's experience. It involves opening the heart's door to feel another's pain or need deeply enough to carry it before God. In doing so, the intercessor participates in the mysterious fellowship of suffering and redemption that characterizes God's covenant people. This process nurtures compassion as both a gift and a discipline, shaping the believer's ongoing formation. Finally, the communal implications of emotional intercession highlight the shared nature of faith. Prayer is shown to be inherently social and relational, connecting individuals into a collective garment of care and responsibility. When the heart prays with compassion, it extends beyond isolation into solidarity—affirming that personal entry into God's presence bears consequences and blessings for the wider community. This communal dimension provides a profound reminder that faith unfolds not in solitude but within the tapestry of relationships. To delve more deeply into the implicit theology of these intercessory prayers, it is essential to recognize that such prayers explicitly acknowledge human dependence on divine grace in the face of brokenness and need. They presuppose a God who is both just and merciful, capable of responding to intercession and moved by the sincere cries of tender hearts. This belief empowers the intercessor with hope and courage, enabling prayers that address monumental issues such as justice, healing, deliverance, and peace. Consider also the relational aspect underscored in the dialogue between God and the intercessor, as seen in Abraham's negotiation with the Lord or Moses's repeated pleas for

Israel's forgiveness. These encounters reveal a God who listens, responds, and invites partnership in the divine work of redemption. Prayer here becomes an act of co-laboring with the divine purpose, and compassion is the language that fuels this sacred collaboration. Moreover, these biblical instances affirm that emotional intercession does not diminish the sovereignty or transcendence of God but rather enlivens the intimacy between Creator and creation. It expresses a faith that can wrestle tenderly with divine will, offering honest lament and pleading that nevertheless trusts in God's overarching goodness. This balance between lament and trust shapes a prayerful posture that is humble yet bold, vulnerable yet resilient. From a psychological perspective, engaging in emotional intercession and compassionate prayer fosters spiritual resilience and emotional well-being. By externalizing grief, anxieties, and hopes through prayer, believers experience a form of catharsis that can alleviate spiritual and emotional burdens. The act of standing in the gap for others cultivates deeper empathy, reduces feelings of isolation, and strengthens communal bonds. The biblical model encourages nurturing a heart attentive not only to personal needs but also to the suffering and growth of others, thus enriching the individual's spiritual maturity. Historically, the practice of intercessory prayer and compassion-oriented prayer has been foundational within the faith communities. Early Christian mystics and monastic traditions upheld intercession as a vital practice, sometimes dedicating entire lives to standing in prayerful solidarity for others. The great reformers and revivalists often appealed to communal intercession as a means to invoke renewal and revival, recognizing that heartfelt, compassionate prayer carries immense spiritual power. The King James Bible, with its majestic language and rhythmic cadence, imparts a solemnity and dignity to these prayers that continue to inspire believers to embrace emotional intercession as a core aspect of their devotional life. Practically, embracing emotional intercession and compassion within prayer life challenges believers to cultivate attentiveness to others. It beckons a prayerfulness that listens keenly to the pains and needs swirling around one's own life and community. This attentiveness is nurtured through regular spiritual disciplines—meditation on Scripture, silent contemplation, and active listening to the Spirit's promptings. It also requires cultivating an interior sensitivity that refuses to harden the heart amid the world's suffering, instead allowing the compassionate love of God to flow outward through prayer. Theologically, these intercessory prayers invite reflection on the nature of the human heart as created in the imago Dei—the image of God. The capacity to feel deeply, to enter into another's distress, and to plead on their behalf reflects not only human empathy but a divine attribute mirrored in humanity. God's compassion is the root from which our own intercessory love springs, suggesting that prayer is an act where human hearts echo divine mercy. Thus, prayerful compassion is not merely a human virtue but a participation in God's own loving nature. In conclusion, emotional intercession and compassion stand as vital pillars within the broader theme of the prayerful heart. Through biblical examples spanning the Old and New Testaments, we observe how the heart functions as a living conduit where faith's whisper becomes a communal voice, carrying the burdens, hopes, and redemption of others before the throne of grace. These prayers overflow with tenderness and fervor, enriching both the spiritual vitality and emotional depth of the believer. They draw us beyond the limited horizon of self-interest into the expansive realm of divine compassion—a realm in which faith is embodied as active love, and prayer becomes a sacred bridge that unites hearts, knits communities, and transforms lives. As readers engage with these profound expressions of intercessory compassion from the King James Bible, they are invited not only to reflect intellectually but to enter the prayerful posture themselves. To cultivate a heart moved by love's urgency, ready to stand in the gap for others, embracing the fullness of human experience in God's presence. In doing so, prayer ceases to be a solitary whisper and becomes a chorus of compassionate voices echoing the divine, reverberating through time and across communities in a symphony of grace.

Gary E. Risenhoover

Cultivating an Embodied Prayer Practice

To cultivate an embodied prayer practice is to open oneself fully—not only in mind and spirit but in body and emotion—to the sacred dialogue that prayer invites. In the realm of spirituality, prayer is often pictured as a purely mental or verbal exercise, a matter of words or silent pleas lifted to heaven. Yet the King James Bible, with its rich tapestry of language and imagery, invites us into a more holistic experience—one where the whole person, including the body and heart, is engaged deeply and authentically. To embrace this fuller approach to prayer is to honor the profound connection between body, emotion, and spirit, fostering a wholeness that speaks more vividly to the human condition and God's intimate presence within it. The embodiment of prayer is not merely a metaphor but a practical, lived reality. It encourages us to notice how the physical posture of prayer, the rhythms of breathing, the movements of the body, and the stirring of emotions interlace to create a sacred space within ourselves. Such awareness offers a bridge from the abstract to the concrete, from the ethereal to the tangible, enriching our spiritual expression and deepening our communion with the Divine.Let us embark on a journey to explore this integration of bodily awareness and emotional openness into the prayerful experience, discovering ways to foster wholeness and authenticity in our spiritual lives.---The Body as a Sacred VesselOur bodies are often treated as mere vessels for our spiritual endeavors, but the Scriptures intimate a more profound relationship. "Know ye not that your body is the temple of the Holy Ghost which is in you?" (1 Corinthians 6:19). This declaration frames the body as sacred, a dwelling place for divine presence. When we approach prayer with this understanding, the very act of bringing our bodies into attentive awareness becomes an act of reverence and worship. In practical terms, cultivating an embodied prayer practice begins with acknowledging the physical self as a participant in spiritual dialogue. How we sit, stand, or bow; how we breathe; even the tone and volume of our spoken words affect how we experience and express prayer. The Psalmist exemplifies this integration, declaring, "Let my prayer be set forth before thee as incense; and the lifting up of my hands as the evening sacrifice!" (Psalm 141:2). Here, the physical gesture of lifting hands becomes an extension of the inner plea, an outward expression that carries spiritual significance. To awaken this awareness, one might begin each prayerful session by observing the posture of the body. Is it tense or relaxed? Open or closed? Does the position invite receptivity or resistance? Small intentional adjustments—a gentle straightening of the spine, a softening of the shoulders, a slight lowering of the gaze—can create an environment where prayer moves from mechanical recitation to embodied encounter. Breathing, often overlooked, is a key conduit between body and spirit. The rhythmic pattern of inhaling and exhaling mirrors the ebb and flow of life itself. Incorporating conscious breathing into prayer, such as slow, deep breaths synchronized with silent or spoken phrases, deepens concentration and presence. The breath becomes a symbol of divine life breathed into us, a sacred tide connecting heaven and earth within our ribs.---Emotional Openness as a Portal to Authentic PrayerPrayer is not confined to words alone; it is profoundly shaped by the emotions that underpin our communication with God. The King James Bible offers countless examples where deep feelings—joy, lamentation, yearning, gratitude—pour forth in prayerful speech. The Psalms, in particular, are vivid testimonies of prayer as heartfelt expression, encompassing the full gamut of human emotion. To cultivate a prayer practice that integrates emotional openness is to invite honesty before God. It means allowing feelings to arise without judgment or suppression and presenting them fully within our spiritual petitions. Indeed, God calls us to bring our whole selves, emotions included, into the sacred space of prayer. As the prophet Jeremiah lamented, "If I say, I will not mention him, nor speak any more in his name; then there is in my heart as it were a burning fire shut up in my bones... and I am weary with forbearing, and I cannot contain" (Jeremiah 20:9). Here, the intensity of feeling becomes both the impetus and the content of prayer itself. Practically, this may mean beginning a prayer moment by naming the emotions present—whether sorrow, gratitude, confusion, or hope. This naming frees the spirit from constriction and invites God's healing and comfort. Journaling can be a helpful tool, in which one writes candidly about emotional states and prayers, allowing thoughts to flow alongside feelings. Silent meditation can further deepen this presence to emotion, offering space to both feel and surrender all within God's tender care. Emotional openness in prayer also means embracing vulnerability, which can be challenging in a world that often prizes stoicism or emotional control. But vulnerability does not denote weakness; rather, it is the courage to stand naked before the Divine, trusting that our raw, imperfect selves are met with grace. This authenticity enriches the prayer experience, transforming it from rote practice into relational encounter.---Movement and Gesture: The Language of the SpiritThe silent eloquence of the body finds profound expression in movement and gesture within prayer. Bowing, kneeling, clasping hands, folding arms, or even walking prayerfully all convey spiritual attitudes and deepen embodied awareness. In the biblical context, gestures hold powerful symbolic weight. Jesus often lifted eyes to heaven or folded His hands in prayer, while other figures prostrated themselves or stretched out their arms in supplication and praise. These physical acts speak directly to the heart, affirming our embodied humanity and symbolizing inner spiritual realities. Integrating such gestures consciously into prayer prompts the mind and heart to align more fully. For example, kneeling is a posture of humility and surrender, visibly acknowledging God's majesty and our need. Standing with arms lifted invites openness and praise, embodying trust and thanksgiving. Even a quiet bow of the head can frame prayer as an act of devotion and contemplation. For those who find seated prayer challenging or static, incorporating gentle movements—a slow walk in nature while reciting a psalm, or a series of gentle stretches to accompany meditative prayers— can anchor prayer in the body's rhythm and the natural world's pulse. These movements help release mental distractions, inviting a deeper flow of presence. Such integration need not become a rigid routine but rather a spontaneous expression of the spirit's yearning. Listening attentively to what the body desires to do in prayer—whether to raise hands, to still oneself, to sway gently—cultivates a responsive, alive prayer rhythm deeply attuned to personal experience and divine prompting.---Silence and Stillness: The Body's Embrace of Divine PresenceAn essential aspect of embodied prayer is embracing silence and stillness, allowing body and soul to rest in God's presence. This does not mean a cold absence of activity but a warm, receptive poise—an open, expectant posture that invites the Divine Spirit to move freely within. Scripture often invokes silence as a sacred space where God's voice is heard most clearly. "Be still, and know that I am God" (Psalm 46:10) encapsulates this ancient wisdom. Stillness is the body's way of ceasing its restless striving, permitting awareness to deepen beyond words into the mysterious presence of God. To cultivate this, begin prayer with moments of quietude: settle into a comfortable posture, close the eyes gently if desired, and allow the breath to slow naturally. Notice the body's sensations without attempting to change them, letting thoughts pass like clouds while resting firmly in the present moment. Many find that silence unveils layers of spiritual insight and emotional clarity inaccessible amid noise. The body softens, tension unwinds, and an interior spaciousness grows— a sacred pause where faith's whisper becomes audible. Stillness also means honoring times when prayer is not verbal or active but simply being with God in trust. This receptive posture refreshes the spirit and reorients the soul toward peace, patience, and grace.---Integrating Prayer into Everyday Life: Embodiment Beyond the AltarEmbodied prayer is not confined to the moments set apart for devotion; it invites integration into the full texture of daily life. The sacred becomes accessible not only in cathedral or sanctuary but in kitchen, street, workplace, and wilderness. Attuning to bodily sensations during the day serves as a prayerful reminder of God's nearness. The rising of the sun, the warmth of a breath, the beat of the heart—all can be invitations to quiet gratitude and mindfulness. Such integration transforms mundane moments into sacramental spaces, where prayer is continuous and fluid. Practically, this can take many forms. Morning stretches can become prayers of awakening. Walking to work can be a pilgrimage, with each footstep a mindful nod to God's sustaining presence. When emotions arise—stress, joy, frustration—pausing briefly to connect breath, emotion, and awareness re-centers us in prayerful presence. Visual or tactile cues, such as a prayer bracelet, a scriptural verse posted nearby, or the simple act of crossing oneself, provide embodied anchors that recall the soul to prayer amid busy days. Over time, these small acts accumulate into a deeply rooted habit of living prayerfully, where body, mind, and spirit move in union.---Obstacles and Encouragements on the Journey to Embodied PrayerThe path to embodied prayer is rich yet often challenging. Modern culture frequently detaches mind and body or regards feelings as liabilities rather than gifts. Such perspectives may cause resistance or discomfort in integrating physical and emotional dimensions of prayer. Common obstacles include embarrassment regarding bodily expression in spiritual contexts, impatience with slow inner work, difficulty tuning into subtle sensations, or fear of emotional overwhelm. Recognizing these challenges with compassion is crucial—self-criticism stifles growth, but gentle encouragement fosters progress. To overcome hindrances, begin with small steps—short periods of embodied prayer, simple breathing exercises, or momentary stillness. Gradually expand these practices, always guided by kindness and curiosity. Community can also be a powerful resource. Participating in group prayers that incorporate movement, or studying scriptural examples aloud with others, can inspire courage and deepen understanding. Moreover, seeking wisdom from spiritual directors or mentors familiar with holistic prayer nurtures sustained engagement.---The Fruit of Embodied Prayer: Wholeness and Authentic Spiritual ExpressionThe ministry of integrating body, emotion, and spirit in prayer bears abundant fruit. Beyond intellectual assent or verbal utterance, embodied prayer invites us to a place of wholeness—a harmonizing of all that we are in God's presence. This wholeness invites healing, as neglected or suppressed aspects of self are welcomed and redeemed. It builds resilience, as prayer becomes a wellspring of strength rooted not only in belief but in the palpable experience of divine love coursing through body and soul. Authentic spiritual expression emerges naturally, no longer confined to external expectations but arising spontaneously from sincere encounter. Prayer becomes a dance between the finite and infinite, where breath, heart, and voice join in a sacred chorus. In this space, faith whispers deeply, the human spirit receives its full dignity, and the divine mystery reveals itself in forms both ancient and immediate—words, tears, gestures, stillness, and breath intertwined.---Practical Exercises for Cultivating Embodied PrayerTo integrate these reflections into daily practice, consider the following exercises:1. Posture Check and Adjustment: Before beginning prayer, notice your posture. Are you comfortable and open? Straighten the spine gently, soften the shoulders, and allow the chest to lift slightly. Close your eyes if it helps focus. Breathe deeply several times, feeling the inhalation fill your body and the exhalation release tension.2. Breath as Prayer: Choose a simple phrase or scripture verse (such as "The Lord is my shepherd" or "Be still and know"). As you inhale, silently say the first part; as you exhale, the second. Repeat this rhythmically, allowing breath and word to merge into one continual prayer.3. Emotion Naming: Before praying aloud or silently, take a moment to identify your predominant feeling. Speak it honestly—confess, rejoice, lament, hope. Bring that feeling before God, trusting that it is welcome and understood.4. Gesture Integration: Incorporate a meaningful physical gesture during prayer—lifting hands in praise, folding them in petition, bowing the head in reverence, or kneeling to cultivate humility. Notice how the movement shifts your internal state.5. Movement Meditation: Engage in slow walking prayer in a quiet place. With each step, recite a short prayer or phrase. Feel the contact of feet on the ground and the movement of the body as integral to the prayerful moment.6. Silent Presence: Set a timer for 5 to 10 minutes. Sit comfortably and breathe naturally. When thoughts or feelings arise, observe them without judgment and return gently to the quiet awareness of God's presence.7. Daily Integration: Choose one daily activity—eating, washing dishes, commuting—and bring conscious bodily awareness and prayerful focus to it. Let each movement, sensation, or breath be a humble offering.---In embracing an embodied prayer practice, we heed an ancient truth restored: that to pray is to enter into union with God as whole beings. The King James Bible, with its majestic words and timeless wisdom, beckons us not only into a mental discourse but into a full-bodied, passionate engagement with the Divine. May this integration of body and emotion enliven your prayer life, drawing you ever deeper into sacred encounter, healing, and transformative grace. Here, in the synergy of breath, feeling, and spirit, the prayerful heart truly awakens—its whispers echoing through flesh and soul, carried gently into eternity's embrace.

Guardian Shades: Angels, Messengers, and Prayer's Echoes

The Ethereal Presence of Angels

From the dawn of sacred scripture to the resonant cadence of prayer uttered in quiet solitude, angels emerge as ethereal presences whose nature defies full human grasp. These celestial beings, shimmering in biblical narrative as messengers and guardians, are more than mere figures of myth or pious imagination; they serve as profound links that bridge the earthly and the heavenly, the visible and the unseen. Their portrayal within the King James Bible reveals them not only as emissaries of divine will but as living, breathing participants in the sacred dialogue of prayer, embodying both protection and intercession. To understand the role of angels as intermediaries is to glimpse the very architecture of spiritual communication itself — an architecture fashioned on the intricate interplay between human yearning and divine response. The biblical account offers a tapestry where angels move gracefully between the realms. From the earliest chapters of Genesis, where the "angel of the Lord" appears as a divine sentinel, to the climactic visions of Revelation, where angelic hosts form the chorus of creation's eternal worship, these beings are enmeshed in the unfolding drama of God's interaction with humanity. Their silhouettes are often described with vivid, luminous imagery — eyes like flames of fire, wings that stir the cosmos, and countenances radiant as lightning. Yet, despite these dazzling descriptions, angels remain enigmatic, distant from human comprehension, their forms both terrifying and reassuring. This duality is essential to their function as intermediaries: they are close enough to the divine to carry messages of hope, judgment, or salvation, yet sufficiently removed to embody transcendence. In the context of prayer, angels assume a pivotal spiritual role, often depicted as witnesses to human petitions or as divine echoes that amplify mortal cries to the heavens. One of the most arresting biblical images is found in the Book of Revelation, where it is said that the prayers of the saints arise before God "as the incense" offered by angels (Revelation 5:8). This metaphor powerfully illustrates the angelic function as conveyors—a fragrant ascension of human longing that transcends the earthly plane, transformed into a pleasing sacrifice to the Most High. The angel, then, is not a passive observer but an active participant, a living bridge that enlivens the theological reality of prayer by transporting its essence into the divine presence. The Genesis narrative also introduces angels as guardians of sacred spaces and sanctuaries. Their presence at the gates of Eden, wielding the flaming sword to bar man's return after the fall, symbolizes an early and profound understanding of their protective role. These guardian angels are envisaged not solely as sentinels against spiritual or physical harm, but also as conduits of divine justice and mercy. In this sense, they guard not only the sanctity of sacred locales but the spiritual integrity of human beings who seek communion with God through prayer. This protective function often extends beyond the immediate context of the scriptural story. The psalmist's heartfelt appeal in Psalm 91, "For he shall give his angels charge over thee, to keep thee in all thy ways," echoes a timeless assurance that angels accompany the faithful, responding to prayer with unseen guardianship throughout life's trials. An exploration of angelic presence in Scripture must also grapple with their complex hierarchies and specific functions. The King James Bible, while often economical in its angelic terminology, hints at various ranks and orders, such as archangels, cherubim, and seraphim, each with a distinct role in divine communication. For example, the archangel Michael appears especially as a warrior and protector of God's people, engaged in cosmic battles against the forces of evil. In contrast, the seraphim are described in Isaiah's vision as hovering above God's throne, their six wings and ceaseless chant "Holy, holy, holy" reverberating the holiness that defines the very nature of God. These distinctions deepen the understanding of angels as creatures uniquely attuned to divine purposes, functioning within the celestial hierarchy to ensure that the prayers of the faithful reach their intended destination and that divine will is executed. Throughout biblical history, angels serve repeatedly as direct, often startling, responders to prayer. Their sudden appearance brings comfort to the faithful, guidance through difficult decisions, or even deliverance from imminent danger. The story of Hagar in Genesis 16 exemplifies this intervention: wandering in the wilderness, she encounters the "angel of the Lord" who not only hears her silent distress but offers reassurance and a promise for her son Ishmael's future. Similarly, the angelic visitation to Mary in the New Testament embodies the epochal transition from anticipation to fulfillment as Gabriel announces the incarnation of Christ. These encounters underscore the angel's role not simply as an external messenger, but as a companion who steps into human experience at pivotal moments, embodying both the invitation to draw near in prayer and the assurance of divine presence. Moreover, the angelic role as "echoing voices" in prayer extends beyond literal biblical episodes to a broader spiritual theology. Angels carry the prayers of believers beyond the audible realm, into the eternal presence of God where time and place dissolve. They amplify the universal echoes of hope, repentance, praise, and supplication that prayer occasions across cultures and epochs. This function resonates strongly with the notion that prayer itself is a language of the soul—a transmission of deepest needs and aspirations that transcends human limitation. Angels, then, are the bridge between human frailty and divine omnipotence, broadcasting voices of yearning with unwavering fidelity to the divine ear. The participatory nature of angels in the prayer experience also reveals a profound symmetry: as humans reach upward in supplication, angels descend as bearers of divine favor and communication. This reciprocity reflects a spiritual ecology in which prayer is not a solitary act but a dynamic encounter involving multiple realms of existence. The shimmering silhouettes imagined in scripture thus carry a richer symbolism: they breathe life into the very atmosphere of prayer, wrapping the human spirit in both mystery and consolation. Unlike abstract spiritual forces, these angelic beings are portrayed as distinct entities whose presence can be perceived in moments of transcendence, heightened awareness, and sacred encounter. Acknowledging angels as witnesses to prayer also enriches the understanding of accountability and authenticity within spiritual practice. The Bible intimates that angels observe the sincerity and disposition of those who pray. This suggests that prayer is not merely a transactional act but one held within a sacred gaze — a divine assembly where angels, as intermediaries, witness the unfolding truth of heart and motive. Such awareness challenges believers and seekers alike to approach prayer with reverence and honesty, recognizing that unseen eyes accompany every utterance, echoing every whispered plea and every heartfelt praise. The presence of angels as intermediaries illuminates the theological truth that communication with God transcends the limitations of humanity. Through angelic mediation, the divine presence becomes more approachable, kindness more tangible, and the mystery less forbidding. In this light, prayer evolves from a solitary monologue into a profound dialogue, facilitated and enriched by those appointed as heavenly messengers. This dynamic interplay unites the transcendent with the immanent, suggesting that within the most personal spiritual moments lie cosmic connections—where angels stir the air, and prayer ascends as a living flame. Biblical reflections on angels also invite a renewed contemplation of their relevance in contemporary spiritual experience. While ancient texts present them in magnificent and sometimes fearsome forms, modern sensibilities can understand angels metaphorically as embodiments of God's care and presence. The "shimmering silhouettes" become symbols that evoke awe, protection, and an ongoing spiritual reality that transcends dogma or ideology. For believers who pray in the quiet solitude of their rooms, or in vast congregations lifted in unified voice, angels represent the unseen company that accompanies every petition and thanksgiving. This enduring presence attests to the universality of prayer as an experience infused with divine attentiveness and cosmic participation. Further, angels as guardians and messengers highlight the intercessory dimension of prayer—where the prayers of one may be carried, amplified, and answered in ways beyond human imagination. The angelic ministry suggests a spiritual collaboration whereby human intention and divine compassion meet, mediated by these celestial intermediaries. This reflects a biblical worldview that prayer is not isolated but embedded within a larger cosmic order, where angels serve as vital agents who translate human longing into divine action. The depiction of angels also challenges contemporary readers to consider the multi-dimensional nature of spiritual reality. The biblical angels, though often described with corporeal traits—wings, eyes, voices—exist primarily as spiritual beings whose essence eludes full human definition. Their role as emissaries between heaven and earth compels a humility in our understanding of prayer: that it is always enacted within a sacred mystery, enlivened by forces beyond sight and sound. By embracing the presence of angels in prayer, one acknowledges that faith is not blind but daring, embracing the unseen dimensions that inform human existence. Indeed, the biblical narrative's recurrent focus on angels as "shimmering silhouettes" can be read not only as literal descriptions but as poetic imagery intended to evoke the luminous, shifting, and intangible nature of these beings. Their presence "breathes life into the atmosphere of prayer" by transforming quiet spaces into sanctuaries of divine encounter. The angels' light is not simply physical brightness but an illumination of the spirit, turning moments of prayer into radiant experiences of connection, hope, and transformation. Moreover, the angelic role emphasizes the relational nature of prayer. Angels witness the intimacy between the human soul and God, reflecting back the trust, dependence, and surrender that characterize prayerful communion. This relational dimension invites believers to perceive themselves not as isolated supplicants but as part of a larger spiritual community that includes heavenly beings. Angels, in this view, become companions who journey alongside the faithful, nurturing the relationship between the divine and human hearts. The scriptural testimony of angels also affirms the dynamic externalization of internal spiritual truths. Prayer often begins as silent meditation or private mourning, yet with angelic mediation it emerges as a celestial event, a sacred transaction that alters realities unseen. This externalization underscores prayer's power to transcend personal boundaries and invoke divine action through heavenly channels. Angels, as messengers, carry the weight and authenticity of prayer into the divine assembly, ensuring that human voices are neither lost nor ignored. An essential dimension of the angelic presence is their dual role as comforters and agents of challenge. In moments of despair, angels appear to soothe and encourage, reminding the faithful of God's abiding care. Conversely, they sometimes bring penetrating messages that call for repentance, reform, or acceptance of divine plans that may be difficult to comprehend. This complexity reflects an angel's function not merely as dispensers of comfort but as cosmic agents who ensure the integrity of prayer's purpose within the larger framework of divine justice and mercy. Taken together, the biblical portrait of angels as intermediaries and guardians within the sphere of prayer suggests a rich theology that extends beyond textual history into lived spiritual reality. Angels are shimmering, luminous agents who both protect and participate in the unfolding drama of human-divine interaction. They hear prayers, carry them forward, respond with guidance, and stand as eternal witnesses to the sacred moment where heaven and earth meet. Their presence beckons believers and seekers alike to embrace prayer not merely as words or rituals but as the echo of life breathed upward and returned in divine response. In closing, angels in the King James Bible stand as both literal and symbolic bridges—silhouettes shimmering in the spiritual atmosphere—who remind humanity that no prayer is uttered in isolation, and no heart's cry fades unheard. They invite us into a cosmos alive with celestial life, where every petition is met with a listening wing, and every surrender is accompanied by a radiant messenger. Their ethereal presence compels us to recognize that prayer is an ever-unfolding conversation held within a divine community, witnessed and nurtured by angels who breathe life into the sacred dialogue between God and mankind.

Messengers of Grace and Hope

Throughout the sacred pages of the King James Bible, angels emerge as luminous conduits of divine presence—messengers whose very beings scatter grace and hope like seeds cast upon the fertile soil of human hearts. Their appearances are neither arbitrary nor incidental; rather, they serve as sacred affirmations of prayer's enduring power and the limitless promise that it carries. The narratives housing these angelic interventions reveal a profound intertwining of the celestial and the terrestrial, where faith and supplication meet God's swift and tender response through these ethereal emissaries. To grasp the vibrancy of such encounters, one must see them not as mere historical accounts but as living metaphors, reflections of a spiritual reality that continues to echo in the soul's quiet chambers. Consider the moment the angel Gabriel visits the Virgin Mary, a scene etched into the collective consciousness as a paragon of hope delivered with gentle strength. "Hail, thou that art highly favoured, the Lord is with thee: blessed art thou among women" (Luke 1:28). In this single, sweeping salutation, the divine speaks through an angel, transforming what might have been a moment of fear into one of radiant promise. Mary's prayer, perhaps unvoiced yet deeply held in her heart, finds voice and answer in Gabriel's words. Here, the angel is more than a herald; he is the very embodiment of grace itself, a bridge joining human trepidation to divine purpose. The light that envelops Gabriel is not just physical brightness but a spiritual glow, illuminating paths uncharted and possibilities yet unseen. In poetic metaphor, these angels resemble a gentle dawn, the quiet breaking of light that heals the darkness's wounds and beckons a new day. Their approach is neither overwhelming nor coercive but filled with a strength as soft as the morning breeze that stirs the leaves yet carries the promise of warmth and renewal. They come as whispers of God's love, traversing the heavens and earth alike, stirring the quiet hopes lodged deep within human souls. To envision them as "messengers of grace and hope" is to recognize that they carry not merely messages, but the very breath of God's compassion and reassurance, breathed into the fabric of creation to rouse the weary and steady the trembling. The story of Daniel in the lion's den further reveals the angelic ministry as a manifestation of divine protection born from prayer's fierce trust. As Daniel's enemies conspired, their venomous intent unable to sway his faithful heart, an angel descended, closing the mouths of lions and shielding him from harm (Daniel 6:22). This scene shimmers with the metaphor of a steadfast sentinel, whose presence transforms a pit of despair into a throne of triumph. The angel's strength is tangible, a radiant barrier that responds directly to Daniel's unwavering prayers, proving that intercession is never powerless but is the very spark that summons divine intervention. Like a mighty oak weathering storms, the angel stands as a living emblem of how prayer commands a guardian force, turning threats into testimonies. Angelic visitors also evoke the imagery of wind—unseen yet felt, swift yet silent—carrying God's purposes across the realms. In Acts 12, Peter's prison chains fall from his wrists as an angel leads him past guards with a light-footed grace, guiding freedom from captivity. The angel's presence here is an invisible current that bends the will of earthly powers, freeing the prisoner not through mortal might but through divine subtlety. This transformative power of prayer, unveiled through angelic intervention, suggests that our petitions send out ripples extending far beyond our own walls. Like a messenger riding the wind, the angel carries with them the assurance that no barrier is impenetrable when covered by earnest prayer and divine favor. Moreover, these messengers often appear when human hope teeters on the edge of despair. The story of Hagar in the wilderness (Genesis 16) paints a poignant portrait of an angel arriving amid desolation, a tender voice cutting through the silence of abandonment. "Lift up thine eyes, and look on the place from whence thou art taken" (Genesis 16:9). This gentle call to recognize God's providence encapsulates the angel's role as a balm for the broken, a vivid symbol of hope rekindled. The angel's message blossoms in a desert of despair much in the way a desert flower bursts forth after rain—unexpected, resilient, breathtaking in its quiet beauty. Through such divine visits, prayer is shown to awaken new life where the world might only see ruin. Visually and spiritually, these angels invite us to contemplate the sacred interplay of light and shadow, where the brightness of grace dances with the shadows of human frailty. They emerge as radiant beings, celestial flames glowing softly yet fiercely against the backdrop of life's darkest moments. Their strength is not of overwhelming force but a delicate might born of devotion to God's plan—an essence akin to a candle's flame steadfast against the night wind, unwavering yet yielding to gentle portions of darkness. It is precisely this balance that invites believers and seekers alike to embrace prayer—not as a mere ritual but as an active dialogue where the divine response is lived and experienced through angelic presence. The angel's function as a divine courier underscores a central truth: prayer is never silent or solitary. It weaves a tapestry into which God threads divine purpose, answered petitions, and celestial assurance. The biblical narrative of Jacob wrestling with the "man" (Genesis 32), commonly understood as an angelic figure, captures this profound interaction. Jacob's struggle becomes a metaphor for the wrestling of the soul in prayer, the tension between human will and divine blessing. At the trail's end, the blessing bestowed upon Jacob signals transformation, protection, and the unfolding of God's covenant. This interaction illustrates that angels are not distant messengers but participants in the inner drama of faith—agents who, through prayer, help us navigate the complexity of doubt, struggle, and hope toward spiritual renewal. Beyond individual encounters, angels collectively symbolize the perpetual activity of the divine in response to the prayers of the faithful. Hebrews 1:14 declares them as "ministering spirits, sent forth to minister for them who shall be heirs of salvation." Such a depiction invokes the poetic image of a vast host—immortal guardians encircling the faithful, their movements like a celestial dance choreographed by God's wisdom, each step resonating with mercy and protection. This cosmic choreography suggests that prayer sends ripples into an unseen realm, calling these servants of grace into motion, amplifying the sense of intimate connection shared between heaven and earth. For the believer and seeker alike, this metaphor breathes life into the abstract concept of prayer's efficacy, transforming it into a tangible, ongoing spiritual reality. In the Psalms, angelic imagery further illustrates the protective and sustaining power accompanying prayer. Psalm 91:11-12 assures that "He shall give His angels charge over thee, to keep thee in all thy ways. They shall bear thee up in their hands, lest thou dash thy foot against a stone." The gentle strength implied here conjures an image both majestic and tender—a celestial embrace cradling the supplicant amid life's trials. The angels' care is depicted not as distant supervision but as an intimate holding, a spiritual support that reflects the loving response to prayer's call. Such poetic imagery conveys the angel's role as an active participant in the journey of faith, a living testament to the promise that no soul goes unheard or unguarded. The New Testament amplifies this angelic motif in the story of Peter's release, as well as in the consistent references to angels rejoicing over repentant sinners (Luke 15:10). Angels here function as celebrants of grace, embodying the hope that prayer and repentance awaken joyous responses in the heavenly realms. Their presence is that of a festive, radiant company welcoming the lost and weary with open arms and lifted voices. This portrayal elevates the angelic role beyond mere guardianship to active participants in divine celebration, reflecting a joyous echo of prayer's transformative power. Sometimes, angels appear as bearers of correction and guidance, tender yet firm in their mission to bring truth and direction. The angel who stops Abraham from sacrificing Isaac (Genesis 22:11-12) is a compelling depiction of divine mercy intervening at the cusp of tragic consequence. This intervention is both a test and a revelation, showing that prayer is a dynamic conversation with God wherein even the most agonizing acts are met with divine understanding and reprieve through angelic deliverance. The angel, a harbinger of mercy and hope, shifts the narrative from one of loss to one of promise, highlighting the profound capacity of prayer to alter destiny through grace's intercession. Throughout these narratives, a consistent theme emerges: angels do not supplant human prayer but rather affirm and amplify its potency. They serve as divine echoes—vibrations in the spiritual ether—that confirm God's attentiveness to the cries of the heart. Their interventions are not mere miracles to be marveled at from afar, but intimate communications that embody hope, encouragement, and the soft strength that prayer holds. In this way, angelic visitations become living metaphors for the invisible yet impactful ways in which divine grace answers our petitions. To feel the presence of these messengers of grace and hope is to sense the whisper of the divine amid the tumult of life, the gentle reinforcement of prayer's promise that one is never alone. Their light beckons the weary to press forward, their touch softens the ache of waiting, and their very being offers a reminder of the sublime dance between humanity and the divine. Through the vivid tapestry of biblical accounts, angels emerge as radiant threads weaving the story of prayer into a greater whole—a tapestry where hope is renewed, grace is unceasing, and the echo of faith reverberates through eternity. In contemplating these messages, one is invited to see prayer not as a distant plea but as a vital spiritual practice illuminated and energized by these celestial messengers. Each angelic intervention underscores the truth that prayer is met not with silence but with a dynamic, ongoing response that bridges heaven and earth. These messengers of grace and hope are the living affirmation that every whispered word, every lifted hand, and every heart laid bare in prayer is held tenderly and answered with a divine embrace that transcends time and circumstance. Thus, as we reflect on the myriad ways angels appear amid the biblical record, their stories knit together a powerful testament: prayer rouses angels to action; prayer is the invisible summons that stirs heaven's host to rally around the fragile yet fervent human spirit. The messages they bear are not merely announcements but living testimonies of God's enduring love, mercy, and providential care—an eternal gift wrapped in the wings of grace and whispered in the breath of hope.

Gary E. Risenhoover

Walking with the Divine Amidst Shadows

In the vast spiritual landscape that unfolds within the pages of the King James Bible, prayer emerges not simply as a vocalized petition or ritual chant, but as a profound encounter—a sacred dialogue where the human soul reaches beyond its mortal confines to touch the divine. Yet, this encounter is rarely solitary or stark. Interwoven among the threads of prayer's tapestry is a figure of immeasurable significance: the angel. These heavenly beings, often described as messengers and guardians, serve as companions who walk alongside the Divine Presence, enveloping prayer in layers of protection, mystery, and unfathomable grace. To walk with the divine amidst shadows—the unseen realms and spiritual trials—is, in many ways, to experience the quiet agency of angels who stand sentinel over the fragile moments when the human heart opens to God. Within this sacred communion, angels are not distant or indifferent figures. They are intimate actors in the divine economy of prayer, bridging the sacred and the temporal. Their presence invites believers and seekers alike into an awareness that prayer transcends the spoken word alone; it is surrounded by a heavenly chorus and guarded by forces whose arms extend into the unseen. In contemplating this alliance, we begin to understand prayer not only as an act of individual devotion but as a journey shared with the divine entourage, a pilgrimage marked by both light and shadow, comfort and mystery, promise and challenge. The biblical narrative itself is saturated with moments where angels move as intermediaries between the human and the divine. Whether delivering God's messages, offering protection, or bearing witness to the unfolding of providence, these beings reveal a profound truth: prayer is enfolded in a cosmic relationship that defies human limitation. The angels' presence alongside the Divine Presence assures those who pray that they are never alone, even amidst darkness or uncertainty. Instead, they are embraced by companioning forces, celestial allies who accompany the soul's ascent through trials and triumphs alike. To explore this final aspect of prayer as depicted in the King James Bible is to invite readers to sense, beyond words, the dynamic and living presence of these guardian shades as they walk in step with the divine. Such reflection unveils prayer's protective and mysterious dimensions, offering a spiritual lens through which to view one's own inner journey, wounds, hopes, and desires. It awakens a consciousness that the sacred is not confined to the seen but extends into realms populated by unseen protectors whose purpose is to uplift, shelter, and whisper assurances that transcend earthly fears. The veil of mystery surrounding angels is, paradoxically, both a source of awe and reassurance. The Bible portrays these beings with an otherworldly majesty that surpasses human comprehension, yet their actions frequently reveal tender compassion and vigilant care for those who seek God. To walk with the divine amidst shadows is to trust in this duality—that the inscrutable and the intimate coexist in the divine economy of prayer. The angels' accompaniment in this spiritual expedition reflects God's own faithfulness, a steadfast presence that neither fails nor falters when the soul calls out in hope, desperation, or reverence. From the earliest chapters of Scripture, the connection between prayer and angelic presence is deeply etched. Consider the patriarchs and prophets who encountered angels as they lifted their voices to heaven: Abraham's intercession for Sodom (Genesis 18), Jacob's wrestling with the angel (Genesis 32), or Daniel's visions accompanied by angelic interpreters (Daniel 9). In these accounts, prayer becomes a shared space where the temporal and heavenly realms converge, and where angels become tangible signs of God's attentive care. The Psalms, the heartfelt songbook of ancient Israel, also reveal the protective mantle of angels over the praying soul. In Psalm 91, the psalmist declares, "He shall give His angels charge over thee, to keep thee in all thy ways." This assurance—embedded within the language of worship and petition—nourishes the soul with the knowledge that divine guardianship attends every step taken in faith. The angels act as sentinels, a divine escort walking with the faithful through the shadows of life's darkest valleys. It is here, in the rich poetry of prayer, that the protective nature of these spiritual beings is made vivid: a promise that divine care is extended through heavenly agency. Yet the mystery deepens when we consider the role of angels in the New Testament, particularly in relation to the prayer of Jesus and the earliest Christian communities. Angels appeared to minister to Him during His time of trial (Luke 22:43), and again to announce His resurrection to the women at the tomb (Matthew 28). These moments reveal angels as participants in the divine plan of salvation, messengers who not only protect but also proclaim hope in the midst of suffering. The early church also found solace in the belief that angels continually intercede and watch over believers, a conviction that shaped communal prayers and personal devotion. What does this mean for the contemporary reader and the seeker today? How might one sense these companioning forces on the often shadowed path of spiritual journeying? The King James Bible's depiction of angels alongside the Divine Presence invites a posture of openness—acknowledging that our prayers are woven into a living tapestry of divine attentiveness. It is an invitation to recognize that prayer creates a spiritual field, charged not only with human longing but animated by heavenly beings who walk with us. Even in moments when God's presence feels shrouded in silence or mystery, the angels stand as tangible reminders that the soul is surrounded, upheld, and never abandoned. This companionship marks a profound shift from viewing prayer as a singular act to experiencing it as an extended communion enriched by divine mystery. Angels become, in this framing, not just figures of ancient texts but living symbols of God's nearness and care. They embody the bridge between human frailty and divine power, carrying echoes of God's promises into the shadowed depths of human existence. To walk with these guardian shades is to journey through a sacred landscape alive with divine presence, where prayer itself becomes an act of participation in the heavenly realm. The protective aspect of angelic presence also reflects a deep spiritual truth about human vulnerability. Prayer emerges often out of need—need for healing, guidance, courage, or deliverance. The angels' watchful vigil suggests that this vulnerability is not met with indifference but with divine solidarity. Through these celestial guardians, the Bible portrays a God who does not abandon the weak, the fearful, or the repentant. Instead, the divine response includes sending forth invisible companions who form a shield around the believer's spirit. This vision calls for a changed understanding of prayer as both a courageous act of surrender and an invitation to receive protection and strength beyond the veil of ordinary perception. Intrinsically linked to this protective role is the mystery that enshrouds angels' identity and purpose. The Bible never exhausts the nature of these beings; they remain, to some extent, beyond human comprehension—a divine enigma. This mystery invites humility in the one who prays, a recognition that the spiritual realm holds wonders beyond grasp and that faith entails trust in these hidden realities. The presence of angels beside the Divine Presence is not an invitation to certainty but to reverent wonder, encouraging an embrace of the unknown within the spiritual experience. Walking with the Divine amidst shadows, then, becomes a metaphor for the spiritual pilgrimage itself—a journey through light and darkness, hope and despair, clarity and mystery. Angels as guardian shades remind us that even when the divine seems distant or silent, unseen companions journey alongside us, carrying our prayers into the heart of the divine, and returning with grace, peace, and sometimes with an urgent nudge toward trust and faithfulness. This awareness also enriches how we understand intercession. Prayer for others, often a lifeline extended beyond the self, enters into a celestial dialogue energized by angelic ministry. Angels not only stand watch over the individual but participate in the sacred economy of intercession, bearing the prayers of many before God's throne. In this way, the communal dimension of prayer is heightened, revealing spiritual connectivity that spans beyond human boundaries. Such a perspective can foster a profound sense of solidarity and hope among believers and seekers—an assurance that no prayer, no matter how faint or faltering, is lost or unheard. In practice, cultivating an awareness of the angels' companioning presence can transform the personal experience of prayer. It invites a posture of attentiveness and openness, where one might slow the hurried mind and listen for the subtle movements within the soul and spirit. The angels' presence, though invisible, can be sensed through moments of unexpected peace, encouragement, or strength in times of trial. This does not require outward signs or miraculous events but rather a cultivated spiritual sensitivity that attunes the heart to the multifaceted ways the divine speaks. Moreover, the shadows through which these heavenly companions walk are not always external trials but interior struggles—the fears, doubts, and wounds that silence the voice of prayer. Here, angels symbolize hope: a promise that these internal deserts are not traversed alone. Their presence incites courage and the steady perseverance required to continue seeking, calling, and trusting in the unseen. The King James Bible's majestic language amplifies this dimension of prayer as a realm where the mortal and the celestial convene. The imagery of angels ascending and descending, of heavenly hosts encamping around the faithful, and of divine messengers executing the purposes of God—all these evoke a spiritual theater that expands the practitioner's awareness beyond self to the cosmic choreography of grace and vigilance. To walk with the divine amidst shadows also encourages a reexamination of how we perceive divine timing and response. In the quiet depths of unanswered or delayed prayers, the biblical narrative and angelic accompaniment remind us that God's acts in the spiritual realm often move in ways beyond immediate understanding. Angels may bear the prayers to God's throne, attend to spiritual battles imperceptible to human eyes, and usher in transformations that unfold across time. Patience, therefore, becomes a spiritual virtue sharpened by the trust that these companioning forces are active, even when visible evidence is absent. This dimension of prayer leads ultimately to a deepened sense of hope—not a naive optimism but a robust assurance grounded in divine fidelity manifested through these guardian shades. The journey, with its shadows and challenges, becomes infused with meaning. No step taken in humility and faith is wasted or overlooked; rather, it is caught up in a divine dance where angels walk beside the pilgrim, encouraging perseverance, nurturing hope, and embodying the presence of a God who neither slumbers nor sleeps. In closing reflection, to sense the presence of angels alongside the Divine Presence is to step into a sacred mystery that invites awe, comfort, and courage. It calls the believer and seeker to embrace prayer not as a solitary act but as a voyage accompanied by heavenly companions whose very existence testifies to God's unceasing care and glory. When shadows gather, these guardian shades walk close, enfolding prayers in a protective embrace that transcends human understanding, assuring the soul that it is always held, always heard, and always beloved. Thus emerges a timeless truth from the King James Bible's portrayal of angelic presence in prayer: that amidst the shadows, we do not walk alone. The divine procession moves with us, angels as faithful escorts in the pilgrimage of the heart. To walk with the divine amid shadows is, then, a sacred invitation—one to behold the mysteries that flourish in the darkness, to trust in unseen aid, and to open oneself fully to the transformative power of prayer held in the hands of heavenly guardians.

Gary E. Risenhoover

Prayers for the Modern Soul: Applying Ancient Wisdom Today

Ancient Prayer in Contemporary Challenge

Amid the relentless pace and complexity of modern life, prayer—a practice rooted deeply in antiquity—can seem at once distant and yet profoundly necessary. The ancient prayers recorded in the King James Bible come to us from a world both remote and remarkably familiar. They encapsulate human experiences that transcend millennia: anguish, hope, yearning, surrender, doubt, and the fierce desire for connection with the divine. In the midst of the 21st-century whirlwind of anxieties, fragmentation, and the pervasive search for meaning, these prayers beckon us to pause, reflect, and align ourselves with a timeless spiritual rhythm. They offer not only consolation but also challenge and guidance, inviting us to overlay their wisdom upon our contemporary landscapes and discover, within their sacred words, a transformative resonance for our own souls. The world we inhabit today is marked by profound contradictions. On one hand, technological advancements and global interconnectivity have expanded awareness like never before; on the other, this very hyperconnectivity fosters unprecedented isolation. Our lives are punctuated by ceaseless distractions, endless demands, and a persistent sense of fragmentation—not only within our external environments but also within our inner selves. Against such a backdrop, the ancient biblical prayers teach us to acknowledge this fragmentation without being overwhelmed by it, to wrestle with our doubts without abandoning faith, and to seek meaning amid chaos. When we hear the voice of King David crying out in Psalm 13, "How long wilt thou forget me, O LORD? for ever? how long wilt thou hide thy face from me?" we recognize the rawness of a heart wrestling with the silence of God in a time of great distress. David's prayer is a vivid outpouring of human vulnerability—a feeling that is no less relevant in our modern experience. Today, many face spiritual desolation amidst mental health struggles, global crises, and personal upheavals. The Psalms remind us that such expressions of confusion, lament, and even anger toward God are not signs of spiritual failure but integral parts of authentic relationship and communication with the divine. They model for us the courage to bring our whole selves—including our fractures—to God in prayer. Expansion of this understanding leads us to view the ancient prayers as more than relics of spiritual history; they become living, breathing conversations with God that mirror the existential quests of our own time. Beyond mere petition or praise, these prayers are invitations into deep spiritual honesty. The prayer of the prophet Habakkuk, for example, questions the presence of injustice and suffering in the world, reflecting an urgent struggle to reconcile faithfulness with observable hardship: "O LORD, how long shall I cry, and thou wilt not hear? even cry out unto thee of violence, and thou wilt not save?" (Habakkuk 1:2). Such prayers resonate today as we confront systemic injustice, environmental degradation, and moral uncertainty on global scales. The ancient question lingers, as relevant now as it was then: how do we uphold faith and hope when the world seems steeped in despair? These biblical petitions do not offer simple answers, but they do invite a posture of surrender and continued trust. Consider the profound shift in Job's prayer journey—a narrative arc that moves from severe questioning to an eventual deeper understanding of divine wisdom beyond human comprehension. Job's cries of pain and despair climax in a recognition of divine sovereignty: "I know that thou canst do every thing, and that no thought can be withholden from thee" (Job 42:2). For modern readers grappling with the apparent randomness of suffering, Job's prayer encapsulates the tension between questioning and submission, reminding us that spiritual resilience involves holding paradox: to mourn deeply, to question boldly, and yet to maintain open-hearted trust. The ancient biblical prayers also speak powerfully to our yearning for meaning in an era often characterized by existential uncertainty. Contemporary society is marked by a proliferation of philosophies, ideologies, and belief systems, each offering differing answers to life's fundamental questions. Yet many still experience a spiritual void—a feeling that, despite this plurality, something essential remains elusive. The Lord's Prayer, recorded in the New Testament, provides a crucial touchstone in this quest. Its words—"Thy kingdom come. Thy will be done in earth, as it is in heaven"—point toward the yearning for a reality aligned with divine order, justice, and peace. This prayer serves as a blueprint for living with intention and a reminder that prayer is an active engagement with the divine purpose in the present moment. Overlaying such ancient wisdom onto the modern canvas invites us to engage prayer not as mere rote recitation but as a dynamic, transformative practice. In moments of profound uncertainty—when the future seems perilous or when inner turmoil threatens to overwhelm—prayer grounded in biblical tradition offers a path to re-center and reorient. Through the Psalms, the prayers of the prophets, and the teaching of Christ, the ancient texts guide us to anchor ourselves in a reality larger than our fears, anxieties, and the fragmentation we observe around us. Moreover, the collective nature of many biblical prayers emphasizes the relational dimension of faith, a counterbalance to the hyper-individualism pervasive in contemporary culture. The prayers of the Old Testament frequently model communal lament, petition, and thanksgiving, highlighting the interconnectedness of individuals within the faith community. For example, the communal supplications in Nehemiah and Ezra during times of national crisis foreground the power of collective prayer as a source of strength and renewal. This communal aspect speaks directly to modern challenges of isolation, alienation, and the fragmentation of social bonds, inviting believers and seekers alike into a shared spiritual journey. The ritual rhythms embedded in ancient prayers also have critical implications for modern life's frenetic pace. The structured prayers of morning and evening, the repetition of sacred words, and the incorporation of silence in ancient worship serve as antidotes to the hurriedness and distraction that mark much of our day-to-day existence. Adopting similar rhythms can offer modern practitioners a framework for cultivating mindfulness, presence, and spiritual attentiveness. In this way, ancient biblical prayer traditions become practical guides for embedding the sacred into the fabric of contemporary life. Confronted by the swell of digital noise, misinformation, and the often overwhelming flood of sensory input, the ancient practice of prayer invites us to create sacred space—both internal and external. The Psalter's repetitive refrains echo the therapeutic power of focus and intention, showing how returning repeatedly to a trusted prayer can calm the storm of the mind. For example, Psalm 23's pastoral imagery offers a profound metaphorical sanctuary amid the turbulence of life: "He maketh me to lie down in green pastures: he leadeth me beside the still waters." In its simplicity and depth, this prayer anchors the soul, reminding the modern worshiper that amid chaos there is refuge, peace, and restoration. It is striking that the prayers recorded in the King James Bible do not shy away from the messiness of reality or the complexity of human emotion. They encompass joyful praise and painful lament, steadfast hope and anguished doubt, communal intercession and intimate supplication. This inclusivity is penetrative for our times; it validates the full spectrum of human experience as worthy of being brought before the divine. Where contemporary culture sometimes pressures individuals toward sanitized optimism or superficial positivity, these ancient prayers invite honesty, vulnerability, and depth. They assure us that bringing our authentic selves—including our fears, frustrations, and confusions—into prayer is itself a sacred act. Furthermore, the biblical portrayal of prayer includes significant elements of spiritual struggle and perseverance, themes that resonate deeply in today's world. The metaphor of wrestling with God, most famously embodied in the story of Jacob, encapsulates the tension of seeking blessing while confronting divine mystery. Jacob's prayerful encounter, where he wrestles through the night until daybreak, concludes with both blessing and transformation. This narrative vividly illustrates that prayer is not always silent or serene; it can be vigorous, challenging, and even confrontational. In contemporary spiritual practice, this reimagining opens space for those whose prayers are marked not by calm certitude but by wrestling, struggle, and bold persistence. In applying ancient prayers to modern challenges, it is essential not to romanticize or simplify the biblical context but to engage with these texts dynamically and thoughtfully. The world of the ancient Israelites and early Christians was rife with its own unique challenges: exile, conquest, cultural upheaval, and spiritual crises. Their prayers arose out of real struggles of survival, identity, and hope. Recognizing this complex backdrop helps us connect more authentically with the texts, appreciating that the spiritual forces at work then—fear, hope, despair, courage—are fundamentally the same forces shaping human hearts today. Technology provides another striking arena where ancient prayer can intersect with contemporary life. In an era where human interactions often occur through screens and algorithms, prayer invites a countercultural return to presence and groundedness. The act of praying the ancient words—whether quietly within or publicly with others—can function as a form of digital detox, a means of stepping away from the ephemeral and superficial to touch something eternal and substantive. Likewise, the discipline of memorizing or reciting biblical prayers can serve as an anchor amidst the shifting tides of online information and distraction. This ancient-contemporary dialogue also highlights the universal accessibility of prayer. Regardless of religious affiliation or theological tradition, the human impulse to seek connection beyond oneself is fundamental. The biblical prayers affirm this universality by expressing experiences and emotions that cross cultural and temporal boundaries. Feelings of abandonment, gratitude, yearning, and surrender are woven throughout the Psalms and prophetic prayers alike, inviting all who encounter them to find a voice for their own spiritual experiences. Moreover, the ethical dimensions embedded in many biblical prayers provide moral compass points amidst the ethical ambiguities of modern society. Prayers asking for justice, mercy, guidance, and humility remind us that prayer is not merely self-centered but is linked to the well-being of others and the broader world. Ancient prayers challenge modern believers to integrate their spirituality with action, towards peacemaking, reconciliation, and the pursuit of justice. They urge us to consider how prayer shapes not simply private devotion but public witness. Amid contemporary mental health challenges, prayer as portrayed in the King James Bible offers both solace and a framework for processing emotional turmoil. The honest expression of fear, anxiety, and grief present in the Psalms can function as spiritual therapy. For instance, Psalm 22 begins with despair—"My God, my God, why hast thou forsaken me?"—yet it leads the prayerer through a journey into hope and trust. In this way, ancient prayer texts provide models for naming pain without becoming captive to it, for embodying resilience through spiritual surrender. The fragmented nature of modern life finds a peculiarly fitting response in the biblical prayer tradition's embrace of ritual and repetition. Ritual grounding, prayer cycles, the cadence of imprecatory and petitionary prayers offer a steady heartbeat beneath the turbulence. This steady rhythm supports the modern soul in its search for coherence and meaning, offering a spiritual scaffold upon which to rebuild wholeness. Through prayer, the fractured self is invited into integration, aligning disparate parts through sacred dialogue. Additionally, prayer's transformative potential as portrayed in biblical literature addresses modern desires for personal growth and spiritual evolution. Many prayers culminate in renewed faith, strengthened resolve, and deepened understanding. The story of Hannah's fervent prayer for a child (1 Samuel 1) reveals how prayer can cultivate patience, fortify hope, and prompt action in unexpected ways. These narratives encourage contemporary prayers to be hopeful endeavors, seeking transformation not only in circumstance but within the prayerer themselves. Engaging ancient biblical prayers in the context of modern life thus becomes an act of spiritual translation—taking the language and experiences of a distant past and making them resonate within current realities. This engagement calls for both intellectual inquiry and heartfelt openness. Scholars who analyze the historical, linguistic, and theological nuances of these prayers deepen our comprehension; simultaneously, contemplative readers allow the words to touch their interior landscapes, bridging time and culture. In summary, the ancient prayers of the King James Bible remain profoundly relevant to the complexities and challenges of contemporary existence. They speak to our deepest anxieties and yearning for meaning, providing a language for lament, praise, petition, and surrender. These prayers invite us to wrestle with divine mystery, to embrace vulnerability, to renew hope, and to seek justice in a fractured world. By overlaying the timeless spiritual wisdom of these prayers upon modern canvases, we enter into an enduring dialogue that enriches our spiritual lives, offering sustenance, courage, and transformation for the modern soul.

Crafting Personal and Communal Devotion

In the vast landscape of spiritual life, prayer remains one of the most intimate and powerful expressions of faith, hope, and connection with the divine. The King James Bible, with its timeless language and profound wisdom, presents prayer not merely as a ritual but as a dynamic relationship—an ongoing conversation that invites both personal reflection and communal encounter. As we journey toward crafting devotion that resonates deeply with the modern soul, it becomes essential to embrace not only the forms and words of biblical prayer but also the attitudes, intentions, and openness that undergird those ancient expressions. This subchapter aims to offer practical guidance for adapting biblical prayer forms and attitudes to personal and community practices, encouraging a devotional life that is at once rooted in sacred tradition and authentic to contemporary realities. How can we, in a world defined by rapid change, diverse cultures, and complex challenges, engage prayer in a way that speaks truthfully to our hearts and binds us meaningfully with others? To explore this, we will consider key aspects of biblical prayer— its posture, language, emotions, and rhythms—and then translate these into tangible steps and creative approaches for modern devotion, emphasizing the balance between structure and spontaneity, silence and speech, solitude and fellowship.### Embracing Authenticity: Prayer as Honest EncounterThe first cornerstone in crafting personal and communal devotion is authenticity. The prayers recorded in the King James Bible—whether from David's heartfelt laments, Hannah's fervent pleas, Solomon's wise supplications, or Jesus' intimate conversations with the Father—are marked by raw honesty. They reveal a spectrum of human emotions: joy, sorrow, doubt, anger, gratitude, confusion, and awe. These biblical prayers teach us that genuine prayer is not performance; it is the courage to bring one's true self before God. For the modern believer or seeker, this means allowing prayer to transcend mere formulaic repetition or cultural habit. It means entering the sacred space of devotion without putting on a mask of false composure or preconceived notions about what prayer "should" look like. In practice, this could begin with a simple commitment: when you pray, embrace whatever emotional or spiritual condition you find yourself in. If your heart is heavy with grief, give space for grief. If your mind is restless with questions, bring those questions honestly into the dialogue. Encouraging honesty also applies to communal prayer. Often, group prayers can become rigid or overly formalized, limiting participation or stifling genuine expression. Creating a community devotional environment that welcomes vulnerability and diversity of voices can transform prayer into a shared encounter of authenticity. This may involve setting norms that honor each person's unique experience—whether through shared silence, spontaneous intercessions, or guided reflections that invite honest sharing.### Adapting Biblical Prayer Forms to Today's Devotional PracticeThe King James Bible reveals several key prayer forms that have served believers through centuries: adoration, confession, thanksgiving, supplication, intercession, meditation, and lament. Each form carries a distinctive purpose and emotional texture, offering a framework upon which contemporary prayer can be shaped. Adapting these biblical forms need not mean slavish copying; rather, it invites creative reinterpretation that resonates with your personal and communal context. 1. Adoration:

Cultivating a Posture of Reverence and Wonder Adoration underscores the recognition and praise of God's holiness, majesty, and loving attributes. Psalms like Psalm 8 and Psalm 145 are exquisite models that express awe and exaltation. For the modern soul, adoration might take the shape of poetic reflection on nature, music that stirs the spirit, or silent reverence amidst daily chaos. Practices such as journaling aspects of the divine that inspire wonder or setting aside moments in nature for quiet contemplation can embody adoration authentically. In community settings, adoration can be nurtured through worship arts—songs, visual imagery, or collective affirmations—that evoke the transcendent and invite collective upliftment. 2. Confession: Opening to Renewal and Healing Confession in biblical prayer invites the acknowledgment of personal and communal shortcomings, fostering humility and reliance on divine grace. It is never simply about guilt but about transformation. The Psalms, especially Psalm 51, offer rich language for expressing repentance. To integrate confession today, personal devotion might encompass reflective writing that names struggles and seeks forgiveness, or guided meditation that gently invites awareness of areas needing healing. Communities might incorporate intentional times of confession, allowing space for silent reflection, spoken words, or shared prayers that emphasize mercy rather than judgement. 3. Thanksgiving: Anchoring in Gratitude Thanksgiving prayers in scripture highlight the importance of recognizing blessings and God's providence. Whether in joyful praise or heartfelt acknowledgment during trials, gratitude shifts the heart's focus towards abundance and faith. Modern practitioners can cultivate thanksgiving by maintaining gratitude journals, consciously noting everyday gifts and answered prayers. Communal devotion might involve sharing testimonies of gratitude or creating "thankfulness circles" where each participant expresses a heartfelt blessing. 4. Supplication and Intercession: Participating in Divine Partnership Supplication is the earnest personal petitioning of God, while intercession extends this petitioning on behalf of others. The biblical witness, from Hannah to Paul, shows the power and intimacy of interceding in prayer. Today, prayer lists can be personalized and refreshed regularly, maintaining connection with the needs closest to heart. Intercessory prayer groups or digital prayer networks can foster communal solidarity, magnifying spiritual care through shared concern. The creativity here may include prayer walks through neighborhoods, prayer chains, or even digital platforms that unite people in real time. 5. Meditation: Listening and Reflecting with Stillness Meditation in biblical tradition, though not always labeled as such, encompasses deep reflection on God's word and presence. Psalm 1 speaks of meditating on the law day and night. This invites a practice of contemplative listening and spiritual absorption. Modern meditation practices can integrate reading and reflecting on scripture passages slowly and with attention, accompanied by silence, breathing exercises, or focused imagery. Group meditation sessions can provide peaceful communal space to rest and receive. 6. Lament: Validating Sorrow and Seeking Comfort One of the most remarkable contributions of biblical prayer is the lament: an honest expression of grief and questioning in the face of suffering. Lament psalms nearly always balance sorrow with trust. In modern devotional life, lament can serve as a healing doorway. Personal lament might involve writing unscripted prayers that vocalize pain, or creative arts like music or poetry to shape grief. Communities may hold "lament services" or prayer vigils where collective sorrow finds a sacred voice, bearing witness to pain while nurturing hope.### Creating a Rhythm: Structuring Devotion for Consistency and FlexibilityAnother vital element in crafting devotion is the rhythm or habit of prayer. The biblical scriptures reveal that prayer was often integrated into daily life—morning and evening, at set festivals, and in moments of crisis. Developing a rhythm that maintains consistency while allowing the flexibility required for authentic expression can ground the modern soul amidst daily distractions. For personal devotion, consider establishing fixed times that gently anchor your prayer life—morning moments of gratitude, midday pauses for supplication, evening reflection in confession and meditation. Utilize tools like prayer journals, reminders, or devotional guides inspired by scripture but adapted to your needs. At the communal level, regular gatherings—whether weekly, monthly, or aligned with liturgical seasons—can sustain group prayer life. Yet it is equally important to permit spontaneous gatherings or brief prayer breaks within larger meetings or events. The flexibility to respond to immediate communal or personal needs fosters an organic and alive devotional culture.### Incorporating Physicality: The Role of Embodiment in PrayerPrayer in the Bible is often embodied. Kneeling, lifting hands, bowing, standing— all physical postures signal attitude, reverence, or urgency. Embodied prayer connects the soul with the body, anchoring spiritual intention in tangible action. For individuals today, integrating physical gestures can deepen prayer's impact. Simple acts such as kneeling to focus attention, lighting a candle to symbolize presence, or walking prayerfully in silence can enrich the experience. In communal settings, collective physical expression—rising, sitting, communal hand-holding or laying on hands during intercession—can create a shared sense of unity and presence. Even mindful breathing or rhythmic chanting as a body can foster spiritual attunement.### Language and Creativity: Cultivating a Prayer Vocabulary for Today. The poetic and majestic language of the King James Bible often inspires reverence, but it can also feel distant or unfamiliar to contemporary readers. Adapting prayer language to one's own voice while honoring the biblical tradition requires thoughtful creativity. Encourage personal devotioners to create their own prayers using scripture as a template—borrowing rhythm, structure, or key phrases but filling them with contemporary language and concerns. This honors continuity with the past while enabling authentic expression. Communities can embrace multilingual or multicultural prayer forms, incorporating songs, readings, and expressions from various traditions to reflect diversity. Creating prayer books or digital resources that blend scripture with locally relevant language invites participation and ownership. Poetic creativity—writing prayers as poems, songs, or visual arts—can also expand the language of devotion, making it vibrant and accessible.### Technology's Role: Prayer in a Digital AgeModern technology offers unprecedented opportunities to sustain and expand devotional life. Prayer apps can provide daily scripture guides, reminders, and journaling spaces. Online prayer communities allow connection beyond geographical limits, sharing intercessory needs and support.However, the digital realm also challenges attentiveness in prayer, risking distraction or superficial engagement. Encouraging intentional use of technology—setting boundaries, choosing quiet times, integrating offline moments—can preserve prayer's depth. Creative practices may include digital "prayer walks," virtual prayer rooms, or coordinated community prayer challenges harnessing social media's connective power.### Navigating Challenges: When Prayer Feels Difficult or DryEven in a rich devotional life, moments come when prayer feels distant, mechanical, or hollow. Recognizing and navigating these seasons is vital. Biblical figures themselves experienced prayer droughts—Job's anguish, David's cries, Jesus' agony in Gethsemane. These affirm that dryness and doubt are part of the spiritual journey. Practical responses include varying prayer practices, introducing silence or music to shift atmosphere, seeking spiritual counsel, or temporarily resting from formal prayer while maintaining openness to divine presence. Communally, holding space to share struggles with prayer fosters mutual encouragement and renewal. Creating prayer "check-in" moments ensures that devotional life remains a safe and supportive process rather than a burden.### Building Bridges: Prayer as a Communal Bond and Social WitnessBeyond personal spirituality, prayer is a vital communal bond and a form of social expression. When communities pray together, they weave relationships of trust, empathy, and shared purpose. Prayer can also serve as a prophetic witness—lifting voices for justice, healing, and peace. Modern applications might include prayer walks through neighborhoods marked by division, interfaith prayer gatherings that promote understanding, or focused prayers for societal issues like poverty, mental health, or environmental stewardship. By framing communal prayer as both an inward connection and outward engagement, devotion expands to reflect God's love in tangible, transformative action.### Encouraging Experimentation: Cultivating a Living Prayer LifeFinally, fostering creativity and experimentation is essential. Prayer should never become stagnant; it is a living, evolving practice. Invite both individuals and communities to try new forms—silent retreats, labyrinth walking, breath prayers, artistic expression, or even movement-based prayer like dance or yoga informed by biblical meditation. Recording and reflecting on these experiences deepens understanding and appreciation, helping discern which forms resonate most authentically. Encouraging openness to change while honoring tradition creates a balanced devotional life—grounded and alive, structured and free, ancient and immediate. In conclusion, crafting personal and communal devotion in today's world involves a thoughtful weaving of biblical wisdom with genuine, creative expression. The forms and attitudes of prayer found in the King James Bible offer a rich treasury from which to draw, but they thrive best when adapted with authenticity, responsiveness, and inclusiveness. By embracing honesty, cultivating multiple prayer forms, establishing rhythm and embodiment, expanding language, wisely using technology, navigating challenges, building communal bonds, and fostering experimentation, individuals and communities alike can nurture devotional lives that nourish the modern soul. Prayer thus becomes more than obligation; it blossoms into a profound encounter—one that echoes the divine within and among us, shaping lives and world with hope, love, and transformation.

Integrating Silence, Ritual, and Reflection

In a world that moves with relentless speed—where distractions abound and the noise of daily life can feel overwhelming—finding moments of stillness may seem almost impossible. Yet, this very stillness holds profound power. It is within quietness that prayer moves beyond words, rituals weave deeper meaning, and reflection becomes a pathway to transformation. To the modern soul, navigating complexities both external and internal, the integration of silence, ritual, and reflection offers a holistic approach that bridges ancient wisdom with contemporary life. This synthesis is not merely an ideal but a practical rhythm of spiritual living, inviting each individual into a sacred dance of presence and purpose. At the heart of this integration lies silence—not simply the absence of sound, but a spiritual quality, a fertile ground where the soul breathes and commune with the Divine becomes intimate and unhurried. The King James Bible, with its majestic language and rich imagery, points repeatedly to the value of silence in communion with God. One recalls Psalm 46:10, "Be still, and know that I am God," an admonition that calls believers to pause and center themselves amid chaos. Silence, then, is the first thread weaving through the fabric of meaningful prayer—it clears away clamor, inviting space where God's voice can emerge not as thunder but as a gentle whisper. However, silence alone cannot carry the full weight of spiritual practice. It must be paired with ritual—those repeated, embodied acts that root prayer in the physical world and tie the temporal to the eternal. Ritual grounds the soul, creating patterns that anchor faith in the shifting sands of everyday life. The Scriptures offer abundant examples: the laying on of hands, the washing of feet, the breaking of bread, even the cadence of repeated prayers such as the Lord's Prayer. These acts do not merely symbolize devotion; they enact it, embodying belief in gestures that engage the whole person—body, mind, and spirit. For the modern practitioner, rituals can take diverse, personal forms beyond traditional liturgy. Lighting a candle in the quiet of morning, folding hands in deliberate pause before a meal, tracing a cross on the forehead, or even the simple act of breathing deeply with intention can become ritualized moments that nurture sacred space within the quotidian. These embodied practices help the soul remember its place in a larger story and invite presence that is active, not passive. Reflection, then, serves as the contemplative hinge between silence and ritual. If silence is the soil and ritual the seed, reflection is the tender care that nurtures growth. Through meditation, journaling, or focused contemplation on Scripture, the modern soul engages in a dialogue with itself and with the Divine. This process encourages the interiorization of faith—allowing the truths encountered in prayer and ritual to permeate the heart's depths rather than remain abstract concepts. The King James Bible itself offers prescriptions for reflection in verses that invite meditation on God's laws and promises. Psalm 1:2 describes the blessed man "whose delight is in the law of the Lord; and in his law doth he meditate day and night." Reflection is thus shown not merely as an ancillary practice but as a vital spiritual discipline that cultivates wisdom, discernment, and transformation. In this light, reflection becomes a mode of listening—listening not only to the Word but to the stirrings within one's own spirit. Together, silence, ritual, and reflection create a triad of spiritual rhythms that can restore balance and deepen connection in a fragmented world. They counteract the centrifugal forces of distraction and superficiality by drawing the soul inward and upward. Yet these rhythms are not rigid or formulaic. Rather, they invite fluidity and personal adaptation—elements particularly essential in contemporary contexts where diverse lifestyles and beliefs converge. To imagine how this integration might unfold in daily life, consider the example of a morning prayer ritual. Rising with the dawn, one might begin in silence—a brief pause to breathe and attune the heart to God's presence. This stillness may last only a few moments but sets a sacred tone. Following this, lighting a candle or opening a treasured book may mark a ritual action, a physical expression of intention. Then comes reflection: reading a passage from Scripture, perhaps from Psalms or the teachings of Jesus, followed by quiet meditation or journaling to capture insights and prayers. The ritual concludes with a spoken benediction or a simple "Amen," grounding the practice and preparing the soul for the day ahead. This pattern illustrates how ancient wisdom lives anew when integrated thoughtfully into modern life—as a daily rhythm that shapes the soul's disposition and empowers faithful living. It also exemplifies an inclusive spirituality, inviting seekers of varied traditions to engage these practices in their own ways without rigid dogma. The recursive nature of these rhythms—cycle after cycle of silence, ritual, reflection—cultivates spiritual resilience. Over time, such practices mold inner landscapes, fostering patience, humility, and openness. The soul learns to recognize the Divine not only in extraordinary moments but in the texture of the ordinary. As Saint Augustine famously said, "God is closer to us than we are to ourselves," a truth made tangible through disciplined attentiveness in prayer. Importantly, the integration of silence, ritual, and reflection does not exclude the messiness of human experience. On the contrary, it offers a container where grief, joy, doubt, and hope can all find expression and transformation. In times of distress, silence can become an anchor; ritual—a steadying gesture; reflection—a means of discernment and healing. Such practices acknowledge the full spectrum of life and lend grace to the journey. Technology, often blamed for modern distraction, can paradoxically serve this integrated approach when wielded with mindfulness. Apps that guide contemplative prayer, digital devotionals, or recorded chants can aid in cultivating silence and reflection. But these tools must always remain servants, not masters, preserving the primacy of embodied experience and interior stillness. Moreover, communal expressions of prayer benefit from the synergy of silence, ritual, and reflection. In congregations, shared rituals deepen bonds and amplify intention, while moments of collective silence open spaces for God's collective voice to unfold. Reflection, whether through sermons or group meditation, extends personal insight into community wisdom. This holistic approach echoes the biblical narrative itself, where prayer is never a mere formula—but a living encounter engaging the whole person. The intertwining of stillness, embodied practice, and meditation mirrors the rhythms of creation—rest and work, word and silence, action and contemplation. By embracing these rhythms, the modern soul partakes in a timeless dance that nurtures faith alive and responsive. And so, the integration of silence, ritual, and reflection calls us beyond compartmentalized spirituality toward a seamless practice that touches every facet of life. It invites a spirituality that is both ancient and urgently contemporary—rooted in the venerable text of the King James Bible, yet adaptable and open to the realities of today's seekers. As such, it becomes a beacon and a refuge, empowering the soul to navigate modern challenges with grace, wisdom, and depth. In concluding this reflection on integration, it is helpful to consider practical suggestions for cultivating these rhythms in everyday life. Begin with intentional times of silence—setting aside even five minutes daily to center breath and mind in stillness. Introduce simple rituals that resonate personally—lighting a candle, grounding posture, or reading sacred text aloud. Commit to reflective practices such as journaling thoughts and prayers or contemplative reading. Over weeks and months, these actions become habits that imbue routine moments with sacredness. The integration of silence, ritual, and reflection need not be grand or complicated. Its power lies in constancy and sincerity. Through faithful engagement with these spiritual rhythms, the modern soul finds itself drawn into a deeper communion with the Divine, discovering that prayer is not merely an activity but a way of being—echoing across time and space, uniting all seekers in an unfolding journey toward wholeness. In embracing this integrated path, readers are invited to experiment, to find their unique expressions of silence, ritual, and reflection, meeting God in the sacred ordinary and the ineffable mystery alike. This holistic approach nurtures not only individual growth but also communal flourishing, fostering a world where the echoes of ancient prayer resound anew in hearts attuned to divine presence.

A Symphony of Light: Concluding the Eternal Dance of Prayer

Synthesis of Themes and Insights

Across the span of these pages, a luminous thread has been woven—a thread that delicately intertwines the myriad facets of prayer as portrayed in the King James Bible. The exploration has delved deeply into the timeless essence of prayer, revealing it not merely as a ritualistic act or a set of prescribed words, but as an eternal and living dialogue between the human spirit and the Divine. This synthesis aims to gather the insights scattered throughout the journey, drawing together the vibrant themes and emotions that have unfolded, and to present a harmonious reflection that echoes the profound nature of prayer as a sacred conversation transcending time and tradition. At the very heart of this exploration lies the recognition of prayer's timeless essence. From the earliest verses of Genesis to the profound laments and praises of the Psalms, and onward to the teachings of Christ and the epistles of Paul, prayer emerges as a persistent and enduring thread woven into the fabric of human existence. It is a continuum—connecting ancient voices to modern hearts, bridging centuries, and transcending cultural boundaries. In the King James Bible, the language of prayer is not confined to one epoch or circumstance; it vibrates with a perennial vitality, affirming that prayer is a constant companion to the believer and seeker alike. This timeless nature is part of what makes prayer universally accessible. It is neither bound by geography nor limited by dogma; prayer exists wherever the human soul reaches beyond itself in search of meaning, solace, guidance, or connection. The King James Bible, with its majestic phrasing and rhythmic cadences, encapsulates this universal longing through poetry and prose alike, inviting every reader—whether steeped in Christian faith or approaching from a diverse spiritual vantage point—to partake in its sacred dialogue. In this, the book highlights prayer not as an exclusive domain but as a shared human heritage, a spiritual practice that transcends the boundaries of creed and culture. The poetic language of the King James Bible, celebrated for its grandeur and solemnity, serves as more than stylistic ornamentation; it functions as a conduit for the sacred, allowing prayer to ascend beyond mere words into a realm of mystery and reverence. Phrases like "The Lord is my shepherd; I shall not want," "Give us this day our daily bread," and "Thy will be done on earth, as it is in heaven" resonate with rhythm and majesty. Such language evokes emotional depth, stirring the soul and enabling prayer to become not only a verbal act but a profoundly felt experience. The deliberate cadence and carefully chosen diction invite believers into a space where words undertake the loftier role of bridging the human to the divine, articulating hopes, fears, praises, and petitions with both humility and grandeur. Embedded in this poetic fabric is the universal spirituality that prayer fosters—a spirituality that is inclusive and expansive. While the King James Bible is anchored in Judeo-Christian revelation, the prayers and dialogues it contains transcend theological particularity, touching on themes that harmonize with the wider human quest for transcendence. Prayer is portrayed as an act of surrender and trust, a moment in which the seeker becomes aware of a presence greater than self, a source of light, grace, and unending love. This universal aspect invites readers across traditions, cultivating a recognition that prayer is less about rigid orthodoxy and more about a heartfelt communion with the sacred mystery that undergirds all life. The emotional journey of prayer, as explored throughout the book, reveals its dynamic and transformative quality. Prayer is not static or monotonous; it encompasses a wide spectrum of human feeling—from deep anguish and pleading to exultant joy and thanksgiving. In the Psalms especially, one witnesses the candid honesty with which biblical writers express their innermost turmoil, despair, gratitude, and hope. These raw emotions do not distance the individual from God; rather, they deepen the connection, illustrating that prayer is a fearless offering of the self in all its complexities before the Divine. This emotional vulnerability invites readers to recognize prayer as a safe space where sorrow and celebration, doubt and faith coexist, ultimately nourishing spiritual resilience and growth. The sacred silence that prayer often inhabits has also been a subtle yet profound theme embraced in the book. In the King James Bible, moments of quiet reverence, pauses for reflection, and the stillness of heart are as significant as spoken petitions. The silence within prayer is not emptiness but a fertile void where clarity, peace, and divine presence may be encountered most intimately. This sacred silence serves as the backdrop against which words of prayer rise and fall, grounding the tempest of human emotion in serene trust. It is in this interplay of sound and silence, speech and stillness, that the true depth of prayer unfolds— revealing it as an eternal dance between the soul and its source. Together, these themes illustrate how prayer functions as both an individual and communal expression. While the book has centered on the personal dialogue between one's heart and God, it has also acknowledged prayer's power to unite communities, generations, and nations. The prayers recorded in the King James Bible, whether uttered by solitary psalmists or gathered congregations, reflect a collective voice that transcends solitary experience. This communal dimension affirms that prayer is a living tradition—an ongoing symphony where countless voices compose a harmony of faith, hope, and love, echoing through the corridors of time. Moreover, the exploration has underscored prayer's multidimensional purpose: as a channel of praise, intercession, confession, petition, thanksgiving, and contemplation. Each mode serves a unique function in the spiritual life, contributing to the wholeness of the dialogue with the Divine. Praise elevates the spirit beyond earthly concerns, confession brings liberation through honest acknowledgment, petition seeks aid and wisdom, thanksgiving cultivates gratitude that transforms perspective, and contemplation engenders profound attunement to God's presence. The King James Bible richly presents these dimensions, inviting readers into a holistic experience of prayer that embraces both action and stillness, speaking and listening. This intricate interplay reflects the inherent tension within prayer between human agency and divine sovereignty. The biblical prayers reveal a beautiful honesty in acknowledging human frailty alongside unwavering trust in God's providence. Through this tension flows the vitality of prayer as a sacred conversation—not a one-sided monologue but a dance of mutual participation. The believer surrenders control and offers desires, yet remains open to transformation by the Divine will. This dynamic embodies the essence of the "eternal dance of prayer" named in the chapter title—the perpetual motion between the finite and infinite, the known and the mysterious, the spoken and the silent. In embracing this eternal dance, the book has also engaged with the paradox of prayer as both an answer and a mystery. While some prayers receive clear responses or tangible outcomes, many remain unanswered or seem prolonged in silence. Yet, the biblical narrative invites the faithful to trust that even unanswered prayers hold meaning and contribute to spiritual maturity. This paradox enriches the understanding of prayer as a practice embedded not only in hope for particular blessings but in a steadfast commitment to relationship with the Divine. Prayer, therefore, becomes an expression of faith itself—a trust in the unseen and the eternal, woven through every plea and praise. The King James Bible's enduring influence and cultural significance also serve as a vital aspect of this synthesis. The historic language and literary craftsmanship continue to shape religious thought, art, literature, and spirituality centuries after its publication. This literary heritage invites reflection on how the text bridges ancient revelation with contemporary experience. The majestic phrasing resonates with modern readers, inviting them into a transcendent encounter that defies linguistic and cultural shifts. Thus, the book has presented prayer not only as a mystical dialogue but as an enduring cultural treasure—a source of inspiration and comfort that continues to illuminate the human soul. Another essential insight to emerge centers on prayer's transformative potential. Throughout the biblical prayers, individuals are changed—not merely in their circumstances but within their very being. Prayer shapes identity, aligns will, calms turmoil, emboldens hope, and fosters love. This transformative power manifests in both divine intervention and internal renewal, underscoring that prayer is as much about transformation of the self as it is about seeking external aid. The King James Bible vividly portrays this process, illustrating how prayer opens the heart to grace and leads the soul toward greater harmony with the divine purpose. Closely tied to transformation is the concept of prayer as an act of surrender. The biblical narratives emphasize the humility of approaching God, the willingness to relinquish personal control, and the courage to trust beyond understanding. This surrender is neither passive resignation nor defeat but an active, courageous opening to divine will—a freeing release that paradoxically restores agency by embracing dependence on God. Through surrender, prayer becomes a profound act of liberation, releasing burdens and inviting peace. This theme, deeply rooted in the scripture's portrayal of prayer, resonates universally with those who have experienced the paradoxical freedom found in yielding to something greater than the self. The emotional vulnerability and surrender inherent in prayer also highlight its role as a source of consolation amidst human suffering. The King James Bible, candid in its depiction of anguish, doubt, and lamentation, reveals prayer as a refuge where pain is voiced and compassion is received. This candid emotionality confirms prayer's therapeutic dimension—its capacity to hold the full spectrum of human experience without judgment, offering solace and strength. The Psalms, Job's dialogues, and Christ's own prayers provide a model for embracing suffering within a sacred framework that acknowledges pain while affirming hope and redemption. Moreover, the universality of prayer illustrated in the text opens pathways for interfaith reflections and ecumenical dialogue. By highlighting prayer's fundamental elements—communication with the sacred, expressions of longing and trust, moments of silence and praise—the book encourages an appreciation of shared spiritual practices across religious traditions. This inclusive vision promotes mutual respect and understanding, suggesting that prayer can function as a bridge between diverse faith communities, fostering peace and unity in a fragmented world. Throughout, the exploration has also maintained a delicate balance between scholarly rigor and heartfelt reflection. The careful exegesis of biblical passages is complemented by meditative insights and personal application, creating a rich tapestry that honors both the intellectual and experiential dimensions of prayer. This approach reinforces prayer's accessibility, inviting readers not merely to study prayer as a distant artifact but to engage with it intimately—as a living, breathing reality capable of shaping hearts and minds today. In summation, the varied themes and insights presented across this work converge to illuminate the radiant complexity and simplicity of prayer embodied in the King James Bible. Prayer emerges as an eternal sacred conversation—a symphony composed of light, silence, emotion, surrender, praise, and petition—that invites humanity into ongoing communion with the Divine. It is a dynamic dance that encompasses all aspects of human existence and reflects the deep yearning for connection and transcendence woven into the soul's fabric. By recognizing prayer's timelessness, embracing its poetic grandeur, honoring its emotional and silent depths, and appreciating its universal spirituality, the reader is invited to participate in the ongoing dialogue that has echoed through millennia. Prayer ceases to be a mere religious formality and becomes a living language of the spirit—a profound expression of humanity's aspirations, vulnerabilities, and hope. As the final chords of this symphony resonate, the echoes of prayer continue to ripple across time and space, inviting every soul to join in the dance. This eternal conversation, vibrant with meaning and grace, remains ever open—ready to receive our words, our silence, and our hearts, connecting all who seek with the boundless light of the Divine.

Invitation to Continued Communion

As we near the close of this journey through the sacred tapestry of prayer woven in the pages of the King James Bible, it is fitting to extend an earnest and heartfelt invitation—an open call to every reader to carry forward the vibrant, living practice of prayer. This is no mere act of repetition, no empty ritual to be performed out of habit or expectation. Rather, it is a perpetual dance of light, an eternal symphony unfolding between human hearts and the Divine Presence that moves just beyond the veil of sight yet within reach of deepest longing. Prayer, as we have explored, is far more than words spoken or thoughts directed heavenward; it is the essence of communion itself. It is the language of the soul reaching out, the beating rhythm by which the human spirit invites and responds to the sacred. From the Psalms that lift the heart in lament and praise, to the quiet surrender of Hannah's whispered hope, to Jesus' own moments of intimate dialogue with the Father, prayer pulses as the lifeblood of faithful living. It is this lifeblood we are now called to cherish and nurture, bringing the dance with the Divine into every moment of our unfolding lives. Imagine prayer as a radiant beam of light—sometimes steady and blazing, sometimes flickering gently like a candle in the evening breeze. This light emanates from within, irradiating outward to touch not only our own souls but others around us. It is an invitation, a bridge, a shimmering pathway where heaven and earth entwine. It transcends circumstance, belief, and theology, bathing all who engage it in a shared experience of hope, peace, and transformation. To carry this flame forward requires more than mere desire; it calls for willingness—willingness to embrace vulnerability, to step into the fullness of our humanity, and to open our hearts without reservation. Prayer is a dance because it involves movement and response: listening as well as speaking, receiving as well as offering. It is a dynamic rhythm, a sacred interplay where both the human and the holy collaborate in an eternal unfolding. Consider, for a moment, the difference that arises when prayer ceases to be a task and becomes instead a living presence within us. We begin to notice the subtle ways the Divine responds—a gentle nudge in our hearts, a sudden peace in the midst of turmoil, the quiet assurance that we are never truly alone. This ongoing communion infuses everyday moments with sanctity, transforming ordinary life into a playground for divine encounter. Yet, this communion is not confined to the private or the hidden; it overflows into the communal, the social. Prayer invites us to join hands with others, to lift collective voices in shared longing and gratitude. In the Scriptures, the community's prayers form a chorus of faith that echoes across generations. From the corporate lamentations in times of exile to the united hallelujahs in times of jubilee, the power of communal prayer emerges as a vivid testament to God's enduring presence among His people. This invitation, therefore, extends not only to the solitary seeker but also to the gathered community, each member contributing to the symphony of light. In this shared dance, individuality is honored even as unity is celebrated—a beautiful paradox that reflects the very nature of the Divine whose essence is both One and Many. To the believer, prayer may be a familiar refuge, a place of rest and renewal. To the seeker, it may be an open door, a threshold toward unknown mysteries. To the doubter, it may be a question posed to the silence, a tentative step into a realm beyond rational understanding. To all, it is an invitation—a sacred beckoning to enter into deeper, richer communion with the Divine Presence that is always extending itself toward us. Importantly, this invitation carries with it both promise and challenge. The promise is that prayer is a source of strength, healing, and transformation; the challenge is that it requires commitment and openness. It asks us to cultivate patience amid unanswered questions, to embrace paradoxes without needing immediate resolution, and to persist in faith even when the divine seems distant. In embracing this dance, we become co-creators with the Divine of a reality suffused with grace and light. Each prayer offered, each breath drawn in sacred intention, becomes a luminous thread in the fabric of creation, weaving hope and love into the world's tapestry. We are invited not to be passive recipients but active participants, dancing the eternal rhythm of longing and fulfillment, surrender and embrace.Let your prayer be not just a practice but a posture—a posture of openness and expectancy that transforms how you see yourself, others, and the world. Allow it to deepen your sensitivity to the sacred in daily life, to sharpen your awareness of God's subtle movements amid the chaos and calm alike. Envision the Divine Presence not as a distant monarch seated on a throne far removed from our troubles, but as a Lover, a Friend, a Constant Companion engaged in a timeless dance with your own heart. This presence responds to the song of your soul, mirrors your joy, holds your pain, and invites your steps into an endless waltz of grace. Remember the words of the Psalmist who proclaimed, "Call upon me in the day of trouble: I will deliver thee, and thou shalt glorify me" (Psalm 50:15). This is no mere promise of rescue; it is a covenant of ongoing relationship, an assurance that prayer is an open channel through which divine help, guidance, and love flow ceaselessly. As you continue this journey beyond these pages, may you carry prayer with you as a lantern for dark roads and a light for bright days. May it be your shelter in storms and your song in seasons of joy. May it ever draw you nearer to the Divine Dance Partner who moves in rhythm with your heart, even when the music seems faint or paused. Cultivate the habit of turning inward often, opening the windows of your soul to invite the breath of the Spirit. Speak honestly and listen expectantly. Let prayer be the breath of your days, the root of your stability, the wings of your hope. In this eternal dance of light, your steps matter. Each moment of prayer is a step toward deeper communion, a step that resonates far beyond what eyes can see or ears can hear. Together with countless seekers and saints throughout history, you join a symphony that has no end—a living, breathing testament to the enduring power of prayer to unite, to heal, and to transform. As you step forth now, take with you the wisdom and wonder discovered here. Let the rhythms and patterns studied become the foundations upon which you build your own sacred practice. Adapt them, shape them, make them your own expression of longing, surrender, and communion. Know that you are never alone in this dance. The Divine Presence is always there, just beyond sight yet palpably near, extending hands of grace and light. The invitation stands open to all— believers, seekers, skeptics alike—to join in this timeless interplay of spirit and soul. May your dance be steady and joyful, your heart open and brave. And may the light of prayer continue to illuminate your path, drawing you ever closer into the embrace of the Divine. Carry this invitation in your heart as both gift and calling. For prayer is the eternal spark that ignites the sacred fire within us, the melody that colors the silence with hope, and the dance of light that never ceases, flowing forth from the Divine through human hearts to the world. Step boldly and gracefully into this dance. The music plays on, the light pulses strong, and the Divine Presence awaits your willing embrace. Welcome to the endless symphony of prayer—an invitation not only to speak but to listen; not only to ask but to receive; not only to reach out but to be held in the everlasting dance of light. Keep dancing. Keep praying. Keep believing. The eternal communion has only just begun.

Closing Meditation: The Dance of Light and Sound

In the vastness of infinite space, where stars weave tapestries of silver threads across the canvas of night, there unfolds a sacred symphony — a dance of light and sound, merging in timeless harmony. This dance is not bound by earthly measures, but flows freely within the spiritual expanse where prayer moves like a river, winding, changing, yet eternal. It is here, in this luminous interplay of vibration and illumination, that we find ourselves drawn into the heart of the divine mystery, invited to listen beyond words and see beyond forms, entering a rhythm older than time itself. Picture the first note rising from the silence, a single ray of light stretching across the horizon of your soul. This light, soft and shimmering, carries the delicate vibration of hope — a pure whisper in the hush of creation. As it touches the darkness, the silence begins to fracture, giving birth to music. It is a music not heard by ears alone but by the very essence of being, resonating within the chambers of the heart and the hidden corners of the spirit. Each pulse, each wave, is a thread in the vast symphony, connecting all who dare to seek union with the unseen source. In the King James Bible, prayer often emerges as both a voice and a light — a sacred sound that rises in the forms of supplication, praise, confession, and thanksgiving, and a radiant flame that never ceases to shine despite the shadows of the world. This dual nature of prayer, its capacity to embody both resonance and illumination, reveals a profound truth: that within every human cry, there is the potential to kindle divine light; in every silent petition, a pattern of sacred sound is formed. Close your eyes now. Envision this cosmic dance. The light is not static; it pulses, undulates, and interlaces with tones that reverberate like distant chimes carried on the wind. These are the echoes of the divine, the primal chant that gave birth to the universe, still unfolding in the whisper of every breath, in the beat of every heart. Here, prayer is not merely an act; it is a living symphony, a dance where the spirit sways in rhythm with eternal harmonies. Feel the vibration of this encounter within you. It begins as a tremor – a gentle stirring beneath your ribs, the flicker of an ember long concealed. As your breath deepens, so does the pulse of the light and sound entwined within you. Each inhalation draws in the radiant energy of grace; each exhalation releases it in waves of love to the world around you. The dance accelerates, becoming a crescendo of light, a cascade of voices raised in sacred song beyond time and place. The theological significance of this imagery beckons us to understand prayer not merely as petition or thanksgiving but as participation — a joining of human expression with the eternal chorus of creation. It affirms the interconnection between all beings, united in the luminous fabric spun from the celestial notes and shafts of light that pulse through existence. To pray, then, is to step into this radiant dance, to synchronize one's own rhythm with the cosmic pulse, to become a living instrument where light transforms sound and sound births light. Consider the psalmist's words: "The heavens declare the glory of God; and the firmament sheweth his handywork" (Psalm 19:1). Here is the auditory made visible, the visible made sacred sound. When we pray, we echo this declaration — we become, in a profound sense, participants in the very testimony of creation's light and sound. Our prayers are threads woven into the endless tapestry, harmonies that rise as a fragrant offering to the sacred presence dwelling within and beyond us. Now, let your mind wander among the stars, imagining each one as a note in the grand melody of being. The night sky hums with the pulse of infinite praise, a continuous outpouring of light that sings without words. This celestial music mirrors the inner song of the seeker, who through prayer finds the rhythm of the divine heartbeat. Just as the stars cannot cease their shining, so too, the spirit's longing, expressed in prayer, is eternal, a perpetual dance inviting connection, healing, and transformation. Observe the interplay of light and shadow in this dance. Shadows are not enemies to be banished but vital contrasts that give form and depth to the illumination. In moments of silence, when prayer feels still or unanswered, the shadows hold space for sacred mystery — the places where the music softly fades only to rise anew, the silences pregnant with expectation and faith. This dialectic of light and dark enriches the symphony, lending it texture and tension, a dynamic that propels the dancer forward into greater depths of surrender and openness. Imagine now the light taking on color — hues of gold, violet, and crimson swirling in radiant arcs. These colors correspond to the notes of spiritual virtues expressed in prayer: the gold of gratitude, the violet of reverent awe, the crimson of fervent love. Each shade is a voice in the celestial choir, a thread woven into the complex harmony of divine communion. When our prayers arise from the heart's purest intentions, these colors blaze forth, illuminating not only our souls but the paths of those around us. In the fullness of this dance, there is also motion, a flowing movement that transcends stillness and sound. Picture a field of wildflowers swaying in the breeze, their petals catching shafts of sunlight as they move in joy. Prayer is like this dance — fluid, responsive, alive. It has its own choreography, sometimes slow and contemplative, sometimes soaring in exuberance. It invites us to trust the rhythm even when we cannot see the next step, to let go of control and be carried by the invisible currents of grace. This surrender, so central to authentic prayer, is the dancer's leap into freedom. To release our grasp on outcomes and to trust the silence between the notes is to open ourselves to transformation. Here the divine whispers in the spaces between sound, the light dances within the pauses, and we are invited to dwell in that sacred tension. This is the eternal dance — a movement that embraces vulnerability, hope, and the abiding presence of love. As the dance unfolds within, so too does a communal chorus arise. Though prayer is intimately personal, it is never solitary. Across time and space, prayers converge, intertwining like woven threads in a vast tapestry. Imagine countless voices joined together, a vast choir singing the song of yearning and praise, their lights merging into a breathtaking aurora. This collective harmony uplifts and sustains the individual soul, reminding us that the dance of light and sound is shared, that we are never truly alone in our seeking. The Apostle Paul's words resonate deeply here: "Likewise the Spirit also helpeth our infirmities: for we know not what we should pray for as we ought: but the Spirit itself maketh intercession for us with groanings which cannot be uttered" (Romans 8:26). This groaning is part of the soundscape of prayer — a raw and wordless music that emerges from the depths of the spirit. It is the echo of divine longing made audible beyond human language, joining the symphony where understanding transcends explanation. It calls us to embrace mystery, to honor the unspeakable, and to listen with hearts attuned to divine melody.Now, draw this passage to an inner stillness. In this moment, the dance slows, the music softens, and the light becomes a gentle glow surrounding you. Embrace the quiet presence that remains after the crescendo — the calm core of being where all vibrations merge into silence, and the dance becomes a sacred pause. Here lies the wellspring of peace, a place where the soul finds its rest and renewal. In this silence, reflect on the journey of prayer you have undertaken — the moments of soaring light and enveloping sound, the times of shadow and color, the communal chorus and the solitary groan. Each has shaped the dance, weaving complexity and beauty into your spirit's response to the divine. Know that this dance is ongoing, an eternal gift flowing through you, inviting you to engage again and anew whenever you breathe. As you begin to reopen your eyes, carry within you the memory of this symphonic encounter. Let it inspire a deeper appreciation for the sacred rhythms at work in your life — rhythms that echo the divine dance of light and sound, that play out in every prayer, every breath, every moment of attentiveness to the holy presence. With this awareness, prayer becomes not only a practice but a living art, a vibrant participation in the cosmic symphony of being. May this closing meditation linger in the chambers of your soul, an eternal flame and a song that will rise ever higher, inviting you to join the dance anew, to celebrate with unfettered joy the sacred interplay of light and sound. In this dance, find your heart aligned with the vastness of creation, your spirit awakened to the divine cadence, and your life transformed by the radiant symphony of prayer. So enter now this space of luminous silence and exuberant celebration, and become one with the dance — a dance that forever draws us home.

—

Concluding: Till We Meet Again

Wow, what a wild ride it's been! As we close this chapter together, I want to thank you for sticking around, for your curiosity, and for diving headfirst into the whirlwind of thoughts, facts, and stories we've explored.

This book was made to spark your imagination, challenge your perspectives, and leave you buzzing with new ideas. If even a fraction of that energy stuck with you, then we've done our job.

Remember, the journey doesn't end here. Think of this book as a launchpad—a place to ignite your passion for discovery and to encourage you to keep asking, exploring, and creating.

I hope these words have fired up a part of your mind and soul that craves more—more knowledge, more adventure, and more breakthroughs. Let that hunger lead you to unexpected places and fascinating conversations.

Thank you for being an incredible reader. Your enthusiasm is the spark that fuels books like this, and for that, I'm endlessly grateful.

So go forth with confidence, armed with new insights and a fresh perspective. The world is waiting for what only you can bring.

Until our paths cross again in the pages of another story, keep dreaming big, thinking boldly, and living vibrantly.

This isn't goodbye—it's a 'see you soon' from one adventurer to another. Thanks for coming along on this journey!

Keep the fire blazing!

Gary E. Risenhoover